"Real business success is not about having *either* great people *or* great organizational processes. It's about having *both*—coming together in a reinforcing upward spiral that continues to create even more of both. That idea lies at the center of this timely collection of insights and provocative thoughts focused on the solvable mystery of effective organizations.

"The forward-looking concepts described here link to two thoughts that have guided actions in our business: 'Fifty percent of a leader's work here is to build the business; the other 50 percent is to build the organization such that they can build the business.' Bob Gandossy and his team have brought together more than 20 different perspectives on what we would regard as those simple truths."

—Ken Murphy, Senior Vice President,
Human Resources and
Administration, Altria Group, Inc.

"*Workforce Wake-Up Call* provides great insights critical to managing the next generation of talent. People leaders across all organizations should embrace these basic tenants, as they take on the challenge of twenty-first-century talent management."

—Kevin Cox, Executive Vice President,
Human Resources, American Express

Workforce Wake-Up Call

Workforce Wake-Up Call

Your Workforce Is Changing, Are You?

Edited by
Robert Gandossy, Elissa Tucker,
and Nidhi Verma

HEWITT ASSOCIATES

WILEY

John Wiley & Sons, Inc.

Published by John Wiley & Sons, Inc., Hoboken, New Jersey.
Published simultaneously in Canada.

For general information on our other products and services or for technical support, please contact our Customer Care Department within the United States at (800) 762-2974, outside the United States at (317) 572-3993 or fax (317) 572-4002.

Wiley also publishes its books in a variety of electronic formats. Some content that appears in print may not be available in electronic books. For more information about Wiley products, visit our web site at www.wiley.com.

Library of Congress Cataloging-in-Publication Data:

Workforce wake-up call : your workforce is changing, are you? / edited by Robert Gandossy, Elissa Tucker, Nidhi Verma.
      p.   cm.
   Includes index.
   ISBN-13: 978-0-471-77348-1 (cloth)
   ISBN-10: 0-471-77348-4 (cloth)
  1. Human capital. 2. Labor market. 3. Leadership. 4. Supervision of employees. 5. Employee motivation. 6. Organizational effectiveness. I. Gandossy, Robert P. II. Tucker, Elissa. III. Verma, Nidhi.
HD4904.7.W67   2006
658.3—dc22

                                          2006003778

CONTENTS

PREFACE

THE CHANGING TALENT LANDSCAPE

HOW QUICKLY things change. Faster than you could say "contested election," the booming 1990s gave way to the economic downturn of the early twenty-first century. Employers who had been scrambling to find enough warm bodies—let alone skilled, knowledgeable bodies—suddenly found themselves faced with widespread workforce reductions. Week after week, layoffs mounted as organizations regretfully shed the very people they had fought so hard to hire in the first place. Even the most highly sought-after workers—IT whiz kids who had practically been able to write their own ticket just a year or two before—were out on the streets, Starbucks coffee in one hand, resume in the other.

In the midst of these dismal times, a number of trends began taking shape, converging on the workplace in a relatively short period of time. And these nascent trends will loom large in the future. Changes in birthrates, retirement trends, and job requirements will drastically reduce the size of the workforce, creating significant skill shortages. Eased trade barriers, communications advances, and the knowledge economy will produce a highly global and virtual workforce. Loosened cultural norms, higher minority birthrates, and relaxed migration barriers will create a vastly diverse workforce. Meanwhile, the knowledge economy, information technologies, and a changed employment contract will give rise to the most autonomous and empowered group of workers ever.

Together, these trends will not only reignite the war for talent, they will drive the most sweeping workforce changes in decades, radically changing the rules for people management in the process. Only by understanding the intricacies of each trend will organizations be able to fully comprehend what the near future holds for them in terms of talent management, allowing them to begin putting appropriate "combat strategies" in place.

UNSTOPPABLE TREND 1: THE INCREDIBLE SHRINKING WORKFORCE

After years of struggling to identify kinder, gentler ways of performing painful workforce reductions, employers find themselves standing on the brink of an immense and potentially long-term struggle to fill job openings. This 180-degree turnabout comes as the result of a host of phenomena, which—when brought together—promise to have a dramatic effect on both the sheer number of available workers, as well as the skill sets of those who remain in the workforce.

Across the world's industrialized nations, working-age populations have shrunk—the combined result of naturally smaller, middle-aged population segments and the growing popularity of early retirement programs. Encouraged by favorable pension schemes and growing affluence, mature people are fleeing the workforce in droves—visions of golf courses, exotic vacations, and hours spent penning the "Great American Novel" dancing in their heads. Across Europe, fully half of the male population aged 55 to 64 has already stopped working,[1] and by 2050, it's estimated that one in three Europeans will have retired.[2] Much sooner, employers will suffer the mass exodus of baby boomers—the roughly 76 million people born between 1946 and 1964. While it would usually make sense to look to the next generation to pick up the slack, that's not an option in this case. That's because Generation X is small (51 million) by comparison, the result of a widespread population bust among developed nations from 1965 to 1976.

The results of this trend will be dramatic. In the United States alone, it is estimated there will be 10 million more jobs than workers by the year 2010.[3] In other developed nations the impact will be felt even sooner and much more intensely, due in part to highly restrictive immigration policies. By the time this trend hits bottom, it is estimated that member nations of the Organization for Economic Cooperation and Development (OECD) will have suffered a combined reduction in their working-age populations of 65 million people.[4]

Some relief will be found in alternate labor pools, such as mature workers, women, and the disabled. The greatest relief, however, will arrive in the form of Generation Y—by definition, those born between 1977 and 1994—which is expected to have fully entered the workforce by the year 2016. Stacking up just shy of 73 million, Generation Y is much closer in size to the baby boomer generation than to Generation X, promising significant relief for worker shortages—at least in terms of numbers.

While the arrival of Generation Y may generate enough warm bodies to make up for the pending dearth of middle-aged and mature workers, that doesn't mean they can simply step in and replace their seasoned predecessors. This new crop of workers may boast more advanced technical skills, but they don't possess the irreplaceable knowledge or experience of the departing boomers. In today's information economy, knowledge is the new currency, and the majority of new jobs require substantial expertise. Unfortunately, growth in worker educational attainment is falling woefully short. Over the next decade, just 23 million people are expected to graduate from U.S.-based colleges. That's seven million shy of the number it's been estimated that organizations will need.[5] As if workforce education wasn't inadequate enough, many organizations are shooting themselves in the foot by cutting back on corporate training programs at the same time. These skill shortages will create an intense global competition for the most valuable talent.

Unstoppable Trend 2: The Anywhere, Anytime Workforce

"Looking for work"—traditionally, that phrase meant searching for a job in the area one calls home, or at the very most within a reasonable commuting distance. These days, it carries a very different connotation, as the geographic boundaries that long surrounded the workforce are crumbling fast. No longer are workers limited to marketing their skills solely within one country or region. Free-market economic reforms and technological advancements have made it possible for people to sell their services to any employer, in any location, anywhere around the globe. Where you are matters little.

Naturally, this trend means different things to different people, depending on their own personal situations. For some, it means a welcome opportunity to globe-trek, working in a number of locations—perhaps for a number of employers—around the world. Indeed, studies have shown worker mobility and migration are on the rise, as people today are far less likely than previous generations to remain in one physical location throughout their careers. Over the past 40 years, in fact, global migration of both less skilled and highly skilled workers has doubled.[6] Among developed nations, the United States is by far the biggest recipient of labor inflows, although other nations are likely to increase their share of migrant labor in an attempt to mitigate the impacts of domestic talent shortages.

That's not to suggest that everyone wants to spend his or her career moving from place to place, dealing with culture shock, language differences, and the other challenges of expatriate life. Many workers have shown themselves to be quite content staying put. A growing number have even gone so far as to become "electronic immigrants," working in another country without actually changing residence, much less citizenship.

Workers aren't the only ones benefiting from crumbling workplace geographic boundaries. Low-cost communication technologies and rising education levels have made it not only possible, but advantageous for organizations to move the work itself around the globe in search of lower operating costs. Consequently, a number of functions, including information technology (IT), human resources (HR), finance, accounting, and call center support, are increasingly being performed in countries in the Asia-Pacific region and Eastern Europe, which boast large populations of college-educated workers, along with low labor and operational costs.

This controversial practice, known as offshoring or strategic sourcing, is primarily an American phenomenon with three-fourths of offshored jobs currently originating in the United States. Other nations are expected to hop on the bandwagon, however, as the trend toward offshoring continues picking up steam. Over the next three years, the number of jobs moved offshore is expected to double. By the end of the decade, that number will grow 30 to 40 percent, as the jobs being sent offshore will become increasingly sophisticated.[7]

Along with the rise in offshoring comes a rise in concerns about its negative impacts on the workforce, as the practice has reportedly boosted worker stress and competition while diminishing worker engagement. These concerns aren't about to put the brakes on the trend, however, as the failure to offshore is increasingly equated with a significantly diminished competitive advantage.

UNSTOPPABLE TREND 3: THE 24/7 VIRTUAL WORKPLACE

Wireless phones, high-speed broadband connections, personal digital assistants; these technological advancements, combined with the growing amount of work products that can be transmitted electronically, have completely redefined the concepts of *workplace* and *workday*. No longer tied to a specific physical location—nor to a fixed work schedule—people are spending an increasing amount of time working in cars or hotel rooms, at client sites or at home, even while on vacation. Freed from their desks and relieved of their traditional nine-to-five schedules, these people switch back and forth from work to nonwork activities in a seemingly effortless fashion. Multitasking like never before, they can be found responding to e-mails while waiting at the dentist's office and logging back in to work after putting the kids to bed.

This trend is definitely on the rise. According to a recent survey, senior executives cited "a significant upsurge in remote working."[8] Over the next two years alone, the number of companies with employees who work from home on a regular basis is expected to rise an astonishing 26 points—from 54 to 80 percent.[9]

As more people begin working from disparate locations, the term *co-worker* is being completely redefined as well. No longer limited to the person in the next cubicle or the office down the hall, a co-worker may be someone located on the opposite side of the planet. Online news groups, discussion forums, and social networks are making many geographic, social, and even corporate barriers obsolete. Increasingly, workers are part of a global talent supply chain, connected via the latest communications technologies, and participating in virtual teams comprised of the best employees from around the world. With ease, they connect and collaborate with colleagues at all levels of the organization—even with the CEO.

Essentially on call 24/7, this next generation workforce sees no limit to their jobs. But while some workers find great satisfaction in this new level of work/life synchronization, it only serves to foster unhealthy workaholic tendencies for others. They are afraid to slow down or disconnect from work for fear of losing job security in an increasingly global labor market. The consequences of such fear-induced dedication can be dire, in that it often produces tired, depressed, mistake-prone, unproductive, resentful employees, who burn out far too soon.[10] This creates quite a challenge for managers, who suddenly find themselves overseeing a workforce they rarely see. Unfortunately, most have been given little, if any, guidance on how to engage a dispersed, virtual, and diverse team.

UNSTOPPABLE TREND 4: THE ULTRADIVERSE WORKFORCE

Still reeling from the on-the-job clashes that took place between baby boomers and Gen Xers? As the saying goes, "You ain't seen nothin' yet!"

These days, there are more generations in the workplace than ever before, as people enter the workforce earlier and stay later. Fully 70 percent of Generation Y members are already in the American workplace in some capacity,[11] and a similar trend has been observed in Europe.[12] At the other end of the spectrum, mature workers—motivated by longer life expectancies, changing cultural expectations, and the availability of knowledge and service work— are staying in the workforce longer. Impelled by the need for income—as well as something to keep them busy—increasing numbers of people in the 50- to 70-year-old range are returning to the workforce. And they're doing so long-term. In the United States, new hires over the age of 55 are staying on the job an average of 15 years after being brought onboard.[13] Fully 80 percent of U.S. boomers expect to keep working past age 65.[14] While older workers in other countries are not yet employed to such an extent, it's only a matter of time before this trend becomes global. While over the long haul this trend will not be enough to solve the talent shortage, it will be enough to change the generational dynamics of the workplace.

For most employers, that translates into the potential for members of three generations—baby boomer, Generation X, and the incoming Generation Y—to all butt heads at once. Already, there's been an increase in discrimination claims, attributed to the unprecedented number of generations in the workplace. In the United States, for example, age discrimination claims rose from 14,000 in 1999 to 20,000 in 2002.[15] In the United Kingdom, age discrimination now ranks as the country's top workplace discrimination claim.[16]

Loosened cultural norms and economic necessity have already led women to enter the workforce in significant numbers. According to the International Labor Organization (ILO), women already represent 40 percent of the global workforce. In the developed world, 70 percent of women are engaged in paid employment. Amazingly, that number stands at 60 percent in the developing world.[17] Across OECD nations, female participation in the labor force is only expected to rise. In the United States, according to the Bureau of Labor Statistics, women's share of the labor force was 46.4 percent in 2004 and is projected to be 46.8 percent in 2014,[18] with a similar trend predicted for most EU-15 member nations.[19]

It's no longer just single women entering the workforce "until the right man comes along," either. Across the board, female participation is up— among both married and single women, as well as those with and without children. As more women enter the workforce, members of both sexes are entering occupations once considered gender-specific. Increasingly, men are taking on traditionally female roles, becoming nurses, secretaries, librarians, nannies, preschool teachers, paralegals, and typists. Women, meanwhile, are participating in all industries, professions, and job levels.

At the same time that the workforce roles of men and women are intermingling, ethnic minority birthrates are increasing, while majority birthrates are declining. As a result, minorities have become the fastest growing segment of the U.S. labor force. If migration patterns and birthrates live up to predictions, Hispanics, African-Americans, and Asian-Americans are expected to make up nearly 40 percent of the American workforce by the year 2025.[20]

The next generation workforce is diverse not only in terms of demographic characteristics, such as age and ethnicity, but also in terms of lifestyle and life patterns. These days, fewer workers are partaking in the traditional progression through life stages—education, work and family, followed by leisure. Instead, they are mixing up the pattern, juggling, repeating, and changing stages, more frequently in a lifetime. Older workers are staying on the job into their retirement years. Workers of all ages are departing their jobs for sabbaticals at different points in their careers. Parents are temporarily leaving the workforce while raising young children. And seasoned workers are going back to school while staying on the job.

UNSTOPPABLE TREND 5:
THE IN-CHARGE WORKFORCE

No longer are people content to stay with one employer from cradle to grave, only to be rewarded with a gold watch and pension upon reaching their golden years. Empowered by technological and economic forces, today's workers, especially those with critical knowledge and skills, have taken the driver's seat when it comes to controlling the direction and substance of their professional lives.

Boasting expertise that is not shared by management—not to mention a wealth of competitive intelligence and business trend information easily accessible via the Internet—they possess the skills and the desire to be self-sufficient on the job, making them the logical decision makers in many areas. Meanwhile, corporate layoffs have pushed many workers into free agency— at least temporarily. As the economy rebounds, many free agents will again seek traditional employment. However, they will now have newfound skills and desires for self-management that they did not possess prior to the economic downturn. This gives them the capacity for greater authority both on the job and in the job market.

These highly sought-after workers are not only ripe for the picking by headhunters and competitors, they are expert job seekers as well. The increasingly knowledge-intensive nature of jobs has given most workers the skills they need to be proficient at finding, evaluating, and responding to employment information on the Web. And there's certainly no shortage of information readily available at the click of a mouse. On the contrary, most workers have access to unprecedented amounts of high-quality employment information, ranging from specific job openings, compensation and benefits comparisons, and career paths. They are even able to obtain inside information on potential employers from current and former employees who've chosen to share the details of their employment experiences online with anyone who cares to read about them.

As employees are no longer limited to one corporation or career path as their sole route to promotion or increased rewards, the act of searching the external job market is, likewise, no longer considered the mark of a problem employee. Indeed, it has come to be viewed as a sign of business acumen. These days it has become the norm for workers to continuously comparison shop the electronic job market for better opportunities. Using their new-found employment intelligence, workers actively bargain with employers and switch jobs when they find a better deal. As the job market improves, this trend is expected to become even more acute. One survey found that 83 percent of workers are "extremely" or "somewhat" likely to search for a new job when the economy gets stronger.[21]

IMPLICATIONS FOR TALENT MANAGEMENT

As the next generation workforce takes hold, traditional talent management practices—designed for an abundant, isolated, homogenous, employer-dependent workforce—will be rendered grossly insufficient, possibly even detrimental to the bottom line. While this scenario may seem daunting, even insurmountable, the good news is that it's not hopeless. There are a number of things that can be done, should be done, and in some cases, are already being done to address the demands of the new workforce. Let's take a close look at these new approaches to talent management and discover how they are already making a difference for several pioneering organizations.

Implication 1: Get the Talent Forecast and Workforce Strategy Right

Managing the next generation of talent effectively requires that organizations use sophisticated talent forecasting techniques to craft talent strategies that build long-term value. To do so, organizations must bid adieu to after-the-fact HR measurement and reactive workforce management and instead embrace such proactive approaches as predictive workforce monitoring and strategic talent decision making to anticipate and fulfill future talent needs.

By definition, workforce monitoring entails tracking broad workplace trends and gathering information on workforce demographics, attitudes, behaviors, and skills. When used properly, it can provide sufficient lead time for acting on opportunities and challenges. At Pacificorp, for example, workforce monitoring revealed that a whopping 80 percent of the workforce would be eligible for retirement within the next 15 years. Because this fact was discovered early, there was adequate time to implement a graduate recruitment and onboarding process for attracting and retaining young talent.[22]

When it comes to taking action on the issues and opportunities identified through workforce monitoring, organizations have a variety of strategic decision-making techniques at their fingertips. By measuring at-risk talent—those employees with a higher likelihood of leaving the organization—business consulting giant Deloitte Consulting determined that it needed to retain 40 percent of its retirement-eligible partners.[23] Decision makers may also employ measures of "pivotal talent," determining how behavioral changes among certain key employee groups could impact productivity in any given quarter. Using this strategy, office furniture manufacturer Steelcase Inc. identified the need to either retain or do succession planning for a top executive with significant expertise and a deep relationship base.[24]

CASE STUDY: FACING FUTURE STAFFING CHALLENGES

The Amerada Hess Corporation faced a potential talent gap that was symptomatic of the entire energy industry. Not only were the majority of its petroleum geologists and engineers rapidly approaching retirement age, but the U.S. education system was not producing enough qualified replacements. The time had come to take action. Seeking to better forecast and plan for future workforce needs, the leading global energy company created the Organizational Capability (OC) function. Dedicated to forecasting and planning for future workforce needs, the OC Group monitors data associated with workforce attrition (for example, education, retirement age, time spent in a given role, experience with

Hess, etc.), as well as prospective talent requirements. They consider how each line of business is evolving and what jobs at Hess will look like in the future. In addition to helping develop current and newly hired employees, the group identifies sources for procuring the best talent, thus helping the lines of business better prepare to meet changing global talent demands.

> —June 2004 interview with Robert Vogel,
> former Director of Organizational Capability,
> and Steve Stulbaum, former manager,
> Human Resource Development and
> Organizational Capability Process,
> Amerada Hess Corporation

Implication 2: Revitalize the Talent Entry Process

When tackling the challenges associated with sourcing the next generation workforce, organizations will have no choice but to abandon the rigid and reactive staffing practices of the past. Instead, they must revitalize their talent entry processes by adopting more flexible, anticipatory talent sourcing strategies and leveraging a broader spectrum of workers and employment relationships. A number of organizations are already ahead of the game, including Home Depot Inc., which has partnered with AARP (formerly the American Association of Retired Persons), Aspira Association, Hispanic Association of Colleges and Universities, and the U.S. Department of Defense, among others, for employee referrals.[25] Monsanto Company has established a Resource Reentry Center that allows full-time employees who have exited the organization in good standing to reapply for part-time positions after six months.[26] And IBM has effectively leveraged the skills of disabled workers, utilizing them in key positions, such as software engineering, marketing, and IT architecture.[27]

Traditional, one-size-fits-all employment offers simply won't work for the new breed of talent. This heavily diversified workforce, in short supply and empowered to switch jobs, will require and—in many cases, demand—customized reward and development offerings. Diversified Brazilian company Semco attracts talent by offering a flexible rewards program in which employees actually determine their own compensation levels. The company keeps amounts in check by providing detailed financial information upon which employees are encouraged to base their salaries.[28]

Organizations will also rely on a variety of nonstandard employment relationships, ranging from part-time work and telecommuting to temporary workers and free agents. JetBlue Airways Corporation demonstrated the value of nonstandard employment by offering remote work opportunities for call center representatives, many of whom are at-home moms working part-time. With this strategy, the low-fare airline eliminated call center expenses, while boosting productivity and retention in what's traditionally a high-turnover position.[29]

CASE STUDY: MAXIMIZING THE VALUE OF OLDER EMPLOYEES

It's hard to imagine that employee loyalty could ever pose a problem, but when retention is so high that the workforce grows old with the company, the prospect of mass retirement becomes all too real. That's the situation faced by SAS Institute Inc., the world's leader in business analytics software. Over the years, management has worked hard to make the Cary, North Carolina–based company the kind of place that people want to work. Employees enjoy a sprawling campus, on-site fitness center, on-site family medical care, two company-sponsored on-site child care facilities, a subsidized on-site café, break rooms stocked with food, private offices for everyone, a 35-hour workweek, and flexible scheduling.

The company has been rewarded handsomely for its efforts—with greater employee loyalty, higher motivation, and higher productivity. In an industry that averages 20 to 25 percent turnover, SAS's turnover rate stands at a meager 3 percent. Granted, this saves a significant amount of money and effort related to hiring. However, it also presents significant challenges related to managing an aging workforce, many of whom have been with the company since its founding in 1976. Jeff Chambers, Vice President of Human Resources, describes the situation aptly: "As the company grows, our population stays here. No one ever leaves. That does pose some challenges over time."

Recognizing the wealth of intellectual capital and corporate memory possessed by SAS's older workers, Chambers has set out to create a win–win relationship for both SAS and its longtime employees. He is testing a new value proposition—providing older workers with attractive retirement options— and trying out ideas such as day care for grandchildren and part-time and seasonal hours.

> —August 2004 interview with Jeff Chambers,
> Vice President of Human Resources, and
> Betty Silver, Director of SAS University,
> SAS Institute Inc., and Ellen Bankert, Mary
> Dean Lee, and Candice Lange, SAS Institute,
> The Wharton Work/Life Roundtable,
> Wharton Work/Life Integration Project,
> University of Pennsylvania, 2000

Implication 3: Treat Talent Well

The new generation of talent is one that will likely experience greater organizational stress, conflict, and dissatisfaction and have more power to take action in the form of changing employers or withholding valuable knowledge and effort. To keep this talent pool working and motivated, organizations will need to go above and beyond in terms of creating work environments where all employees are respected, valued and provided meaningful work.

Threats to employee engagement are mounting, as the next generation workforce faces immense stress resulting from global competition for jobs, growing responsibility for their own careers, and expanding life choices. Recognizing the adverse implications of stress on employee productivity leaders need to reinvent the work style and schedule by offering employees more choice of where and when to do their work. Semco president Ricardo Semler explains the practice: "People want to work when work is not the enemy of personal freedom and legitimate self-interest."[30] Thus sprouts up programs like Cigna Insurance's E★Work, allowing employees to "work wherever work occurs," whether it's at home, the office, or even a coffee shop.[31]

At the same time, organizations seeking to motivate and retain their talent will need to build unifying and compassionate cultures that minimize self-interest and promote collectivist values, while rewarding collaborative contributions and minimizing stress caused by work/life conflict. Emphasizing commonalities among workers—such as the need to make a living and the desire to participate in fulfilling work—organizations will reinforce organizational belonging over individual difference. At Cincinnati Bell Inc., for example, diversity is not emphasized because it calls attention to worker differences, as opposed to worker similarities. Likewise, the telecom provider does not use employee affinity groups because they highlight divisions between employees and take away from the company's culture of inclusion.[32]

Implication 4: Embrace New Age Leadership

No longer solely the privilege of executives and managers, leadership will increasingly be viewed as an action any worker or group of workers can take to meet the needs of a specific business situation. This is already the preeminent operating philosophy at The AES Corporation, one of the world's largest electric companies, where one of the biggest decisions in company history— to buy a power station—was not made by the CEO or the board of directors, but by an employee whose tenure with AES stood at less than two years.[33]

Likewise, Whole Foods Market Inc., the world's largest retailer of natural and organic foods, operates under a similar philosophy: "Decisions should be made closest to the place they will be carried out, should directly involve the people affected, and should leave out people who aren't involved."[34]

Some organizations will go beyond decentralization to incorporate elements of democracy into their decision-making practices. At Whole Foods, all new-hire candidates work a 30-day trial period in one of the store's departments. The entire department then votes on whether to employ the candidate.[35] At Semco, meanwhile, each department has a representative on the board of trustees. Furthermore, at each board meeting, two of Semco's nine board seats are available for any employee who signs up.[36]

At many organizations, this kind of decentralized decision making will give way to much less hierarchical organizational structures, such as that which already exists at W. L. Gore & Associates Inc., manufacturer of Gore-Tex fabric. Founder Bill Gore created a flat, lattice organization in which there are no chains of command or predetermined channels of communication. Titles are nonexistent, beyond that of president and secretary of the company—both of which are required by law. Management is everyone's job, and Gore employees "manage" by finding other employees willing to work with them.[37]

With the advent of distributed leadership, a radically transformed leadership model is emerging in which executives and managers stop commanding and start promoting a common organizational mission, using their passion for the business to excite employees and ensuring that employees understand how they can contribute to the organizational mission.

FINAL FOCUS

The workforce is in the midst of an unstoppable and dramatic transformation. In the coming years, organizations will confront challenges related to demographic trends, global mobility, diversity, work/life issues, technology changes, and a virtual workforce. Competition will be global; capital will be abundant; leaders will be developed swiftly; and talented people will be keen to change jobs frequently. These changes will influence how work is performed, where it is performed and what skills are required. While other resources will be abundant, the most important resource of all—talent—will become increasingly scarce. Organizations must ask themselves: Are we prepared for this new global workforce revolution? Do we have the right strategies in place?

Recognizing the inevitable and profound changes that will impact the workforce of the future, we embarked on a major research effort to identify the trends and characteristics of the emerging workforce. Our research revealed that as corporations redefine their rules of engagement to face these seismic business challenges they will also need to be prepared for the new global workforce revolution.

This book provides rich insights into the real workforce challenges facing the organizations in the twenty-first century and offers a coherent and focused approach on its implications for talent management. It draws from the experience of the field's premier trailblazers to present a typology of strategies and solutions for successfully confronting new talent challenges to drive productivity and growth. The chapters in this book are organized by common themes or related concepts into four broad sections represented as having talent management implications in this preface. These sections are:

- Get the Talent Forecast and Workforce Strategy Right.
- Revitalize the Talent Entry Processes.
- Treat Talent Well.
- Embrace New Age Leadership.

We hope that the chapters provide new thinking and jolt your perception on the key talent imperatives that should be the focus as you lead your organization into the future.

—Robert Gandossy, Elissa Tucker, and Nidhi Verma

ACKNOWLEDGMENTS

The Greek epic poet Homer once said that "Light is the task where many share the toil." Indeed, it required many hands to make this light work.

Any topic that is as broad as this one incurs many debts. We wish to thank the hard work and generosity of all those who made it possible—approving the concept, writing compelling chapters, managing author contributions, addressing legal issues, proofreading, publishing, and much, much more.

First and foremost, we are indebted to our authors. We have engaged leading thought leaders with a global perspective on a very complex and challenging issue—the emerging workforce. We'd like to thank them for sharing their thoughts in this book.

We'd also like to thank Matt Holt and his team at John Wiley & Sons, Inc. At Hewitt, we'd like to offer our gratitude to John Anderson for his leadership and trust in our ability to make it happen. Once again, we are thankful to Don Minner for always supporting us and helping in countless ways. Diana Reace helped with the editing and made her research team available to pitch in when they were needed. Dan Dreger and Kim Duffey helped pave the way on legal matters. Others at Hewitt who helped with the many things that go into an effort like this include Julie Offord, Karen Wong, Suzanne Zagata-Meraz, Silvana Medvegy, and Robin Guarnieri.

Special thanks once again go to Julie Cook Ramirez. We've worked with Julie for a number of years now and her writing and editing have been outstanding.

Royalties for this book will be donated to The Drucker Foundation and Junior Achievement. We'd like to thank them all for the good they do for many.

The spirit of open collaboration and collegiality are the greatest strengths of Hewitt Associates and this could not have been more evident on this project. Thank you all for helping us create this light for the business and HR community.

RPG
ET
NV

INTRODUCTION

ABUNDANCE, ASIA, AND AUTOMATION

DANIEL H. PINK

RETURN WITH me to the thrilling days of yesteryear—the 1970s, the decade of my childhood. When I was a kid, middle-class parents in the United States typically dished out the same plate of advice to their children: Get good grades, go to college, and pursue a profession that will deliver a decent standard of living and perhaps a dollop of prestige. If you were good at math and science, you should become a doctor. If you were better at English and history, become a lawyer. If blood grossed you out and your verbal skills needed work, become an accountant. A bit later, as computers appeared on desktops and CEOs on magazine covers, the youngsters who were really good at math and science chose high tech, while many others flocked to business school, thinking that success was spelled "M.B.A."

Lawyers, doctors, accountants, engineers, and executives. The great Peter Drucker gave this cadre of professionals an enduring, if somewhat wonky, name: "knowledge workers." Knowledge workers are "people who get paid for putting to work what one learns in school rather than for their physical strength or manual skill," Drucker wrote. What distinguished this group from the rest of the workforce was their "ability to acquire and to apply theoretical and analytic knowledge." (In other words, they excelled at left-brained or L-directed thinking.) They might never become a majority, said Drucker, but they nonetheless "will give the emerging knowledge society its character, its leadership, its social profile."[1]

Drucker, as was his habit, was spot-on. Knowledge workers and their thinking style have indeed shaped the character, leadership, and social profile of the modern age. Consider the tollbooths that any middle-class American must pass on his way to the land of knowledge work. Here are some examples: the PSAT, the SAT, the GMAT, the LSAT, the MCAT. Notice any similarity beyond the final two initials? These instruments all measure what is essentially undiluted L-directed thinking. They require logic and analysis—and reward test takers for zeroing in, computer-like, on a single correct answer. The exercise is linear, sequential, and bounded by time. You answer one question with one right answer. Then you move to the next question and the next and the next until time runs out. These tests have become important gatekeepers for entry into meritocratic, middle-class society. They've created an SAT-ocracy—a regime in which access to the good life depends on the ability to reason logically, sequentially, and speedily. And this is not just an American phenomenon. From entrance exams in the United Kingdom to cram schools in Japan, most developed nations have devoted considerable time and treasure to producing left-brained knowledge workers.

This arrangement has been a rousing success. It has broken the stranglehold of aristocratic privilege and opened educational and professional opportunities to a diverse set of people. It has propelled the world economy and lifted living standards. But the SAT-ocracy is now in its dying days. The L-directed thinking it nurtures and rewards still matters, of course. But it's no longer enough. Today, we're moving into an era in which right-brained (R-directed) thinking will increasingly determine who gets ahead.

To some of you, this is delightful news. To others, it sounds like a crock. This chapter is mainly for the latter group of readers—those who followed your parents' advice and scored well on those aptitude tests. To persuade you that what I'm saying is sound, let me explain the reasons for this shift using the left-brain, mechanistic language of cause and effect. The effect: the diminished relative importance of L-directed thinking and the corresponding increased importance of R-directed thinking. The causes: abundance, Asia, and automation.

ABUNDANCE

Another vignette from the 1970s: Every August my mother would take my brother, my sister, and me to buy clothes for the new school year. That inevitably meant a trip to Eastland Mall, one of three big shopping centers in central Ohio. Inside the mall we'd visit a national department store such as Sears or JCPenney or a local one such as Lazarus, where the children's department featured maybe a dozen racks of clothing from which to choose. The rest of the mall consisted of about 30 other stores, smaller in size and selection, lined up between the department store anchors. Like most Americans of the time, we considered Eastland and those other climate-controlled enclosed shopping centers the very zenith of modern plenty.

My own kids would consider it underwhelming. Within a 20-minute drive of our home in Washington, D.C., are about 40 different mega-shopping sites—the size, selection, and scope of which didn't exist 30 years ago. Take Potomac Yards, which sits on Route 1 in northern Virginia. One Saturday morning in August, my wife and I and our three children drove there for our own back-to-school shopping excursion. We began at the giant store on the far end of the site. In the women's section of that store, we chose from Mossimo designer tops and sweaters, Merona blazers, Isaac Mizrahi jackets, and Liz Lange designer maternity wear. The kids' clothing section was equally vast and almost as hip. The Italian designer Mossimo had a full line of children's wear—including velour pants and jacket sets for our two girls. The choices were preposterously more interesting, more attractive, and more bountiful than the clothing I chose from back in the 1970s. But there was something even more noteworthy about this stylish kiddie garb when I compared it to the more pedestrian fashions of my youth: The clothes cost less, because we weren't at some swank boutique. My family and I were shopping at Target. That velour Mossimo ensemble? $14.99. Those women's designer tops? $9.99. My wife's new suede Isaac Mizrahi jacket? $49.00. A few aisles away were home furnishings, created by designer Todd Oldham and less expensive than what my parents used to pick up at Sears. Throughout the store were acres of good-looking, low-cost merchandise.

And Target was just one of an array of Potomac Yards stores catering to a mostly middle-class clientele. Next door we could visit Staples, a 20,000-square-foot box selling 7,500 different school and office supplies. (There are more than 1,500 Staples stores like it in the United States and Europe.) Next to Staples was the equally cavernous PETsMART, one of more than 600 such pet supply stores in the United States and Canada, each one of which, on an average day, sells $15,000 worth of merchandise for nonhumans.[2] This particular outlet even had its own pet-grooming studio. Next to PETsMART was Best Buy, an electronics emporium with a retail floor that's larger than the entire block on which my family lives. One section was devoted to home theater equipment, which displayed an arms race of televisions—plasma, high-definition, flat-panel—that began with a 42-inch screen and escalated to 47-inch, 50-inch, 54-inch, 56-inch, and 65-inch versions. In the telephone section were, by my count, 39 different varieties of cordless phones. And these four stores constituted only about one-third of the entire shopping facility.

But what's so remarkable about Potomac Yards is how utterly unremarkable it is. You can find a similar swath of consumer bounty just about anyplace in the United States—and, increasingly, in Europe and sections of Asia as well. These shopping meccas are but one visible example of an extraordinary change in modern life. For most of history, our lives were defined by scarcity. Today, the defining feature of social, economic, and cultural life in much of the world is abundance.

Our left brains have made us rich. Powered by armies of Drucker's knowledge workers, the information economy has produced a standard of living in much of the developed world that would have been unfathomable to our great-grandparents.

A few examples of our abundant era:

- During much of the twentieth century, the aspiration of most middle-class Americans was to own a home and a car. Now more than two out of three Americans own the homes in which they live. (In fact, some 13 percent of homes purchased today are second homes.)[3] As for autos, today the United States has more cars than licensed drivers—which means that, on average, everybody who can drive has a car of his own.[4]
- Self-storage—a business devoted to providing people a place to house their extra stuff—has become a $17 billion annual industry in the United States, larger than the motion picture business. What's more, the industry is growing at an even faster rate in other countries.[5]
- When we can't store our many things, we just throw them away. As business writer Polly LaBarre notes, "The United States spends more on trash bags than 90 other countries spend on everything. In other words, the receptacles of our waste cost more than all of the goods consumed by nearly half of the world's nations."[6]

But abundance has produced an ironic result: the very triumph of L-directed thinking has lessened its significance. The prosperity it has unleashed has placed a premium on less rational, more R-directed sensibilities—beauty, spirituality, emotion. For businesses, it's no longer enough to create a product that's reasonably priced and adequately functional. It must also be beautiful, unique, and meaningful, abiding by what author Virginia Postrel calls "the aesthetic imperative."[7] Perhaps the most telling example of this change, as our family outing to Target demonstrated, is the new middle-class obsession with design. World-famous designers such as the ones I mentioned earlier, as well as titans such as Karim Rashid and Philippe Starck, now design all manner of goods for this quintessentially middle-class, middle-brow, middle-American store. Target and other retailers have sold nearly three million units of Rashid's Garbo molded polypropylene wastebasket. A designer wastebasket! Try explaining that one to your left brain.

Or how about the item that I purchased during that same Target trip? It's a toilet brush—a toilet brush designed by Michael Graves, a Princeton University architecture professor and one of the most renowned architects and product designers in the world. The cost: $5.99. Only against a backdrop of abundance could so many people seek beautiful trash cans and toilet brushes—converting mundane, utilitarian products into objects of desire.

In an age of abundance, appealing only to rational, logical, and functional needs is woefully insufficient. Engineers must figure out how to get things to work. But if those things are not also pleasing to the eye or compelling to the soul, few will buy them. There are too many other options. Mastery of design, empathy, play, and other seemingly "soft" aptitudes is now the main way for individuals and firms to stand out in a crowded marketplace.

Abundance elevates R-directed thinking another important way as well. When I'm on my deathbed, it's unlikely that I'll look back on my life and say, "Well, I've made some mistakes. But at least I snagged one of those Michael Graves toilet brushes back in 2004." Abundance has brought beautiful things to our lives, but that bevy of material goods has not necessarily made us much happier. The paradox of prosperity is that while living standards have risen steadily decade after decade, personal, family, and life satisfaction haven't budged. That's why more people—liberated by prosperity but not fulfilled by it—are resolving the paradox by searching for meaning. As Columbia University's Andrew Delbanco puts it, "The most striking feature of contemporary culture is the unslaked craving for transcendence."[8]

Visit any moderately prosperous community in the advanced world and along with the plenteous shopping opportunities, you can glimpse this quest for transcendence in action. From the mainstream embrace of once exotic practices such as yoga and meditation to the rise of spirituality in the workplace and evangelical themes in books and movies, the pursuit of purpose and meaning has become an integral part of our lives. People everywhere have moved from focusing on the day-to-day text of their lives to the broader context. Of course, material wealth hasn't reached everyone in the developed world, not to mention vast numbers in the less developed world. But abundance has freed literally hundreds of millions of people from the struggle for survival and, as Nobel Prize-winning economist Robert William Fogel writes, "made it possible to extend the quest for self-realization from a minute fraction of the population to almost the whole of it."[9]

On the off chance that you're still not convinced, let me offer one last and illuminating statistic. Electric lighting was rare a century ago, but today it's commonplace. Lightbulbs are cheap. Electricity is ubiquitous. Candles? Who needs them? Apparently, lots of people. In the United States, candles are a $2.4-billion-a-year business[10]—for reasons that stretch beyond the logical need for luminosity to a prosperous country's more inchoate desire for beauty and transcendence.

ASIA

Four people I met while researching this book are the very embodiment of the knowledge worker ethic I described at the outset of this chapter. Like many bright middle-class kids, they followed their parents' advice. They did well in high school, went on to earn either an engineering or computer science degree from a good university, and now work at a large software company, helping to write computer code for North American banks and airlines. For their high-tech work, none of these six people earns more than $14,000 a year.

Knowledge workers, meet your new competition: Srividya, Lalit, Kavita, and Kamal of Mumbai, India.

In recent years, few issues have generated more controversy or stoked more anxiety than outsourcing. These four programmers and their counterparts throughout India, the Philippines, and China are scaring the bejesus out of software engineers and other left-brain professionals in North America and Europe, triggering protests, boycotts, and plenty of political posturing. The computer programming they do, while not the most sophisticated that multinational companies need, is the sort of work that until recently was done almost exclusively in the United States—and that provided comfortable white-collar salaries of upward of $70,000 a year. Now 25-year-old Indians are doing it—just as well, if not better; just as fast, if not faster—for the wages of a Taco Bell counter jockey. Yet their pay, while paltry by Western standards, is roughly 25 times what the typical Indian earns—and affords them an upper middle-class lifestyle with vacations and their own apartments.

The programmers I met in Mumbai are but four well-educated drops in a global tsunami. Each year, India's colleges and universities produce about 350,000 engineering graduates.[11] That's one reason that more than half of the Fortune 500 companies now outsource software work to India."[12] For instance, about 48 percent of General Electric (GE)'s software is developed in India. The company employs a whopping 20,000 people there (and has even posted signs in its Indian offices reading "Trespassers will be recruited"). Hewlett-Packard employs several thousand software engineers in India. Siemens employs 3,000 computer programmers in India and is moving another 15,000 such jobs overseas. Oracle has a 5,000-person Indian staff. The large Indian information technology (IT) consultancy Wipro employs some 17,000 engineers who do work for Home Depot, Nokia, and Sony. And the list goes on. As the chief executive of GE India told London's *Financial Times*: "Any job that is English-based in markets such as the U.S., the U.K., and Australia can be done in India. The only limit is your imagination."[13] Indeed, active imaginations have already expanded India's professional ranks well beyond computer programmers. Financial services firms such as Lehman Brothers, Bear Stearns, Morgan Stanley, and JPMorgan Chase have contracted out number crunching and financial analysis to Indian MBAs.[14] The financial news service Reuters has offshored low-level editorial jobs. And throughout India, you'll find chartered accountants who prepare American tax returns, lawyers who do legal research for American lawsuits, and radiologists who read CAT scans for American hospitals.

But it's not just India. L-directed white-collar work of all sorts is migrating to other parts of the world as well. Motorola, Nortel, and Intel operate software development centers in Russia, where Boeing has also sent a large portion of its aerospace engineering work. The computer services giant Electronic Data Systems has software developers in Egypt, Brazil, and Poland. Meanwhile, Hungarian architects are drawing basic blueprints for California design firms. Philippine accountants are performing audits for CapGemini Ernst & Young. And the Dutch firm Philips Electronics N.V. employs some 700 engineers in China, a nation that is now producing nearly as many engineering graduates each year as the United States.[15]

The main reason is money. In the United States, a typical chip designer earns about $7,000 per month; in India, she earns about $1,000. In the United States, a typical aerospace engineer earns about $6,000 each month:

in Russia, his monthly salary is closer to $650. And while an accountant in the United States can earn $5,000 a month, an accountant in the Philippines brings in about $300 a month, no small sum in a country where the annual per capita income is $500.[16]

For these battalions of international knowledge workers, this new world order is a dream. But for white-collar, left-brain workers in Europe and North America, the implications are more nightmarish. For example:

- One out of 10 jobs in the U.S. computer, software, and IT industry will move overseas in the next two years. One in four IT jobs will be off-shored by 2010.[17]
- According to Forrester Research, "at least 3.3 million white-collar jobs and $136 billion in wages will shift from the U.S. to low-cost countries like India, China, and Russia" by 2015.[18]
- Nations such as Japan, Germany, and the United Kingdom will see similar job loss. The United Kingdom alone will lose some 25,000 IT jobs and upwards of 30,000 finance positions to India and other developing nations in the next few years. By 2015, Europe will lose 1.2 million jobs to offshore locales.[19]

Much of the anxiety over this issue outstrips the reality. We are not all going to lose our jobs tomorrow. Outsourcing is overhyped in the short term. But it's underhyped in the long term. As the cost of communicating with the other side of the globe falls essentially to zero, and as developing nations continue to mint millions of extremely capable knowledge workers, the working lives of North Americans, Europeans, and Japanese people will change dramatically. If standardized, routine L-directed work such as many kinds of financial analysis, radiology, and computer programming can be done for a lot less overseas and delivered to clients instantly via fiber-optic links, that's where the work will go. This upheaval will be difficult for many, but it's ultimately not much different from transitions we've weathered before. This is precisely what happened to routine mass production jobs, which moved across the oceans in the second half of the twentieth century. And just as those American factory workers had to master a new set of skills and learn how to bend pixels instead of steel, many of today's knowledge workers will likewise have to command a new set of aptitudes. They'll need to do what workers abroad cannot do equally well for much less money—using R-directed abilities such as forging relationships rather than executing transactions, tackling novel challenges instead of solving routine problems, and synthesizing the big picture rather than analyzing a single component.

AUTOMATION

Meet two more people. One is an iconic figure who may have been real. The other is a real human being who, perhaps to his regret, may become iconic.

The first is the fellow immortalized on a U.S. postage stamp.

As most American schoolchildren could tell you, John Henry was a steel-driving man. Born with a hammer in his hand, he was a figure of immense strength and integrity. (Alas, nobody is certain whether he was an actual person. Many historians believe he was a former slave who worked on the railroads after the Civil War, though none have been able to verify his existence.) He was part of a team of workers who smashed through mountains to clear tunnels for laying railroad tracks. But John Henry was no ordinary laborer. He could drive steel faster and more powerfully than any man alive, and his prowess soon became the stuff of legend.

One day, the tale goes, a salesman arrived at the workers' camp bearing a new steam-powered drill that he claimed could outperform even the strongest man. John Henry scoffed at the notion that gears and grease were any match for human muscle. So he proposed a contest—man versus machine—to see which could blast through a mountainside the fastest.

The next afternoon, the race began—the steam drill on the right, John Henry on the left. The machine took the lead, but John Henry quickly rallied. Chunks of rocks fell as the duo bored through their tunnels. Before long, John Henry had closed in on his competitor. And in an instant before the end of the race, he surged past the steam drill and broke through the other side of the mountain first. His fellow workers cheered. But John Henry, exhausted by the superhuman effort, collapsed. Then he died. The story spread. In ballads and books, John Henry's demise became a parable of the industrial age: Machines could now do some things better than human beings, and as a result a measure of human dignity had been sacrificed.

Now meet our second figure. Garry Kasparov is a chess grand master—the finest chess player of his generation and perhaps the greatest of all time. He's also the John Henry of our new age—a person whose seemingly superhuman prowess has been surpassed by a machine.

Kasparov won his first chess world championship in 1985, around the same time that several research teams began developing computer programs that could play chess. Over the next decade, Kasparov never lost a match. And in 1996, he defeated what was then the world's most powerful chess computer.

But in 1997, Kasparov took on an even more powerful machine, a 1.4-ton IBM supercomputer called Deep Blue, in a six-game match that some dubbed "the brain's last stand."[20] To the surprise of many, Deep Blue defeated Kasparov, the consequences of which the cover of *Inside Chess* magazine reduced to a single word: "Armageddon!"[21] Seeking vengeance—for himself and for all flesh-and-blood L-directed thinkers—Kasparov then arranged a rematch against another computer, Deep Junior, a still more potent Israeli computer that had thrice won the world computer chess championship.

Chess is in many ways the quintessential left-brain activity. It leaves relatively little room for emotion—and depends heavily on memory, rational thinking, and brute calculation, three things at which computers excel. Kasparov says that when he looks at the board, he can examine between one and three moves per second. Deep Junior is, uh, slightly more impressive. Each second, it analyzes between two and three million possible moves. Yet Kasparov believed that human beings had other advantages that would level the 64-square playing field.

On Super Bowl Sunday 2003, Kasparov strutted into the posh New York Downtown Athletic Club to begin another epic contest between man and machine—a six-game match with a million-dollar purse. Hundreds of fans watched in person. Millions more followed the action on the Internet. Kasparov won game one and settled for a draw in game two. In game three, he started strong, but on the edge of victory, he fell into one of Deep Junior's traps and lost. In game four, Kasparov played haltingly and eked out another draw, still so distraught over blowing game three that he admitted that he "couldn't sleep and lost confidence."[22] Game five was another draw, leaving the outcome of the match to the sixth and final game.

Kasparov quickly took the lead. As *Newsweek* later reported, "Against any human player, he would have moved aggressively and gone for the win. But he wasn't playing against a human." In his tentativeness, he made a slight mistake and that left him devastated in a way that an unfeeling machine would never be. Worse, having yielded the advantage he had no hope—as he would have had against a human—that his well-programmed opponent might make its own mistake and let him back in the game. The realization paralyzed even the great Kasparov, and it haunted him for the rest of the match.[23]

In the end, he settled for a draw—in this game and the entire match.[24]

Human beings have much to recommend, but when it comes to chess—and increasingly other endeavors that depend heavily on rule-based logic, calculation, and sequential thinking—computers are simply better, faster, and stronger. What's more, computers don't become fatigued. They don't get headaches. They don't choke under pressure or sulk over losses. They don't worry what the audience thinks or care what the press will say. They don't space out. They don't slip up. And that has humbled even the notoriously egomaniacal grand master. In 1987, Kasparov, then the chess world's enfant terrible, boasted: "No computer can ever beat me."[25] Today, Kasparov, now our modern John Henry, says: "I give us only a few years. Then they'll win every match, and we may have to struggle to win even a single game."[26]

Last century, machines proved they could replace human backs. This century, new technologies are proving they can replace human left brains. Management meta-guru Tom Peters puts it nicely, saying that for white-collar workers "software is a forklift for the mind." It won't eliminate every left-brain job. But it will destroy many and reshape the rest. Any job that depends on routines—that can be reduced to a set of rules or broken down into a set of repeatable steps—is at risk. If a $500-a-month Indian chartered accountant doesn't swipe your comfortable accounting job, TurboTax will.

Consider three heavily L-directed professions: computer programmers, physicians, and lawyers. "In the old days," says computer scientist Vernor Vinge, "anybody with even routine skills could get a job as a programmer. That isn't true anymore. The routine functions are increasingly being turned over to machines."[27] Indeed, a small British company called Appligenics has created software that can write software. Whereas a typical human being—whether the Indians I met or their higher-paid counterparts in the United States—can write about 400 lines of computer code per day, Appligenics applications can do the same work in less than a second.[28] The result: as the scut work gets off-loaded, engineers and programmers will have to master different aptitudes, relying more on creativity than competence, more on tacit knowledge than technical manuals, and more on fashioning the big picture than sweating the details.

Automation is also changing the work of many doctors. Much of medical diagnosis amounts to following a series of decision trees—Is it a dry cough or a productive one? Is the T-cell count above or below a certain level?—and honing in on the answer. Computers can process the binary logic of decision trees with a swiftness and accuracy humans can't begin to approach. So an array of software and online programs has emerged allowing patients to answer a series of questions on their computer screens and arrive at a preliminary diagnosis without the assistance of a physician. Health care consumers have begun to use such tools both to "figure out their risk of serious diseases—such as heart failure, coronary artery disease, and some of the most common cancers—[and] to make life-and-death treatment decisions once they are diagnosed," reports the *Wall Street Journal*.[29] At the same time, there has been an explosion of electronic databases of medical and health information. In a typical year, about 100 million people worldwide go online for health and medical information and visit more than 23,000 medical web sites.[30] As patients self-diagnose and tap the same reservoir of information available to physicians, these tools are transforming the doctor's role from omniscient purveyor of solutions to empathic adviser on options. Of course, the day-to-day work of physicians often involves challenges too complex for software alone—and we'll still rely on experienced doctors to diagnose unusual diseases. But these developments are changing the emphasis of many medical practices—away from routine, analytical, and information-based work and toward empathy, narrative medicine, and holistic care.

A similar pattern is unfolding in the legal profession. Dozens of inexpensive information and advice services are reshaping law practice. For instance, CompleteCase.com, which calls itself "the premier online uncontested divorce service center," will handle your divorce for a mere $249. At the same time, the Web is cracking the information monopoly that has long been the source of many lawyers' high incomes and professional mystique. Attorneys charge an average of $180 per hour. But many web sites—for instance, Lawvantage.com and MyCounsel.com—now offer basic legal forms and other documents for as little as $14.95. As *The New York Times* reports, "Instead of asking lawyers to draft contracts at a cost of several thousand dollars," clients now find the proper forms online—and then take "the generic documents to lawyers, who customize them at a cost of several hundred dollars apiece." The result, says the *Times*, is that the legal industry "may be on the verge of fundamental changes . . . [that] could reduce the demand for traditional services and force lawyers to lower fees."[31] The attorneys who remain will be those who can tackle far more complex problems and those who can provide something that databases and software cannot—counseling, mediation, courtroom storytelling, and other services that depend on R-directed thinking.

To recap, three forces are tilting the scales in favor of R-directed thinking. Abundance has satisfied, and even oversatisfied, the material needs of millions—boosting the significance of beauty and emotion and accelerating individuals' search for meaning. Asia is now performing large amounts of routine, white-collar, L-directed work at significantly lower costs, thereby forcing knowledge workers in the advanced world to master abilities that can't be shipped overseas. And automation has begun to affect this generation's white-collar workers in much the same way it did last generation's blue-collar workers, requiring L-directed professionals to develop aptitudes that computers can't do better, faster, or cheaper.

So what happens next? What happens to us as our lives get clipped by automation and Asia—and reconfigured by abundance?

PART I

GET THE TALENT FORECAST
AND WORKFORCE STRATEGY RIGHT

THE TALENT landscape has gone through significant transformation in recent years. A declining birth rate among virtually all developed nations has laid the foundation for a serious labor shortage, which inches closer day by day. Meanwhile, job dissatisfaction and employee alienation are on the rise, as fewer employees report feeling engaged at work and able to trust their management. At the same time, we've witnessed a rapid rise in outsourcing and offshoring, trends that certainly haven't helped employees feel any more secure about their jobs. All the while, organizations cling to conventional wisdom about people management, when conditions are clearly calling for a new direction in human capital planning. Unfortunately, most human resources (HR) and business leaders are not adequately equipped to predict and plan for the future.

In this section, the contributors call us to look beyond traditional people management strategies like behavioral studies and benchmarking, as typically practiced, arguing that "it is impossible to copy your way to the top." They contend that HR and business leaders must aspire to foresee trends in demographics, economics, technology, and politics, and consider how they might impact the future of business and employment. Rather than solely embracing best practices, they should develop best insights or best models by adopting an attitude open to learning, inquiry, and continually testing ideas. Doing so will also help them better recognize emerging problems, set appropriate priorities, and mobilize effective preventive responses.

CHAPTER 1

SOME HALF-TRUTHS
ABOUT MANAGING PEOPLE

A CALL FOR EVIDENCE-BASED MANAGEMENT

JEFFREY PFEFFER

THE WORLD of people management has changed dramatically in recent years. Virtually all industrialized economies now face a declining birth rate—in many places, below population replacement level, in fact. This means that not only are there likely to be shortages of labor in the coming decades, but the age composition of populations is shifting dramatically to a higher proportion of older people.

As if a looming worker shortage wasn't enough, job dissatisfaction and employee alienation are on the rise as well. Fewer employees report being engaged in their work, trusting their management, and being willing to provide the kind of discretionary effort and ideas that will help companies compete in a world of increasingly global competition. These changes in job attitudes and employee engagement aren't merely an American phenomenon, either. In fact, they pervade most industrialized economies.

Meanwhile, outsourcing and offshoring—the global search for best value in products, components, and business services—is accelerating, implying that

---

Some of the ideas in this chapter come from work with Robert I. Sutton on our forthcoming book, *Hard Facts, Dangerous Half-Truths, and Total Nonsense: Profiting from Evidence-Based Management* (Boston: Harvard Business School Press, 2006).

competition for both physical products and intellectual and creative services is intensifying.

In the midst of all this profound change, many companies continue clinging to conventional wisdom about how to manage human capital, and much of this conventional wisdom has become embedded in common management practices. Truth be told, much of it is either wrong or, at best, a half-truth—sometimes it's correct, but often it's at least partly incorrect. Because people tend to act on the basis of mental models, whether correct or fallacious, half-truths, bad assumptions, and incorrect models of organizational and human performance get in the way of companies living up to their full potentials.

BENCHMARKING IS GOOD?

Many companies have taken what is essentially a great idea—trying to learn from the experiences of others—and implemented benchmarking programs that aren't particularly helpful. Benchmarking, as it is often practiced, has several issues. The first, and perhaps most fundamental, is that by copying others, it is difficult, if not impossible, to come up with a unique approach, strategy, or business model that will differentiate one organization from the pack. In other words, benchmarking is a great way to become as successful as other companies, but it is unlikely to make an organization the leader because it is impossible to copy your way to the top.

Traditional benchmarking also involves finding and copying an apparently successful company. As reported several years ago in *Fortune* magazine, companies trying to reproduce Toyota's success in productivity and quality would implement some of the same things that Toyota did—cords to stop the production process when defects were discovered, statistical process control charts, just-in-time inventory systems, and so forth. They failed to grasp that quality is not about a set of techniques. It is a way of thinking about the business, its customers, and its people. As one participant in an executive program said, "Instead of copying what others *do*, we need to understand how they *think*."

Benchmarking also falls short because it is often undertaken in a very casual way. Companies fail to ask the tough questions with regard to what really contributes to the other company's performance and whether the same things that work for that particular company would work as well or be as effective in another environment. Consider this argument in terms of your personal health. If you were ill, you wouldn't simply take the same pills as another person or undergo the identical medical procedures that had worked for them. On the contrary, learning from others requires fitting the diagnosis to the specific issues and circumstances, not just blindly copying what others are doing.

LABOR RATES DETERMINE LABOR COSTS?

In the face of intense competitive pressure, many companies have become fixated on reducing costs. In the process, they have confused cost reduction with profit enhancement. An organization merely seeking to reduce its costs may easily accomplish this goal simply by closing down. After all, costs don't get any lower than zero.

Furthermore, many managers have confused reducing *total costs* with reducing *labor costs* and further conflated reducing *labor costs* with the objective of reducing the *rate of pay* earned by people. Let's turn to the airline industry for a particularly notorious example of this confused thinking and its deleterious effects.

In the spring of 2004, United Airlines and US Airways, both in bankruptcy, began yet another round of asking their workforces to take further pay cuts. At the time, I was fortunate to meet a former United pilot and Stanford graduate, who explained the numerous ways by which pilots could drive costs up or down, merely by varying their behavior. She further noted that cutting pilot pay might not be such a great idea if it sparked resentment, disengagement, and an unwillingness to help the company prosper. The same pilot told me about a web site, www.airlinepilotpay.com, that detailed the wage rates of pilots and first officers with varying years of service, flying different aircraft for different carriers. These data came from their contracts, among other sources.

How about a little test? First, let's take five top airlines: Southwest Airlines, consistently profitable for the past 30-plus years; United and US Airways, in bankruptcy and losing loads of money; Alaska, a West Coast carrier that is sometimes profitable, sometimes not, but definitely is doing better than United and US Airways; and Frontier, a discount carrier with a major hub in Denver. Now, let's take five representative wage rates—they happen to be for pilots with 10 years of service flying Boeing 737s or comparable Airbus models, but the rates of pay are, in fact, correlated with the hourly wage earned by first officers and by pilots with other amounts of seniority: $143 per hour,

$149, $151, $175, and $194. Which wage rate goes with which airline? Do you think Southwest and Frontier are lowest, and US Airways and United are highest, particularly prior to the additional rounds of wage cuts?

Actually, Southwest comes in at $175, Alaska at $194, Frontier at $151, and United and US Airways at $143 and $149 per hour, respectively. If you're wondering how that could be, consider these two simple words: discretionary effort. When people feel as if they are being unfairly compensated and badly treated, they will find ways to retaliate that will actually drive costs higher.

The same pilot, now working for JetBlue, told me there are substantial differences in fuel consumption for the same aircraft model flying the same routes or distances, and that JetBlue was much more efficient than many of its competitors in its fuel utilization. Once again, the same two words apply: discretionary effort. When people are motivated to use their intelligence and experience to make things work better, they will think of ways to reduce costs and enhance productivity. And when they are disengaged and resentful, almost no amount of wage cutting will be enough to produce good outcomes.

Labor rates are not the same as labor costs. Labor costs depend on two things: how much people are paid *and* what those people do—in other words, their productivity. What's more, labor costs are not the same as total costs, which include many components besides labor. Moreover, cost is not the sole basis for competitive success. There's also service, quality, and innovation. Southwest and JetBlue owe their success not just to having more productive employees; they also offer service that consumers consistently rate as superior to that of United and US Airways.

The reality of these facts at a country level means that Japan, with relatively high wages, runs a trade *surplus* with China, even though China has much lower wages on average. And the European Union, believe it or not, with its unionized, regulated labor markets and comparatively high wage and benefit bills, actually runs an enormous trade *surplus* with the United States. For companies or countries, therefore, solving problems of competitiveness begins by getting the facts straight and building more sophisticated models of performance and productivity that place less emphasis on the importance of pay rates or possibly even labor costs.

WORKING MORE HOURS INCREASES PRODUCTIVITY?

People are consistently amazed that SAS Institute, the largest privately owned software company in the world, a company that boasts sales of over $1.3 billion, can be successful with a 35- to 40-hour workweek. Likewise, people marvel that European Aeronautic Defense and Space Company (EADS), which owns 80 percent of Airbus and operates in Europe's defense and space industry, remains competitive, despite giving employees four to eight weeks of vacation time. Not only is EADS proving them wrong, but Airbus is winning the competition with Boeing—and not just thanks to government subsidies, either.

There is an implicit idea that hours equal output. The more hours people put in, the more they—and their organizations—accomplish. This concept dates back to the days of agricultural production when the only way to plow more was to work in the fields longer. It carried on through the days of physical production when there was closer connection between hours and output. These days, however, the connection between hours and performance is much less clear because increasingly we are dealing with creativity, innovation, and intellectual work, rather than sheer physical labor.

Over the years, working long hours became sort of a loyalty test. As a result, few people have taken advantage of policies that potentially provide flexibility, such as flexible schedules, voluntary job sharing or part-time work, and maternity or paternity leaves. Simply put, they are afraid their managers will think they aren't diligent employees. Apparently, their fears are justified. Holding aside the fact that these family-unfriendly—and frankly, people-unfriendly—attitudes make recruitment and retention more difficult, the relationship between hours and output is unlikely to be that strong for work that requires creativity and innovation.

What working long hours *does* produce is fatigue, exhaustion, and burnout. One of the reasons that SAS Institute's software has fewer bugs is that programmers aren't working when they are tired, and thus, more prone to making mistakes. Because programmers make fewer errors, the company can save on the number of checkers it uses. One of the important lessons of the quality movement is that it is almost invariably more costly to discover and correct mistakes once they are made than it is to prevent them in the first place. This is true whether we are talking about software or physical products. Consequently, to the extent that long hours equal more mistakes, it is unlikely that putting in more hours does much to enhance output or performance.

As Leslie Perlow reminds us, the "hero" culture of long hours inadvertently rewards saving and fixing problems, rather than preventing them. The idea that the only way to be successful as a company is to have everyone working all the time not only is inconsistent with the evidence, but it's also inconsistent with attracting and retaining people by keeping them motivated and creative.

INTERNAL COMPETITION ENHANCES PERFORMANCE?

Many of us first encounter the forced curve ranking system in school, when we are graded on the curve. It's no wonder so many organizations have embraced it, as it has been recommended by no less than the likes of Jack Welch, formerly of General Electric; Andy Grove, the former chairman and CEO of Intel; and many others, including the McKinsey consultants in the *War for Talent* book by Ed Michaels, Helen Handfield-Jones, and Beth Axelrod (Harvard Business School Publishing, 2001). In reality, however, it is premised on several assumptions, all of which don't survive scrutiny.

The forced curve system posits that people do better when they are in competition with each other. Granted, people do tend to run or swim faster or pole-vault higher when they are competing with others than when they are alone. However, those situations have two important characteristics: (1) there is no interdependence in an individual's performance—what a given person achieves depends solely on that person's own effort and ability; and (2) the activities are already well-learned, so there is no need to acquire new knowledge or skills. In fact, the evidence is quite clear that competition *impedes* learning new things, and that competition against others discourages cooperation.

Thus, companies find that they spend millions of dollars on intranets and libraries to encourage knowledge sharing and breaking down silos, only to find there is often much less sharing of information and cooperation than desired. That's because it is the culture of trust and cooperation and not the formal mechanisms that affect whether people help and learn from each other. The evidence also indicates that not only do most people dislike the forced curve systems, but they resent their imposition and often work to undermine them. Even Lincoln Electric and General Electric, both proponents of internal competition and ranking, also do things in other elements of their culture and reward systems to encourage cooperation. Meanwhile, Southwest consistently outperforms its competitors by building a culture of cooperation and teamwork, eschewing the use of individual incentives, and using the word *family* repeatedly in its descriptions of the spirit it is trying to build. After all, sibling rivalry and internal competition among family members is seldom recommended as a way to build more effective and successful families. Why should it work any better in the work environment?

TOWARD AN EVIDENCE-BASED HUMAN RESOURCE MANAGEMENT

At its best, human resources would be the research and development function for the human system of the company, bringing into the organization both theories and evidence to enhance effectiveness. Human resources professionals would be less quick to embrace conventional wisdom with its many half-truths and to chase after so-called best practices. Instead, HR managers—indeed, *all* managers—would try to develop "best insights" or "best models" and understanding. This focus and activity could add a lot of value to companies.

Although information and innovation in the financial markets quickly diffuse, better ways of organizing and managing often provide competitive advantage over decades, as the cases of Southwest Airlines and Toyota so nicely illustrate. That is because it is apparently difficult to copy the philosophy and mental models of business that form the foundation that differentiates one organization from another. But it is possible to learn how to build more effective human systems by adopting an attitude open to learning, inquiry, and continually testing ideas. This is precisely the behavior of Billy Beane, general manager of the Oakland Athletics, as described in the book *Moneyball* by Michael Lewis (W. W. Norton & Company, 2001). It would be useful for leaders in all functions to aspire to practice evidence-based management—acting on the basis of the best available knowledge and insight, instead of operating on the basis of casual benchmarking, incorrect assumptions, or rigid belief and ideology, or copying what has been done in the past.

The evidence-based medicine movement and the idea of using evidence to build more effective educational practices are both further along than the systematic application of evidence in management. But even in medicine and education, there is resistance to learning from experiments and experience. We are often wedded to our past ways of thinking and believing. But it is only by thinking differently and with more insight that organizations can act in ways to build more sustained competitive advantage.

CHAPTER 2

PREDICTABLE SURPRISES

THE DISASTERS
YOU SHOULD HAVE SEEN COMING

MICHAEL D. WATKINS AND MAX H. BAZERMAN

APRIL 29, 1995, was not a good day for Royal Dutch/Shell. That morning, a small group of Greenpeace activists boarded and occupied the Brent Spar, an obsolete oil-storage platform in the North Sea that Shell's United Kingdom arm was planning to sink. The activists brought with them members of the European media fully equipped to publicize the drama, and announced that they were intent on blocking Shell's decision to junk the Spar, arguing that the small amounts of low-level radioactive residues in its storage tanks would damage the environment. Greenpeace timed the operation for maximum effect—just one month before European Union environmental ministers were scheduled to meet and discuss North Sea pollution issues.

Shell rushed to court, successfully suing Greenpeace for trespassing. In the full glare of the media spotlight, the activists were forcibly removed from the platform. For weeks afterward, as the cameras continued to roll, Shell blasted

Greenpeace boats with water cannons to prevent the group from reoccupying the Spar. It was a public relations nightmare and it only got worse. Opposition to Shell's plans—and to Shell itself—mounted throughout Europe. In Germany, a boycott of Shell gas stations was organized, and many of them were firebombed or otherwise vandalized. Pilloried in the press and criticized by governments, Shell finally retreated. It announced on June 20 that it was abandoning its plan to sink the Spar.

Shell's uncoordinated, reactionary, and ultimately futile response to the Greenpeace protest revealed a lack of foresight and planning. The attack on the Spar had clearly come as a surprise to the company. But should it have? Shell actually had all the information it needed to predict what would transpire. The company's own security advisers entertained the possibility that environmental activists might try to block the sinking. Other oil companies, fearing a backlash, had protested Shell's plans when they were originally announced. Greenpeace had a history of occupying environmentally sensitive structures. And the Spar was nothing if not an obvious target: Weighing 14,500 tons, it was one of the largest offshore structures in the world and only one of a few North Sea platforms containing big storage tanks with toxic residues.

But, even with all the warning signs, Shell never saw the calamity coming. Unfortunately, its experience is all too common in the business world. Despite thoughtful managers and robust planning processes, even the best-run companies are frequently caught unaware by disastrous events—events that should have been anticipated and prepared for. Such *predictable surprises*, as we call them, take many forms, from financial scandals to disruptions in operations, from organizational upheavals to product failures. Some result in short-term losses or distractions. Some cause damage that takes years to repair. And some are truly catastrophic—the events of September 11, 2001, are a tragic example of a predictable surprise.

The bad news is that all companies—including your own—are vulnerable to predictable surprises. In fact, if you're like most executives, you could probably point to at least one potential crisis or disaster that hasn't been given enough attention—a major customer that's in financial trouble, for instance, or an overseas plant that could be a terrorist target. But there's good news as well. In studying predictable surprises that have taken place in business and government, we have found that organizations' inability to prepare for them can be traced to three kinds of barriers: psychological, organizational, and political. Executives might not be able to eliminate those barriers entirely, but they can take practical steps to lower them substantially. And given the extraordinarily high stakes involved, taking those steps should be recognized as a core responsibility of every business leader.

THREE WAYS TO FAIL

It's all too easy, of course, to play Monday morning quarterback when things go terribly wrong. That's not our intent here. We readily admit that many surprises are unpredictable—that some bolts out of the blue really do come out of the blue—and in those cases leaders shouldn't be blamed for a lack of foresight. Nor should they be blamed if they've taken all reasonable preventive measures against a looming crisis. But if a damaging event happens that was foreseeable and preventable, no excuses should be brooked. The leaders' feet need to be held to the fire.

So how can you tell the difference between a true surprise and one that should have been predicted? Anticipating and avoiding business disasters isn't just a matter of doing better environmental scanning or contingency planning. It requires a number of steps, from recognizing the threat, to making it a priority in the organization, to actually mobilizing the resources required to stop it. We term this the "RPM process": recognition, prioritization, mobilization. Failure at any of these three stages will leave a company vulnerable to potentially devastating predictable surprises. (See the sidebar "Are You to Blame?" for a further discussion of the RPM process.)

ARE YOU TO BLAME?

Predictable surprises arise out of failures of recognition, prioritization, or mobilization. The best way to figure out whether a disaster could have been avoided is to ask the following:

Did the leader recognize the threat? Some disasters can't be foreseen. No one, for instance, could have predicted that the HIV virus would jump the species barrier to infect humans on such a vast scale. But in examining the unforeseen disasters that strike companies, we've found that the vast majority should have been predicted. The way to determine whether a failure of recognition occurred is to assess whether the organization's leader marshaled resources to scan the environment for emerging threats. That includes ascertaining whether he did a reasonable job of analyzing and interpreting the data. If not, then the leader should be held accountable.

Did the leader prioritize appropriately? Predictable surprises also occur when a threat is recognized but not given priority. Failures of prioritization are particularly common, as business leaders are typically beset by many competing demands on their attention. How can they possibly distinguish the surprise that will happen from the myriad potential surprises that won't happen? The answer is that they can't make such distinctions with 100 percent accuracy. Uncertainty exists—high-probability disasters sometimes do not occur and low-probability ones sometimes do. If, therefore, a leader performs careful cost-benefit analyses and gives priority to those threats that represent the highest costs, he should not be held accountable for a failure of prioritization.

Did the leader mobilize effectively? When a threat has been deemed serious, the leader is obligated to mobilize to try to prevent it. If he takes precautionary measures commensurate with the risks involved, he should not be held accountable. Nor should he be blamed if he lacked the resources needed to mount an effective response.

Lapses in recognition occur when leaders remain oblivious to an emerging threat or problem—a lack of attention that can plague even the most skilled executives. After European Commission (EC) regulators refused to approve General Electric's $42 billion acquisition of Honeywell in 2001, for example, Jack Welch was quoted as saying, "You are never too old to be surprised." Welch is a famously hard-nosed executive and if anyone could have been expected to do his homework, it would have been he. But was Welch correct in viewing the decision as a true surprise, an event that couldn't have been foreseen? The evidence suggests he was not. *The Economist* reported at the time that there were many warning flags of the EC's intent to scuttle the deal. For some time, the magazine pointed out, a philosophical gap had been widening between Europe and the United States over the regulation of mergers. And Mario Monti, the recently appointed head of the EC's competition authority, was widely believed to be looking for an opportunity to assert Continental independence.

It seems the real reason Welch was surprised is that he just didn't pay enough attention. According to the Associated Press, when GE's CEO and his counterpart at Honeywell, Michael Bonsignore, were rushing to close the deal (United Technologies also was eager to acquire Honeywell), they "reportedly never held initial consultations with their Brussels lawyers who specialize in European competition concerns." Welch appeared to assume that the merger would sail through the antitrust review. But while it did pass easily through the U.S. review—no doubt further reinforcing his confidence—it smashed on the rocks in Europe. Had Welch recognized the potential for a negative decision ahead of time, he almost certainly would have managed the merger negotiations and antitrust consultations differently—and Honeywell might well be a part of GE today.

Failures of prioritization arise when potential threats are recognized by leaders but not deemed sufficiently serious to warrant immediate attention. Monsanto fell into this trap in late 1999 when CEO Robert Shapiro and his advisers failed to concentrate on winning public acceptance of genetically modified (GM) foods in Europe. Betting the company on a life sciences vision, Shapiro had sold or spun off Monsanto's traditional chemical businesses and moved aggressively to acquire seed companies. Dazzled by the seemingly vast commercial opportunities of genetically modified plants, the company pressed forward with launches of GM food products in Europe, giving far too little weight to the fact that Europeans were still reeling from the mad cow disease crisis, reports of dioxin-contaminated chicken, and numerous other food-related concerns. By focusing on technical and strategic challenges, not on the hard work of winning hearts and minds, Shapiro ultimately lost his company. He was forced to sell Monsanto to Pharmacia-Upjohn, which bought it for its pharmaceutical division, valuing the agricultural biotechnology operations at essentially zero.

Breaks in the third link in the chain—failures of mobilization—occur when leaders recognize and give adequate priority to a looming problem but fail to respond effectively. When the Securities and Exchange Commission (SEC) tried to reform the U.S. accounting system—well before the collapses of Enron and WorldCom—the Big Five accounting firms fiercely lobbied Congress to block new regulations that would have limited auditors' ability to provide consulting services. Appearing at congressional hearings in 2000, accounting firm CEOs assured legislators that no real problem existed. Joseph Berardino, then the managing partner of Arthur Andersen, stated in written testimony that "the future of the accounting profession is bright and will remain bright—as long as the commission does not force us into an outdated role trapped in the old economy. Unfortunately, the proposed rule on auditor independence threatens to do exactly that." The Big Five also spent millions of dollars urging members of Congress to threaten the SEC leadership with budget cuts if it imposed limits on auditor services. The lobbying worked. The SEC backed off, and the all-too-predictable accounting scandals soon began to unfold.

It's important to note that the leadership failure here lies not just with the SEC but also with the accounting firms, which were well aware that their addiction to consulting fees was compromising their independence as auditors.

Also culpable were political leaders—Republicans and Democrats, in the executive branch and in Congress—who lacked the courage to risk political damage and take a stand on the issue.

Sometimes, leaders actually set themselves up for predictable surprises. A classic example is the 1998 decision by a coalition of 39 pharmaceutical companies to sue the government of South Africa over its attempt to reduce the cost of HIV drugs through parallel importation (buying pharmaceuticals in countries with lower prices and then importing them) and compulsory licensing (requiring patent holders to allow others to manufacture and sell their drugs at far lower cost). The companies feared that the precedent set by the South African move would undermine their control over valuable intellectual property in the developing world. But the suit sparked international outrage against the industry, prompting a very public and unflattering look at drug firms' profit margins and industry practices, which the press juxtaposed against the grim realities of AIDS in southern Africa. In response, governmental and nongovernmental organizations formed a coalition that ultimately won big public health exemptions on international intellectual property protection in developing countries. By mobilizing to win the narrow legal battle in South Africa and not focusing on the broader context, the industry suffered a severe setback.

WHY WE'RE VULNERABLE

When we studied examples of predictable surprises occurring at every stage of the RPM process, we found that they share similar causes. Some of those causes are psychological—cognitive defects that leave individuals blind to approaching threats. Others are organizational—barriers within companies that impede communication and dilute accountability. Still others are political—flaws in decision making that result from granting too much influence to special interests. Alone or in combination, these three kinds of vulnerabilities can sabotage any company at any time. All of them, as you'll see, were apparent in Shell's failure to anticipate the Brent Spar controversy.

Psychological Vulnerabilities

The human mind is a notoriously imperfect instrument. Extensive research has shown that the way we process information is subject to a slew of flaws—

scholars call them cognitive biases—that can lead us to ignore or underestimate approaching disasters. Here are a few of the most common.

We tend to harbor illusions that things are better than they really are. We assume that potential problems won't actually materialize or that their consequences won't be severe enough to merit preventive measures. "We'll get by," we tell ourselves.

We give great weight to evidence that supports our preconceptions and discount evidence that calls those preconceptions into question.

We pay too little heed to what other people are doing. As a result, we overlook our vulnerability to predictable surprises resulting from others' decisions and actions.

We are creatures of the present. We try to maintain the status quo while downplaying the importance of the future, which undermines our motivation and courage to act now to prevent some distant disaster. We'd rather avoid a little pain today than a lot of pain tomorrow.

Most of us don't feel compelled to prevent a problem that we have not personally experienced or that has not been made real to us through pictures or other vivid information. We act only after we've experienced significant harm or are able to graphically imagine ourselves, or those close to us, in peril.

All of these biases share something in common: They are self-serving. We tend to see the world as we'd like it to be rather than as it truly is. Much of Shell's failure to anticipate the disastrous response to its decision to sink the Brent Spar can be traced to the self-serving biases of its people—to their unshakable belief that they were right. Shell was an engineering company run by executives trained to make decisions through rigorous technical and economic analysis. Having reviewed more than 30 independent studies and arrived at what they believed was the correct answer about the Spar, and having received approval from the British government to sink it, executives at Shell UK were utterly confident that their decision made the most sense, and they assumed that every reasonable person would see the issue their way. They were unprepared to deal with a group of true believers who opposed any dumping on principle and who were skilled at making emotional arguments that resonated with the public. In the contest for people's hearts and minds, emotion easily defeated analysis—much to the consternation of Shell executives. Even well after it was obvious that they were losing the battle, the leaders of Shell UK still couldn't back away from a failing course of action.

Self-serving bias can be particularly destructive when there are conflicts of interest. Think of the many business scandals that arose after the Internet bubble burst. Although corruption certainly played a role in these disasters, the more fundamental cause was a series of biased judgments. Professional auditors distorted their accounting in ways that served the interests of their clients. Analysts on Wall Street gave overly positive assessments of companies that were clients of their firms' investment banking arms. Corporate directors failed to pay enough attention to the actions of the CEOs who appointed and paid them. Many of these auditors, analysts, and board members knew that the bubble would burst, but their unconscious biases prevented them from fully acknowledging the consequences or taking preventive action. (For an in-depth discussion of how biases distort accounting results, see "Why Good Accountants Do Bad Audits," by Max H. Bazerman, George Loewenstein, and Don A. Moore, in the November 2002 issue of *Harvard Business Review*.)

Organizational Vulnerabilities

The very structure of business organizations, particularly those that are large and complex, makes it difficult to anticipate predictable surprises. Because companies are usually divided into organizational silos, the information that leaders need to see to assess an approaching threat is often fragmented. Various people have various pieces of the puzzle, but no one has them all. In theory, corporate management should play the role of synthesizer, bringing together the fragmented information in order to see the big picture. But the barriers to this happening are great. Information is filtered as it moves up through hierarchies—sensitive or embarrassing information is withheld or glossed over. And those at the top inevitably receive incomplete and distorted data. That's exactly what happened in the months and years leading up to September 11. Various government agencies had pieces of information on terrorists' methods and plans that, had they been combined, would have pointed to the type of attack that was carried out against the World Trade Center and the Pentagon. Tragically, the information remained fragmented. (For more on September 11, see the sidebar "9/11: The Surprise That Shouldn't Have Been.")

Organizational silos not only disperse information, they also disperse responsibility. In some cases, everyone assumes that someone else is taking responsibility, and so no one ever acts. In other cases, one part of an organization is vested with too much responsibility for a particular issue. Other parts of the organization, including those with important information or perspectives, aren't consulted or are even actively pushed out of the decision-making process. The result? Too narrow a perspective is brought to bear on the issue, and potential problems go unrecognized or are given too little priority.

9/11: THE SURPRISE THAT SHOULDN'T HAVE BEEN

When fanatics commandeered jetliners on September 11, 2001, and steered them into buildings full of people, it came as a horrifying shock to most of the world. But however difficult it might have been to imagine individuals carrying out such an act, it shouldn't have been a surprise. Portents had been building up for years. It was well known that Islamic militants were willing to become martyrs for their cause and that their hatred and aggression toward the United States had been mounting throughout the 1990s. In 1993, terrorists set off a car bomb under the World Trade Center in an attempt to destroy the building. In 1995, other terrorists hijacked an Air France plane and made an aborted attempt to fly it into the Eiffel Tower. Also in 1995, the U.S. government learned of a failed Islamic terrorist plot to simultaneously hijack 11 U.S. commercial airplanes over the Pacific Ocean and then crash a light plane filled with explosives into the CIA's headquarters near Washington, DC. Meanwhile, dozens of federal reports, including one issued by then Vice President Al Gore's special commission on aviation security, provided comprehensive evidence that the U.S. aviation security system was full of holes. Anyone who flew on a regular basis knew how simple it was to board an airplane with items, such as small knives, that could be used as weapons.

But despite the signals, no precautionary measures were taken. The failure can be traced to lapses in recognition, prioritization, and mobilization. Information that might have been pieced together to highlight the precise contours of the threat remained fragmented among the FBI, the CIA, and other governmental agencies. No one gave priority to plugging the security holes in the aviation system because, psychologically, the substantial and certain short-term costs of fixing the problems loomed far larger than the uncertain long-term costs of inaction. And the organizations responsible for airline security, the airlines, had the wrong incentives, desiring faster, lower-cost screening to boost profitability. Inevitably, plans to fix the system fell afoul of concerted political lobbying by the airline industry.

Put another way, decision makers focus on an "impact horizon" that is too narrow, neglecting the implications for key constituencies. This sort of organizational parochialism was clearly evident within Shell. The company failed to see that sinking the Spar would set a precedent for dealing with other obsolete structures in the North Sea and that it was probably the worst structure to start with given its size and toxic residues. The company's decentralized management structure, made up of autonomous national business units, worked well when dealing with routine problems such as customizing marketing efforts to local customers. But it worked very badly when dealing with crises that crossed national lines. The Brent Spar was located in the British part of the North Sea, so responsibility for disposing of it was naturally vested with Shell UK. Shell UK, in turn, dealt with the British government to get the necessary permissions and consulted with British environmental groups. But Greenpeace changed the game by focusing its public relations attack not in Britain but in Germany. The German Shell operating company had not been involved in the process and had no part in the decision to dump the Spar. But it became the target of most of the pressure—financial and political—from Greenpeace. Indeed, the chairman of Shell Germany, Peter Duncan, remarked publicly that he first heard about the planned sinking of the Spar "more or less from the television." Once the crisis broke, Shell's decentralized structure inhibited the company from coordinating crisis response activities and notifying employees of decisions and events. Senior Shell managers outside the UK publicly criticized both the disposal plans and each other through the press.

Political Vulnerabilities

Finally, predictable surprises can emerge out of systemic flaws in decision-making processes. Imbalances of power, for example, may lead executives to overvalue the interests of one group while slighting those of other equally important groups. Such imbalances tend to be particularly damaging during the mobilization phase, when vested interests can slow or block action intended to resolve a growing problem. A case in point is the U.S. Congress, where single-interest groups, such as the National Rifle Association or AARP, wield disproportionate influence. Through a combination of focused contributions to reelection campaigns, well-connected lobbyists, nurtured relationships with committee chairpeople and staff members, and intimate knowledge of leverage points in key processes, special-interest groups routinely stall or torpedo policy changes, even when there is a broad consensus that action is needed.

We saw this dynamic play out after Enron collapsed and WorldCom and other companies restated their financial results. Following an early burst of enthusiasm for seriously tightening corporate governance rules, Congress retreated in the face of intense lobbying by an array of business groups. In the critical area of auditing, for example, accounting industry lobbyists succeeded in watering down the Sarbanes-Oxley Act on corporate responsibility, enabling independent auditors to continue to provide consulting and other lucrative services to audit clients and to be rehired indefinitely by the clients, as well as allowing audit firm staffers to take jobs with their clients. Efforts to reform pension laws to help protect workers from future Enron-like debacles were also beaten back by lobbyists representing employers. As a result, companies and investors remain vulnerable to damaging new surprises.

Companies are all too often oblivious to the dynamics of governmental systems. Shell, for example, failed to anticipate and shape European political responses to its Brent Spar plan. Company officials had finalized the disposal plan after four years of study and quiet negotiations with the British government, which approved the dumping. After signing on to the Shell plan, the British government notified the other European governments with oil development and other interests in the North Sea. These governments raised no objections at that time, but the absence of objections is by no means the same as active support. As Greenpeace applied more pressure on the Continent, the German government responded by openly undercutting the UK's decision to allow Shell to sink the Spar. Through public criticism and direct requests, Germany pressured the UK to reverse its decision. Not building a broad consensus—with governments and with other oil companies—on how to deal with aging North Sea oil rigs cost Shell dearly.

Political vulnerabilities can also crop up within companies. Sanford Weill, the chairman of Citigroup, recently came under fire for apparently using corporate resources to provide personal assistance to Jack Grubman, a star analyst at Citi's Salomon Smith Barney. Weill allegedly helped get Grubman's children into a prestigious day care center in return for issuing a more favorable report on AT&T, a very important client of Salomon's investment banking unit. But broader organizational politics also appear to have played a role in Weill's actions. As *The Economist* reported, "There is much speculation, and some e-mail evidence, that the recommendation helped to win support for Mr. Weill's successful ousting of Citigroup's co-CEO, John Reed from Michael Armstrong, AT&T's chief executive, who also happened to sit on Citi's board." The resulting damage to the reputations of Weill and his company was entirely predictable.

WHAT YOU CAN DO

"Prediction is very difficult," physicist Niels Bohr once said, "especially about the future." Difficult, yes. Impossible, no. Even though many organizations are caught unprepared for disasters they should have seen coming, many have successfully recognized approaching crises and taken evasive action. In the public sector, for example, governments, corporations, and charitable organizations banded together to curtail the use of chlorofluorocarbon (CFC) refrigerants and aerosol propellants once it became clear they were damaging the ozone layer. In the business arena, leaders are today sponsoring what we call "surprise-avoidance initiatives" on topics ranging from genomics research and stem cell biology to Internet security to the reform of corporate governance.

Individual companies can learn a lot from such efforts. We have distilled from our own research a set of practical steps that managers can take to better recognize emerging problems, set appropriate priorities, and mobilize an effective preventive response. The first step is the simplest: Ask yourself and your colleagues, "What predictable surprises are currently brewing in our organization?" This may seem like an obvious question, but it's rarely asked. People at various levels in organizations, from the top to the bottom, are often aware of approaching storms but choose to keep silent, often out of a fear of rocking the boat or being seen as troublemakers. By actively encouraging people to speak up, executives can bring to the surface many problems that might otherwise go unmentioned.

Some threats, of course, are invisible to insiders. To ferret out these potential dangers, companies should use two proven techniques—scenario planning and risk assessment. In scenario planning, a knowledgeable and creative group of people from inside and outside the organization is convened to review company strategies, digest available information on external trends, and identify critical business drivers and potential flash points. (It's essential to include outsiders in this group as a counterweight to the self-serving biases of employees.) Based on this analysis, the group constructs a plausible set of scenarios for potential surprises that could emerge over, say, the coming two years. These scenarios form the basis for the design of preventive and preparatory measures. This exercise should include scenarios that, while unlikely, would have a very large impact on the organization if they occurred. A full scenario-planning exercise should be conducted annually, and formal updates of changes in the organization and its environment should be scheduled every quarter.

Rigorous risk analysis—combining a systematic assessment of the probabilities of future events and an estimation of the costs and benefits of particular outcomes—can be invaluable in overcoming the biases that afflict organizations in estimating the likelihood of unpleasant events. It can be useful not just in setting priorities but in sifting through alternative responses. During the Cuban Missile Crisis in 1962, for example, U.S. military leaders wanted to attack. Fortunately, however, President John F. Kennedy organized a decision-making process that examined in detail the risks of available options. Two groups, each including government officials and outside experts, were organized to flesh out two particular alternatives, attack and blockade, and assess their associated risks and rewards. Based on the analysis, Kennedy eventually decided to conduct a blockade. Recently, Kennedy's Secretary of Defense Robert McNamara made it clear that if the United States had invaded, the consequences might well have been catastrophic. Even if American forces had quickly destroyed all the weapons known to exist in Cuba, several U.S. cities could still have been struck by nuclear missiles—missiles that the military were unaware of at the time.

At its best, risk analysis combines subjective and objective evaluations. Teams of experts, like the ones Kennedy relied on, can be organized to make regular qualitative assessments of conditions and threats. At the same time, decision analysis has developed useful techniques for helping individuals and organizations to more effectively assess the probabilities of future events and their potential consequences. (John Hammond, Ralph Keeney, and Howard Raiffa's book *Smart Choices* [Harvard Business School Press, 1999] provides a particularly good overview of this field.)

Organizational vulnerabilities are often the toughest to overcome. But whereas it's rarely possible to eradicate all the internal barriers within an organization, it is possible to counter their effects by establishing cross-company systems to gather intelligence. Typically, this requires that leaders create one or more cross-functional teams responsible for collecting and synthesizing relevant information from all corners of the business. Some companies use what are called action-learning groups—teams of future leaders who meet to share data and analyze key business challenges. Also required is a change in incentives to get employees to see beyond their parochial interests and begin to share information freely. In the case of the Brent Spar fiasco, the leaders of Shell UK and Shell Germany were each focused exclusively on their own bottom lines and as a result pursued conflicting parochial interests—to the detriment of the company as a whole. Had a broader system of measures and rewards been in place, one that provided incentives to balance corporate and local interests, Shell would have been better protected against internal in-fighting and miscommunication.

Finally, executives need to build good networks—both informal advice networks and formal coalitions—for influencing political decisions. Leaders' beliefs and impressions about the potential challenges facing their organizations are based, in large measure, on their intuition. By organizing a set of knowledgeable advisers, drawn from both inside and outside the company, leaders can test and refine their early impressions and help counter their own unconscious biases. Hank McKinnell, the CEO of Pfizer, is a good example of a leader who routinely calls on a group of external advisers to avoid predictable surprises. One of McKinnell's most valuable "leadership counselors" is Dan Ciampa, former CEO of consulting firm Rath & Strong. By serving as both a sounding board and an adviser on key issues and decisions, Ciampa is reportedly instrumental in helping McKinnell avoid undesirable outcomes.

And when managers have to mobilize people outside their direct lines of control to confront a difficult problem—as is almost always necessary—they need to build formal coalitions. Coalition building is particularly important for getting anything done in highly politicized environments like the U.S. Congress. But it is important in business, too. Sometimes, executives have to make major organizational changes to guard against a potential disaster. Such changes always create winners and losers and generate overt and covert resistance. To prevail, leaders must be able to consolidate their supporters, neutralize their opponents, and persuade fence-sitters to back the changes. That requires, in turn, that they be good at figuring out who wields influence, inside and outside the organization, and then use that knowledge to build support and momentum for their cause.

Taking these steps will help you get an effective RPM process up and running in your company. Once the process is in place, you'll need to shift your attention to speeding it up and making it more responsive. Events move swiftly, and they can quickly spin out of control—as Shell found out. If you're unable to stay ahead of a potential disaster as it unfolds, you'll be stuck in a reactive mode. You'll become a victim of circumstances rather than a master of your own destiny.

CHAPTER 3

HUMAN CAPITAL INVESTMENTS FOR PARETO-OPTIMAL RETURNS

SAMIR J. RAZA AND MARK C. UBELHART

ASKED TO describe their companies' key business objectives, most executives would say something along the lines of changing the face of technology, helping people invest for their futures, devising new treatments for life-threatening illnesses, or responding to consumer demands for easy-to-use products that enable people to keep up with the busy pace of life. These pronouncements are generally true in most cases, but fall a few steps short of why companies are really in business and what ultimately determines success or failure. When it comes down to it, the most basic, fundamental concern of all organizations is to deliver on the expectations of key stakeholders.

Executives do not typically make direct reference to stakeholder expectations, perhaps on account of a commonly held misperception that the interests of key stakeholders are *necessarily* at odds. In other words, actions that benefit one group of stakeholders conflict with the interests of others. This is not surprising, since business solutions that make all stakeholders better off—investors, customers, and employees—are not easily identified. The objective of this chapter is to discuss such solutions, referred to as *Pareto-optimal* solutions, in the context of human capital investments.

Very often the misperception about conflicting stakeholder interests results in a myopic approach to human capital investment decisions. A company may compromise long-term investments in its people, for example, in order to boost short-term earnings, often incorrectly equated to shareholder value. Such shortsighted decisions are inevitable in the absence of an explicit framework to enable a direct evaluation of short-term cost versus long-term benefit. After all, it is much harder to be myopically focused on short-term gains when the long-term consequences are visible and concrete.

Imagine that you are an executive at a leading services firm. Faced with intense earnings pressure, you've been asked to focus on the firm's cost structure, which is predominantly related to people costs. You consider the alternatives: layoffs, reductions in training and development, hiring freeze, pay cuts, decrease in benefits, and so on. At the same time, you think about the risks: loss of employee morale, loss of talent, and quite possibly, a domino effect resulting in poor business performance. You consider cutting back on a rich benefits program, but hesitate going down this path not knowing what impact it will have on employee morale and your ability to attract and retain talent. Another option is to put more emphasis on variable pay as a means to manage employee cost. You wonder if you should also differentiate more in rewards based on individual or team performance, and if so, by how much?

With little to guide or support the decision-making process, you are unsure what to do. How do you determine what decisions will enhance your ability to attract, motivate, and retain key talent, sustain employee morale, and facilitate the redeployment of noncritical talent, while also meeting your cost reduction targets? Myopic decisions that focus on short-term cost reductions could result in loss of critical talent at all levels of the organization, with a tremendous detrimental impact on long-term shareholder value. If you had a crystal ball you might ask: "Is there a way to reduce costs that also facilitates the right talent mix, while having a demonstrable positive impact on shareholder value?"

Thus far, credible answers to such questions have been difficult to come by. Traditional financial planning frameworks offer little to guide human capital investments, even though payroll and benefits typically constitute 30 to 70 percent[1] of operating expenses. That doesn't include the vast expenditures for training, recruiting, and other people-related activities, which add substantially to the cost. Despite the magnitude of these investments, most companies find themselves operating without a compass when it comes to people issues. Decisions are generally supported by benchmark surveys or behavioral studies, which are not sufficient for making the connection to optimal solutions and impact on shareholder value. Granted, benchmarking information can be useful to the extent that knowledge of what other organizations are doing can help identify suitable directions for a given firm. Underneath best practice data, however, there are fundamental organizational characteristics that are not always apparent. Likewise, behavioral studies provide an understanding of employee response to policy decisions, but generally lack a connection to shareholder value or guidance toward prioritization of investment dollars.

The solution lies in gathering conceptual and empirical evidence to guide decisions that result in a positive impact on shareholder value. For our purposes, shareholder value refers to the present value of long-term cash flows that will likely emanate as a result of management actions. Realization of future cash flows depends heavily on the right level of investment in talent, customers, and various other forms of business assets. Some investments pay off in the near term, while others generate returns over the long run. Above all else, it's important to note that shareholder value is contingent on value created for other key stakeholders, namely *high-performing employees* and *high-value customers*.

By definition, Pareto optimality refers to actions that result in all key stakeholders being at least as well off as—if not better off than—they were before. While appealing in concept, the challenge has been the absence of a conceptual framework, factual data, and empirical evidence to guide management toward what constitutes such decisions. Newer directions in human capital planning have now emerged that focus on building the necessary organizational principles and a value-based mind-set, guided by factual information to determine where and how much to invest in human capital. This next level of insight comes from predictive analytics—a new frontier for human capital decisions.

HUMAN CAPITAL FORESIGHT

To address the need for rigorous fact-based analysis, Hewitt Associates LLC has developed the Human Capital Foresight™ (HCF™) methodology. Using data from 20 million people employed by more than 1,000 companies, in effect a microcosm of the U.S. labor market, HCF identifies the optimal areas of investment—for both a company and its business units—and the degree to which such investments are consistent with greater shareholder value. The goal is to provide guidance on people issues, enabling firms to create more value than their peers in good times and lose less value than their peers in times of economic hardship. This, in a nutshell, is known as *beating the fade*—the tendency to trend toward average performance.

Utilizing factual data from several sources, HCF combines multiple years of employee demographics, employee transitions, employment history, compensation, company-specific people practices, and behavioral information derived from engagement surveys.[2] The combined data offers a unique set of observed patterns of employee performance, behaviors, and transitions in response to people practices at respective companies. In effect, the data allows us to observe not only movement of employees across firms over multiple years, but also whether employees joining or leaving a firm—at all levels—are those who are deemed pivotal to business success. The employee data is then weighed against company-specific financial results over several years. In all, HCF offers an opportunity to develop and test several hypotheses on human capital policy, prioritization of investments, and long-term economic value.

A FOCUS ON EMPLOYEE TRANSITIONS AND A FIRM'S TALENT QUOTIENT (TQ)

Within any organization, there are those employees who bring more value to the business than the rest. These high-impact employees may be thought of as pivotal to the company's success. The HCF proxy for identifying pivotal employees is based on how a company chooses to invest incremental compensation dollars, in the form of top-quartile pay progression relative to others in the organization. This measurement is adjusted by age, tenure, and pay level. A company's ability to attract and retain these pivotal employees is measured by means of a metric, a firm's Talent Quotient (TQ™). TQ captures the ratio of pivotal employees joining or leaving a firm relative to all employees joining or leaving, respectively. A score of 100 implies that a firm is attracting or retaining pivotal employees at the same rate as other employees. A score greater than 100 implies that the firm is recruiting and retaining a disproportionately greater number of pivotal employees.

TQ is unique in that it is derived from factual data representing *employee response to management decisions*. It is benchmarkable across companies after adjustments for industry and demographics and a demonstrable driver of business performance. In an environment seeking credible metrics tied to business performance, TQ is expected to become part of internal reporting.

For public companies, it may very well become a standard part of external reporting as well.

As a business-planning tool we do not consider TQ an objective in itself, but rather a key driver of economic value creation. To complete the circle, the long-term benefit of TQ improvement is weighed against implementation costs to ensure that an optimal balance is achieved. These comments convey a few conceptual underpinnings that help unravel the complex relationships that characterize human capital issues.

The factors that drive TQ are numerous, and in several ways interdependent. Consider the impact of employee pay programs on the ability of an organization to attract, retain, and motivate talent. Pay is undoubtedly a key factor, but generally not independent of a firm's leadership, benefit programs, career opportunity, and employee relationships. Some balance among these drivers would likely deliver the most optimal results for TQ. Empirical methods such as Classification and Regression Tree (CART) are employed for this purpose.

HCF seeks to *optimize* human capital investment and TQ so as to *maximize* long-term value. Thus, planned people investments should be structured in a way that seeks the right balance between the extremes of policy choices and between long-term benefits versus costs. Once again, CART enables the identification of these optimal points or sweet spots with reasonable accuracy.

The challenge lies in the determination of optimal investments from a practical, policy-oriented standpoint. Employee costs are clearly visible and draw the most attention, but the value of human capital investments is not as easily traced back to these investments. Consequently, HR's role in the strategic planning process is ambiguous. To help clear up such ambiguity, we develop empirical methods to calibrate these relationships significantly better than was previously possible.

THE LINK TO CASH FLOW AND SHAREHOLDER RETURNS

The cause-and-effect relationship between human capital metrics and long-term financial performance is complex. Granted, there is evidence to suggest that well-developed employee programs have a significant impact on business results. However, there is also truth in the counterargument that financial performance, which allows a firm to invest in people, explains the ability of an organization to attract, motivate, and retain talent.

This circular and reinforcing relationship leads to an interesting notion that we refer to as the *success spiral*. Simply put, companies that invest in talent have the potential to generate financial success, which in turn generates funds to further invest in talent, hence continuing to build on their success. Conversely, the *death spiral* refers to situations where companies respond to market downturns or other financial pressures by cutting back on people investments. This results in the departure of pivotal employees and reinforces the likelihood of future poor performance and financial distress.

Empirical techniques allow us to separate the circular relationships to develop sensitivity estimates of a unit change in TQ, adjusted for industry and demographics, to the corresponding change in financial results. We look at the impact of improvements in TQ to the corresponding impact on a key financial metric, Cash Flow Return on Investment (CFROI®),[3] a sophisticated measure of performance developed by CSFB HOLT. Based on a sample of 115 firms with several years of data, preliminary results suggest a significant difference in financial performance over multiple years in favor of high-TQ firms relative to those that score low on this metric.

To develop business-specific insights, factors such as *labor*, *capital*, and *knowledge* intensity are considered. Financial services firms, which are typically characterized as having a high degree of knowledge intensity, show on average over twice the increase in cash flow relative to the all-industry average. This suggests a much higher TQ leverage in knowledge-driven industries. No doubt there is some variance around these point estimates specific to the time period, industry, and company in question. However, stability in results over multiple time periods has statistical implication that is worthy of consideration.

HCF REPORTING AND MANAGEMENT DECISIONS

Key findings of HCF analyses are captured in optimization charts, which show where a company falls on each policy metric relative to the optimal position or sweet spot. Once again, the sweet spot is the metric value that results in the maximum contribution to the company's overall TQ.

Remember the hypothetical services firm depicted earlier in this chapter? Management was struggling to find ways to contain costs, but at the same time was concerned about the impact on talent, morale, productivity, and the consequent effect on business results. In view of the HCF approach, let's consider few policy directions that would help this firm reduce overall employee costs, improve talent retention (TQ), and propose these changes with a significant positive impact on long-term shareholder value, much like any other capital budgeting or planning approach.

For a services firm, a large proportion of operating cost is tied up in compensation and benefits. Therefore let's consider the following policy areas: pay at risk and total benefits. From a compensation design perspective, the right balance of fixed versus variable pay has a sizable impact on the firm's cost structure. However, other than benchmark data on common practice, there is scarce information to guide the right balance for fixed versus variable pay that would be suitable to a given firm.

In Figure 3.1, the solid circle is indicative of a company's current position for the pay-at-risk metric. The most optimal level, or sweet spot, is represented by the highest point indicated by concentric circles. The number shown above each bar is the incremental TQ impact attained by moving the level of pay at risk from a firm's current position to that indicated for each vertical bar. As discussed before, these are estimated improvements that will vary by firm-specific circumstances.

Clearly, the company has a very high emphasis on salary (or fixed pay) relative to the optimal point to maximize TQ. This is true at both executive and

Figure 3.1
Optimization Charts: Metric—
Pay at Risk as Percentage of Total Compensation

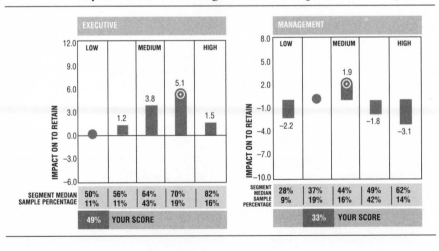

management levels. Changing the mix of pay can be accomplished over time; it is generally not something that is accomplished overnight. Since variable pay is typically tied to performance, moving toward the sweet spot results in significantly lower compensation-related costs when overall performance is below par. If variable pay is structured correctly, high performers may still come out ahead. Overall, this presents a significant opportunity to manage compensation-related costs while improving the firm's TQ. Higher TQ is related to higher cash flow performance in quantifiable terms. This is what Pareto-optimal solutions are about.

A second opportunity for this firm is in managing benefits expenses. Employee benefits involve large dollar costs, but the return on this investment is not usually apparent. The optimization chart looking at this firm's total benefits program is shown in Figure 3.2.

The results shown in Figure 3.2 suggest that this firm lies marginally below the sweet spot. If the company invests more heavily in benefits, the marginal increase in TQ would likely not be justified by the cost of doing so. Instead, scarce funds may be freed up by selective trimming of the benefits program. The chart suggests that a reduction in benefits is expected to have a relatively small TQ impact. Moving toward the median level will make available significant amounts of cash, which can be reinvested in higher-return areas.

Figure 3.2
Optimization Charts: Metric—All Benefits as Percentage of Median

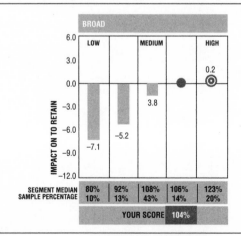

Note: The metric examines the value of employer-paid benefits as a percentage of median employer-paid benefits across all companies, industry adjusted.

Such analysis offers the management of our hypothetical services firm new directions for changes to employee policies and investments, while accomplishing the three criteria previously indicated: cost reduction, talent retention, and positive impact on shareholder value.

Along these lines, several other categories of metrics relating to pay, incentives, benefits, career paths, leadership, diversity, and the like are tested for firm-specific direction toward optimal investment. Actual policy changes will require a careful analysis of cost versus benefit supported by the type of analysis shown earlier. However, the business case for these changes is now on even ground with financial planning and budgeting for other types of investments.

The relative impact of all metrics is shown in a prioritization chart (Figure 3.3). For a given firm, the chart refers to the impact of changes in each policy metric from current level to the optimal levels suggested by HCF methodology and the estimated cash flow impact of the policy change. Information from employee engagement surveys is used to supplement the HCF analysis.

There may be situations where a change in policy, for greater differentiation in bonus payouts, may have a significant positive impact on TQ, implying a favorable response from pivotal employees, but not necessarily favored by

Figure 3.3
Sample Optimization Chart: Prioritization

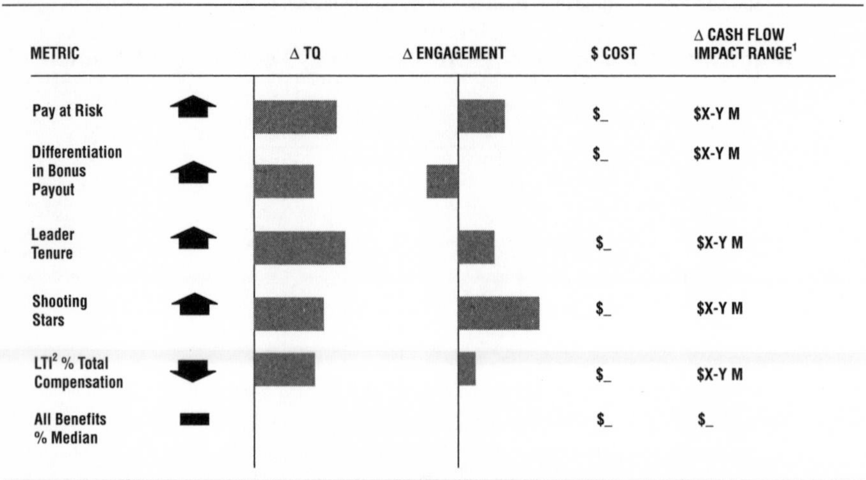

METRIC	Δ TQ	Δ ENGAGEMENT	$ COST	Δ CASH FLOW IMPACT RANGE[1]
Pay at Risk			$_	$X-Y M
Differentiation in Bonus Payout			$_	$X-Y M
Leader Tenure			$_	$X-Y M
Shooting Stars			$_	$X-Y M
LTI[2] % Total Compensation			$_	$X-Y M
All Benefits % Median			$_	$_

[1]The cash flow impact takes into account both the estimated benefit and direct costs associated with policy changes toward the sweet spot. Note that the estimated cash flow for different metrics is not necessarily additive. The total cash flow impact is estimated on a case-by-case basis.
[2]LTI–Long-term incentive

the broader employee population. Such information is valuable to management to move towards the right balance on each policy metric in view of firm-specific business needs.

Most decisions are ultimately based on a combination of factual data, judgment, and other business considerations. HCF offers insights that are relatively unique and with a tangible link to business results—a strong complement to management decision-making.

REAL EXAMPLES (INITIAL STAGE CLIENT APPLICATIONS)

Table 3.1 summarizes partial results actually obtained by applying the methodology. First and foremost, TQ results for particular employee segments

Table 3.1
Applying Human Capital Foresight Methodology

Company	TQ Results	Context	Indicators	Investment Priorities
A	Subpar for employees with $50,000 to $200,000 in salary	Problematic bench strength for organic growth, echoed by investor concerns and low market multiple	Combination of pay at risk and differentiation of pay increases far beyond sweet spot, together with low security benefits	Cost-effective increase in benefits, coupled with changes in performance the management and lower pay at risk
B	Subpar for employees with salaries $125,000 and higher	High return, but no growth business with uncertain future and staffing model out of sync with current circumstances	Lack of bonus differentiation, not enough pay at risk, and long-term incentive opportunity	Consolidation of responsibilities and organization restructuring with differentiated and enhanced incentive opportunities
C	Subpar for employees with salaries over $200,000	New concentrated ownership and transition issues, imposing several restrictions on executive participation in future business value creation	Long-term incentives far below sweet spot	Making business case for enhanced long-term incentives, armed with cost/benefit analysis aimed at TQ improvement

are revealed, highlighting human capital "profitability" issues—that is, degree of retention of pivotal employees. Then the business context is described, followed by the indicators that signal where to focus attention. Finally, the investment priorities are cited to be used in a complete cost/benefit analysis.

FUTURE DIRECTIONS

Anchored in predictive analytics, Human Capital Foresight provides organizations with a framework for making confident decisions on people investments and policy decisions. The growth in multiprocess outsourcing has made available vast databases that offer an opportunity to further enhance the depth and breadth of predictive analytics. In short, HCF is a leading-edge solution to questions that have long eluded HR professionals. So far, we have seen but the tip of the iceberg. What it signals, however, is a change in direction that holds significant promise for the future.

ACKNOWLEDGMENT

The authors would like to acknowledge contribution from Krishna Gopinathan, CEO of Global Analytics, for analytical support toward this research.

CHAPTER 4

USING WORKFORCE ANALYTICS TO MAKE STRATEGIC TALENT DECISIONS

MATT SCHUYLER

A LEAN, engaged, and productive workforce can be a key component of an organization's competitive advantage. By making the workforce leaner, business units and staff groups in an organization can make significant strides in reducing cost gaps relative to leading competitors. To successfully operate a lean organization, the workforce needs to be highly productive and engaged.

An organization's commitment to having a highly talented workforce is an important first step in building a lean, engaged, and productive team. Yet talent alone is not enough. A comprehensive, integrated approach is required to maximize the contributions of each individual. Workforce planning is a way of developing a lean organization design, and then engaging and aligning the talent within the organization. This chapter describes the workforce planning process that drives breakthrough organizational productivity through a lean, agile, and engaged workforce.

WORKFORCE PLANNING FRAMEWORK

Workforce planning is the proactive, methodical process to develop integrated, long-term organizational solutions that are aligned to business goals.

49

Effective workforce planning incorporates the many factors that affect workforce productivity.

First, each business unit or functional group needs the right workforce to meet business goals. This includes:

- *Right size.* To be lean, organizations need to determine the right workforce size required to meet future business goals. Capital One has developed sophisticated models to forecast the workforce capacity required in call center and other line operation functions. In addition, the company developed a new methodology to forecast the right workforce size for exempt knowledge workers using an objective, information-driven approach. This approach forecasts future workload demand based on business goals and uses that information to estimate the required workforce size for both the exempt and nonexempt workforce.
- *Right structure.* An efficient organizational design contributes to better financial performance and improves agility in decision-making. The organization structure should provide scalability aligned with business growth, be in tune with the needs of the customer, and ensure that process handoffs between different departments are seamless. The shape of the organization should emphasize flatness over multiple levels of hierarchy to provide broader roles and the timely flow of communication through the organization. Developing organizational design principles for the shape and structure of the organization allows business leaders to design an efficient organization tailored to business needs.
- *Right level of engagement.* An engaged workforce drives customer loyalty and financial performance. External research studies have shown that by increasing an employee's level of engagement, organizations can significantly improve employee performance as well as reduce attrition risk. A structured approach to assess workforce engagement helps to identify critical segments of the employee population, delineate actions that improve their engagement levels, and reduce turnover.

Second, the business unit needs the right infrastructure to support the workforce, including:

- *Right processes.* In designing work processes from scratch, the ability to deliver high-quality output in the shortest cycle time should be emphasized. For existing processes, continuous process improvement will help businesses develop more efficient ways of performing the work. This can be achieved by applying techniques such as process management, LEAN, and six sigma. In addition, workflow technology solutions can automate and streamline the delivery of work. Streamlined processes often lead to increased employee satisfaction with the work as well as higher customer satisfaction.

- *Right work space.* The work environment can have a significant influence on workforce productivity. Reconfiguring the work space can yield higher group performance at lower costs. For example, Capital One's corporate real estate department designed a Future of Work environment to encourage collaboration and allow greater mobility. Future of Work is characterized by open floor plans, designated work spaces for collaboration, and flexible project rooms to support project-based team assignments. Initial reactions to the Future of Work space have been very positive, with more than 85 percent of employees preferring the new work environment compared to the traditional cubicle-style work spaces.

- *Right technology.* Personal productivity tools such as wireless-enabled laptops, BlackBerry devices, and voice and video over Internet technology enable associates to work from anywhere. Collaboration tools such as instant messaging, Web conferencing, and communities of practice help the workforce stay connected across businesses and geographies. Enterprise-wide systems such as a corporate portal and document management system further support employee productivity by providing a common infrastructure platform. They also enhance the ability to target relevant employee segments and provide them with the right information at the right time.

In the past, these organizational elements were addressed individually. An integrated approach ensures more consistency and alignment across the organization.

PREREQUISITES FOR DESIGNING THE RIGHT WORKFORCE

The workforce plan should be thoughtfully aligned to business needs. Before designing the right workforce, the organization should clearly define its strategy. This includes articulating the long-term vision and clearly defining future business goals. Working backwards from future goals, there should be a well-defined plan to achieve the endgame vision while also focusing on short-term objectives. Understanding the work performed within the organization, specifying the interaction of the organization with other internal and external entities to deliver the work, and defining the key organizational metrics for success are also prerequisites to designing the right workforce.

DEVELOPING THE RIGHT SIZE

The right size module of the workforce planning process assesses how business goals influence the size of the organization. Three elements of organization size are assessed:

1. *Organizational size.* This is the total number of workforce resources required to deliver the workload necessary to meet business needs. Workforce size includes both internal employees as well as external resources and both exempt and nonexempt resources.
2. *Staffing mix.* This is the ratio of internal to external resources. Organizational productivity can be enhanced by retaining core, critical work processes in-house, and for all other work, leveraging external resources for expertise and better economics. External resources can be further broken down into on-site and off-site temporary labor and contractors, and domestic and offshore outsourced resources.
3. *Skills mix.* Business strategy shifts sometimes necessitate some new skills and capabilities in the organization. Conversely, they might also reduce the need for certain existing skills. By identifying skill gaps and prioritizing them, the human resources team can help the organization proactively take steps to close skill gaps through hiring, training, and the use of external experts and consultants.

To arrive at the right size for the organization, begin with a thorough understanding of the as-is state for the organization including a detailed activity-based assessment of the current workload, a determination of the business drivers of workload, and an understanding of the type and size of resources required to deliver current work activities. Next, project the to-be state by using future business goals. Forecast the future workload demand and the intended growth in workforce productivity to determine the required future workforce size.

Designing the Right Structure

Design the organization to have an efficient and effective shape and structure, following these parameters:

- *Shape.* To design an efficient organization with minimal layering, a key organizational design parameter is span of control. Span of control is a measure of managerial leverage in the internal organization and is defined by the number of direct subordinates for each manager. The organization size and the span of control dictate the number of organizational layers within the organization. For a given organization size, a higher span of control would result in fewer layers and a flatter organization. An additional determinant of the shape of the organization is the manager-to-nonmanager ratio at each layer in the organization.
- *Structure.* The organization structure is used to optimize the coordination, management control, and task orientation of a group. Companies do not follow a single structural model throughout the organization. At different levels and at different cycles of growth within the organization, different models may be used. Business units may organize by product, geography, or customer or a combination thereof. Departments may also organize based on workflows by function or process.

The selection of the right organization structure is a complex process and does not have a specific formula. Work with the business units to develop an organization structure that is aligned with the business strategy, processes, management systems, and culture of the organization.

Achieving the Right Level of Engagement

Achieving the right size and structure is still not sufficient to achieve success. Employees must also be engaged—that is, they must truly act as business owners and give their discretionary effort. Discretionary effort refers to employees going above and beyond typical duties. For example, highly engaged employees may show discretionary effort by volunteering to help team members or take the initiative to improve work processes. In contrast, low engagement levels can significantly reduce productivity and put execution of strategy at risk. Engaged employees drive customer loyalty and financial performance. They are also less likely to leave the organization. Focus on the areas of employees' concern, and identify the levers that are driving the low engagement based on the following model.

Capital One has developed an index to track associate engagement across rational and emotional dimensions. Both of these components play an important role in shaping overall employee engagement with the organization. Rational engagement is assessed by measuring the extent to which associates feel they achieve work/life balance, have access to development opportunities, and are rewarded appropriately for their efforts. (See Table 4.1.)

Emotional engagement is assessed by measuring the strength of associates' identification with the corporate mission, the strength of relationships between associates, and the extent to which associates feel their feedback is leveraged by the organization. (See Table 4.2.)

Capital One measures and tracks associate levels of engagement throughout the organization by administering these questions in the Corporate All-Associate Survey. Responses to these questions help identify overall associate engagement and identify the primary rational and emotional levers to raise engagement levels across the organization.

Engagement levels are mapped within an organization to identify areas of concern. The engagement "heat map" in Figure 4.1 is based on the breakouts available in Capital One's Corporate All-Associate Survey. The chart is a disguised representation of engagement levels within a business unit.

Table 4.1
Measuring Rational Engagement

• My job makes good use of my talents.	• My job is interesting and challenging.	• As an individual, I feel valued at Capital One.
• Maintaining a healthy balance between work and home life is supported by manager.	• My manager is committed to my career development.	• I am satisfied with the recognition of my team's contributions.
• I maintain a healthy balance between work and home.	• There are many opportunities currently available to me across company.	• I am satisfied with the performance management process.
• I am interested in taking advantage of flexible work arrangements.	• I am satisfied with training.	• Compared to other organizations, I am fairly paid.

Source: Capital One.

Table 4.2
Measuring Emotional Engagement

- Capital One behaves ethically when dealing with associates.
- I am satisfied with company culture.
- We live the value of integrity.
- Capital One lives up to its brand promise.

- How would you rate Capital One compared with other organizations you know about?
- I am motivated to go above and beyond what is expected of me.
- I am excited about future of Capital One.
- I am satisfied with my job security.

- I feel well informed about important issues and changes at Capital One.
- Executive leadership clearly articulates business direction.
- My manager is interested in me as an individual.
- Associates share ideas to improve work.

Source: Capital One.

Figure 4.1
Measure: Organizational "Heat Map" of Engagement

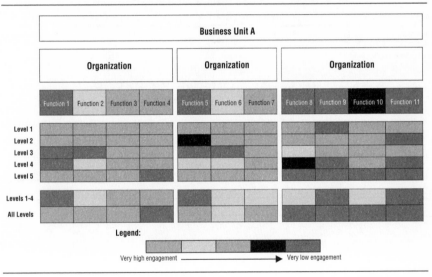

There are numerous tangible benefits to increasing the proportion of engaged employees. These include:

- *Higher employee productivity.* Engaged employees are less likely to miss work;[1] they attend four additional days of work per year.
- *Lower recruiting and training costs.* Engaged employees change jobs at a lower rate, thereby avoiding the cost of recruiting and training (learning curve required).
- *A more loyal customer base.* According to *The Loyalty Effect*,[2] engaged employees can help increase customer loyalty by more than 5 percent through better customer service.
- *Reduced health care costs.* Work is five times more likely to impact health of disengaged employees[3] and thus, the higher the proportion of engaged employees, the lower the average health care cost.

There are also significant discretionary efforts made by engaged employees. This benefit is more difficult to track, but independent research[4] shows that a lift of up to 57 percent is possible when an employee is converted from strongly disengaged to strongly engaged.

ASSESSING THE IMPACT ON THE WORKFORCE

Before finalizing design of the right workforce, assess the potential impact of any organizational changes on the workforce. A recently concluded Capital One "Associate Value Proposition" study found that organizational changes influence many of the factors these employees care about. Areas of employee interest include workload, job security, empowerment (robust job roles), career advancement, and movement opportunities. The study concluded that no one proposition works for any organization. Propose various organizational options to the leadership team and evaluate the potential impact of those options on employees to illustrate any trade-offs that need to be addressed by senior leaders. Attributes used to evaluate workforce impact include hiring needs, promotions, attrition, morale, costs, and productivity. By proactively assessing the impact on the workforce, the trade-offs inherent in any organizational design can be understood and resolved.

For example, consider the trade-offs between promotion rates and attrition. For promotions to occur, new openings must exist at higher levels in the organization. In an organization with flat or declining head count, openings occur only when employees leave the company. These openings can be filled either through external hiring or through promotions. Therefore, to achieve a high rate of promotions, either the attrition rate has to be high or external hires need to be kept to a minimum when openings occur. Business leaders need to resolve the promotion-attrition-hiring trade-off by establishing organizational guidelines and adhering to them in a disciplined manner. For example, set limits on the ceiling for attrition rates and the floor for promotion rates, and preferentially fill openings through promotions rather than external hiring.

Thus, the workforce planning process can help business leaders size and design the organization in line with business strategy. In addition, leaders can understand and resolve, in advance, any potential workforce impact in implementing the design.

APPLYING WORKFORCE PLANNING

Here is an effective five-step process for a typical workforce planning project (see Figure 4.2).

1. *Create baseline and engage senior leaders.* Baseline data on the current state of the organization as well as historic trends are collected. Engage senior business leaders in a conversation to understand business strategy and the organizational design and employee engagement requirements to deliver on business goals.
2. *Identify productivity breakthrough opportunities.* Based on the organizational requirements and the current state of the organization, conduct a gap analysis. Build the business case for organizational design changes based on the gap analysis. Obtain senior leadership team commitment and the resources required to develop the workforce plan.

Figure 4.2
Five-Step Process for a Typical Workforce Planning Project

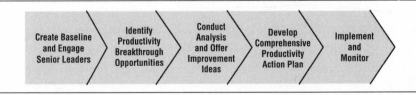

3. *Conduct analysis and offer improvement ideas.* Identify alternative paths the organization can take. Model the organization design's impact on the workforce to assess any trade-offs senior leaders must understand and address. Identify the critical drivers of employee engagement, and suggest specific actions that can improve the level of engagement.

4. *Develop comprehensive productivity action plan.* In this step, the workforce plan is validated and approved by senior leaders. Specific and time-bound actions and goals are finalized. Key metrics are also identified to track progress against the action plan.

5. *Implement and monitor.* Work in conjunction with business leaders to implement design changes and employee engagement initiatives. Conduct periodic progress reviews and make adjustments to the action plan based on changing business plans and feedback received on regular employee surveys.

REQUIRED RESOURCES

It is essential for the success of a workforce planning effort that participants work as a cross-functional team to promote the organization's interests. Consider the model depicted in Figure 4.3.

TRACKING PROGRESS

Successful implementation of the workforce plan requires continuous focus on the key performance indicators. Identify and acknowledge the differences across diversified businesses, and use workforce metrics to help business leaders understand key performance characteristics relevant to their workforces. This enables them to make informed decisions based on where they have been and where they want to go.

Establishing and monitoring key metrics ensure that leaders can meet business objectives, strengthen the workforce, and preserve the elements of the organization's people strategy. Based on business-specific needs, key metrics can be identified and progress against them can be monitored to meet right size, right structure, and right level of engagement goals. Human resources consultants can use these metrics to inform business leaders of progress made against goals established during the workforce planning project. Adjustments can also be made based on changes in business strategy.

Figure 4.3
Cross-Functional Team

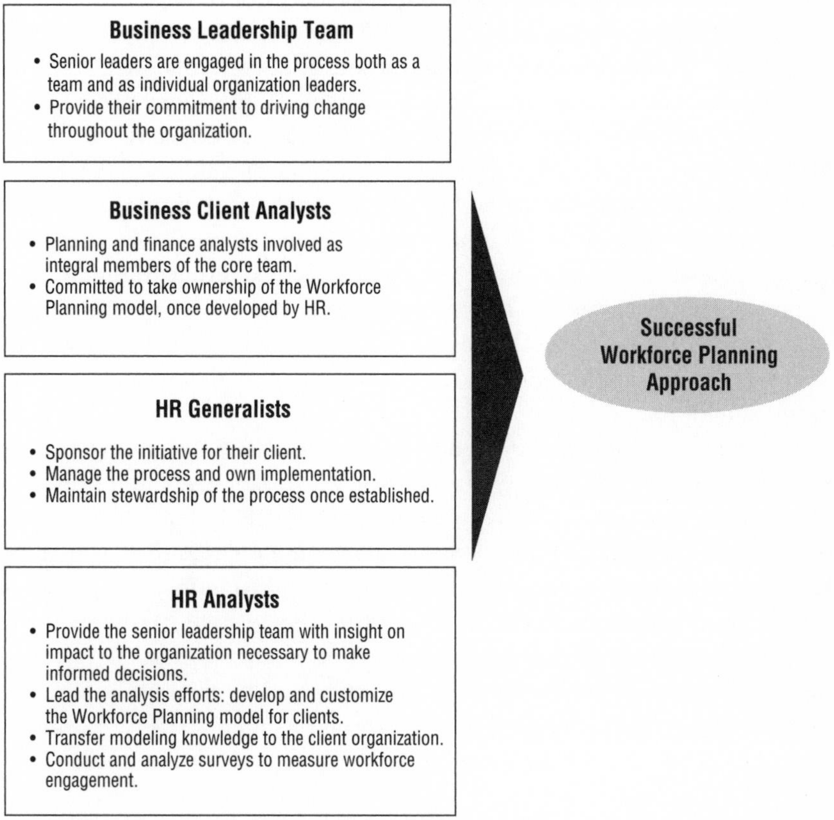

Business Leadership Team

- Senior leaders are engaged in the process both as a team and as individual organization leaders.
- Provide their commitment to driving change throughout the organization.

Business Client Analysts

- Planning and finance analysts involved as integral members of the core team.
- Committed to take ownership of the Workforce Planning model, once developed by HR.

HR Generalists

- Sponsor the initiative for their client.
- Manage the process and own implementation.
- Maintain stewardship of the process once established.

HR Analysts

- Provide the senior leadership team with insight on impact to the organization necessary to make informed decisions.
- Lead the analysis efforts: develop and customize the Workforce Planning model for clients.
- Transfer modeling knowledge to the client organization.
- Conduct and analyze surveys to measure workforce engagement.

Successful Workforce Planning Approach

REPRESENTATIVE METRICS

- *Right size.* Track the size of the organization both in terms of trend over the years as well as the variance against plan, using total workforce head count and head count variance metrics.
- *Right structure.* The focus here is on organizational design metrics, goals of which are determined by the business unit's senior leadership during the workforce planning process. They drive hiring and promotion decisions, as well as definition of managerial and stretch roles. Metrics

include span of control, percentage of managers at each organizational level, and promotion-to-hiring ratios.

• *Right level of engagement.* Employee engagement levels can be raised by identifying employee populations with low engagement and determining the engagement elements and associated levers that will have the most impact. Metrics such as engagement profile (percent engaged), morale, and attrition rates can be identified to track progress.

Workforce planning is a methodical process to design the right workforce required to drive breakthrough improvements in workforce productivity. This scalable, consistent process has been applied across several business units within Capital One as well as in corporate staff groups including information technology, finance, and legal. This work has yielded efficient organization designs, improved employee productivity, and enhanced ability to proactively engage employees.

Designing, developing, and monitoring the workforce are not one-time projects. As the business strategy changes, the organizational design principles and employee engagement strategy should be revisited. In that regard, workforce planning is similar to other business planning processes such as strategic planning and budget planning and should be integrated with those processes.

Strategic workforce metrics can be customized to each business unit or functional group's needs and then monitored on a regular basis. By tracking progress against organizational design principles and by frequently revisiting whether they remain appropriate to the business unit's strategy, workforce planning will become a vital, living process that creates a lean, agile, and engaged workforce.

PART II

Revitalize the
Talent Entry Processes

As EXPERTS debate whether we stand on the cusp of another war for talent, there remains no doubt as to the myriad of challenges posed by the next generation of talent. Today's workforce is highly diverse and ever changing. Gone are the good old days of lifetime employment with expectations of secure, stable jobs. These days, shorter tenures are the norm, particularly among the growing legions of knowledge workers who apply their specialized expertise to solve problems, generate ideas, and create new products and services. At the same time, we've witnessed a rapid growth in nontraditional employment relationships, such as telecommuting, job sharing, free agency, and other virtual arrangements. Employment flexibility has become the new management mantra, as the growing number of temporary, seasonal, and contract workers raises awareness of the need for a "new deal" that emphasizes a new mix of intrinsic and extrinsic rewards.

In the midst of all this change, organizations are finding the traditional approach to employment relationships—generic and one-way in nature—no longer meets the needs of employees or employers. A dramatically changed workforce requires smart, bold solutions. In this section, the authors advocate replacing the traditional one-size-fits-all employment relationship with more customized people management practices. They also dispel the notion that mobile knowledge workers are merely itinerant wanderers with little, if any, sense of commitment, arguing that they have proven themselves to be committed, loyal employees. Also included is advice on adopting a new relationship-based approach to employee orientation.

CHAPTER 5

CUTTING THROUGH THE FOG

NAVIGATING THE MESSY WARS FOR TALENT

HELEN HANDFIELD-JONES

CONTRADICTORY VOICES are arguing about the war for talent. Some experts claim a worker shortage is looming, while others say the workforce is continuing to grow. Likewise, their prescriptions for how to build a strong talent pool are all over the map. What's a businessperson to make of this confusing debate?

As is often the case when experts disagree, there is some truth on all sides. As one of the authors of *The War for Talent* (Harvard Business School Publishing, 2001), I feel some responsibility to make sense of the apparently conflicting advice. In the process, I will take my share of the blame for the confusion, while attempting to dispel the fog.

We can make sense of the war for talent only if we look at one type of worker at a time. There are many different kinds of workers, and each type has a distinct market with its own demand/supply dynamics. To craft an effective talent strategy, organizations need to understand these differences and design a talent management approach that is appropriate for each type.

Our original *War for Talent* research focused on business leadership talent—managers who lead companies, divisions, business units, or functions. In the late 1990s, many organizations were shocked to see some of their talented business leaders jump ship to join dot-coms. At the same time, we watched the extraordinary gyrations in the market for information technology (IT) talent. Collectively, we woke up to the emerging war for talent.

Obviously, business leaders and software designers are just two specific kinds of talent. What about nurses, scientists, industrial electricians, and so many others? Are the same forces affecting them? And what about flight attendants, retail sales staff, and hospital porters? Do the same talent management approaches apply to them, too?

DIFFERENT KINDS OF WORKERS

In the broadest sense, there are three types of workers: those in talent-intensive roles, specialized-skill roles, and low-skilled roles. Granted, this framework is a simplification—there are many roles that don't fit neatly into one of these categories. However, it helps us see the different dynamics at play and understand a range of different people management strategies that might be appropriate. In other words, it can help us navigate the war for talent.

Let's start with those people in talent-intensive roles—portfolio managers, research scientists, museum curators, and the like. In these roles, there is a huge difference between the value creation of a high performer and that of an average performer. Performance differs widely because these are highly complex roles that require a high degree of creativity, judgment, and tacit knowledge, along with very sophisticated skills. The top investment bankers, best CEOs, and elite software designers achieve levels of performance that have twice, three times, even ten times the impact of average performers. In statistical terms, talent-intensive roles have fractal-like distributions, where the people at the top end of the distribution curve have many more times the output than those at the center of the curve. Bill Gates captured this concept when he said, "If it weren't for 20 key people, Microsoft wouldn't be the company it is today." Those 20 people probably performed at fractal-like levels—and as a result, Microsoft outperformed the competition by the astonishing multiples we are all familiar with.

In these talent-intensive roles, one individual can have a huge influence on an organization's success. The quality of the fashion designers at an haute couture enterprise can make or break that business, for example. Likewise, the quality of the consultants is what makes strategy consulting firms successful. And the quality of the senior executives can mean the difference between winning and losing for most companies.

Talent-intensive professions require a high degree of innate talent and many years of education, development, and experience. There is also a high dropout rate as people grow into the most senior levels of these professions. Only one in ten law students makes it to senior partner at the top-tier law firms, and many high-potential business managers derail before they make it to the top executive ranks. Since relatively few people have the ability and desire to excel in these talent-intensive roles and it takes many years to grow them, the supply of talent-intensive workers is constrained and the best are rare indeed.

At first glance, specialized-skill workers look a lot like talent-intensive workers. They are highly educated, talented professionals, after all. There are some important differences, however. Because these roles tend to follow more prescribed methods and require less creativity, there isn't as much performance difference between individuals. And the level of innate talent required isn't as high. With the right education and training, many people could become a capable nurse, librarian, or accountant. Specialized-skill workers require several years of education or training, but since a vast array of experience isn't necessary, they can function very capably soon after graduation. Professional accreditation goes a long way in telling you who will perform capably in these specialized-skill roles, since the required knowledge and skills can be taught, tested, and verified.

At the other end of the spectrum are workers in low-skilled roles. Among this population, there is only a small difference in the performance of individuals in the same environment. Granted, there can be large differences in the performance of the workforce from one company to another or from one division to another, but that has more to do with the culture and management processes than with individual ability. It doesn't require high levels of innate talent to perform well as an assembly line worker, retail sales associate, or administrative assistant. A large portion of the workforce could be trained to do these roles relatively easily. And the training doesn't take long. After a few days or months, a new flight attendant, hospital porter, or call center worker is ready to go.

MANY DIFFERENT WARS FOR TALENT

At the heart of this entire issue lies one central question: is there or is there not a war for talent? To answer this question, we first need to understand the underlying forces that impact labor markets and how these forces affect each kind of worker. These forces include the rising value of intangibles, workforce demographics, increased mobility of workers, increasingly global talent pools, and fluctuations in demand forces for certain kinds of workers.

Many authors have described the rising value of intangibles in our economy. In recent decades, the main source of value creation has shifted from tangibles, such as capital, factories, and geography, to intangibles, such as brands, relationships, and innovation. Of course, people, particularly talent-intensive workers, are the primary source of those intangibles. Thus, the high dependence on talent is not only true for professional service firms, but increasingly for all industries and sectors.

Workforce demographics are an often cited—and often misunderstood—factor in the mess we call the war for talent. Fortunately, Peter Cappelli has helped clear up some of the misconceptions. He points out that the total workforce in the United States and Canada will not be shrinking anytime soon, although it is growing at a much slower rate than it did over the past two decades. Therefore, the idea that a widespread worker shortage in these countries will lead to a widespread talent war is overplayed.[1] More significant than the total size of the workforce, however, will be the changing age mix within the workforce. For roles that are typically filled by a certain age group, the peaks and valleys of baby booms and busts can be a significant factor easing or exacerbating the competition for a specific type of talent.

The new deal between employee and employer has increased worker mobility and created new challenges for companies. Individuals are much more inclined to jump ship for a better opportunity than they were in the days of the loyalty-for-security deal. And the market mechanisms of Internet recruiting and search firms have oiled the gears to make the talent market more transparent and fluid. In this new environment, companies not only have to hire more people to replenish the pool, but they have to work harder than ever to continuously retain their best people.

Talent pools also are becoming more global. Of course, immigration has always been an important labor source for Canada and the United States, and it will continue to be so. However, integrating the higher-skilled people whom employers need today is proving to be more difficult. Issues like accreditation, cultural differences, and language are more challenging for pharmacists and doctors than for bricklayers and carpenters. In addition to importing workers, companies can now offshore jobs to markets with more abundant and less expensive talent. Granted, offshoring has been happening for many years with manufacturing jobs, but the Internet has opened the doors for many knowledge-based jobs to be offshored as well. As many employers have discovered, tapping foreign labor pools can quickly alleviate talent supply constraints.

Fluctuations in demand for workers can be sudden and substantial. Thus, demand forces often become the dominant factor in the dynamics of a particular labor market. Certainly the overall business cycle has a major impact on many labor markets, sometimes in very dramatic ways. The market for newly minted MBAs experienced a terrible boom-bust cycle as the consulting and investment firms faced unprecedented competition for the top half of the class. At the peak of the dot-com boom, afraid that many students would rush to join the "new economy" companies, these consulting and investment firms made more than their usual number of offers. But the bubble burst before offers were accepted or declined, and these firms were stuck with large numbers of new recruits pouring in their doors just as the demand for their services softened with the overall economy. After two years of recruiting frenzy, many of these firms didn't even go to campus the next two years.

These five factors come together in different ways to create a war for talent, or more precisely, many little wars for talent. A war for talent exists when the demand for a particular type of worker outstrips the supply. The greater the supply deficiency, the more intense the war for talent. The longer it takes to develop a particular type of worker, the longer that war for talent will last. The more mission-critical the role is for an organization, the more seriously a war for talent threatens that organization's success.

Talent-Intensive Workers: An Ongoing War

Talent-intensive workers always find themselves at the heart of the war because of the differential quality of performance, the rarity of the innate talent, and the long time it takes to develop a seasoned pro. And recent forces have only served to intensify this differential. We can see the impact that the rising value of intangibles and increased talent mobility has had on compensation levels. In his article "Capital vs. Talent: The Battle That's Reshaping Business,"[2] Roger Martin explores cases where owners have had to give a larger share of the economic profit to talented workers. One of the most striking examples can be found in Hollywood, where stars frequently walk away with tens of millions of dollars even as studio owners take a loss. All of the examples Martin cites are in talent-intensive roles, such as CEOs, investment bankers, and product developers. This big shift of wealth from capital to talent will not be occurring for low-skilled workers or even for specialized-skill workers because they don't have the same kind of differential impact that those in talent-intensive roles do. A film studio may have to pay a high rate to makeup artists if they are in short supply, but it will never come close to what a star like Johnny Depp can command.

The battle for business leadership talent is shaped by these general forces, but there are other, more specific forces at work as well. The primary driver of the war for leadership talent is demand for higher-quality leaders at all levels in organizations. Leading a company, division, or business unit has never been more challenging. Technological innovations, industry structural changes, globalization, and the expectation of the capital markets for double-digit growth are putting enormous demands on today's leaders. Most companies are hungry to upgrade the quality of leadership talent deep in their organizations—not just the top 10 executives, but the top 50, 100, or 500.

At the same time, as demand for highly capable executives is increasing, there are challenges on the supply side as well. Companies have been riding the swell of baby boomers who are now 45 to 65 years old, the typical age for senior leadership roles. A few years from now, however, these baby boomers will be retiring in large numbers—as many as 30 to 60 percent of senior managers in mature companies. Much to their dismay, many companies are finding that their internal pipeline hasn't been geared up to produce enough next-generation leaders. Not only is the 25- to 40-year-old group less numerous in the external talent market, but this generation often grew up in organizations that had cut back entry-level intake, downsized and delayered middle management ranks, and cut back (or eliminated) their leadership development programs.

The worst of the leadership talent crunch is coming over the next decade. It will hit some companies harder than others, but the whole pool will be affected as companies short on leadership talent recruit more heavily from those who have developed a stronger internal supply. And since business leaders are mission-critical, talent-intensive roles that are impossible to outsource or offshore, the stakes are high indeed.

Specialized-Skill Workers: Isolated Battles

The competition for specialized-skill workers varies greatly from one type to another—some have a severe war for talent, while others don't, depending on the specific demand/supply forces at play. Because these roles require very specific technical knowledge and because it takes a long time before new workers come onstream, they are very susceptible to supply constraints. Offshoring can be a good way to quickly tap an additional supply of workers (lower-cost workers at that), but this strategy works only for certain kinds of jobs (programmers, engineers, accountants) and not for others (nurses, industrial electricians, teachers).

Peter Cappelli proposes that it is impossible to have a sustained disequilibrium in a specific talent pool. If demand outstrips supply, he argues, the "price" will go up, which will motivate more people to enter the field and more companies to reduce the number of people they need. This is true in the long term, but try telling your CEO that he or she need not worry because the talent they need today will become readily available in five or seven years. The companies that respond quickly and effectively to talent shortages will get a larger share of this scarce resource and, even more important, a larger share of the best people in this talent pool.

To illustrate how the demand/supply dynamics can vary from one field to another, let's look at four types of specialized-skill workers: one with a deep long-lasting war for talent; one with an approaching war for talent; one with no war for talent; and one with wild gyrations in supply and demand.

The talent market for nurses has experienced both demand increases and supply constraints, causing a chronic long-term war for talent. The aging population is relentlessly increasing the demand for health care services at the same time as supply is weak. A generation ago, intelligent, career-minded women flocked to nursing and teaching. Now, they can just as easily become engineers, doctors, or scientists. The number of years a nurse works has gotten shorter, too, with most nurses now entering the workforce at 30 and retiring at 55. The natural mechanisms that would correct for such a long-lasting supply shortfall have been hampered by pressures on the public health system. Hospitals have been operating under crushing budget constraints for many years, causing them to constrain the number of positions and hold wages down. Absenteeism is high, people are dropping out of the profession, and too few new people are attracted to it. Sure, immigration is helping, but not enough. Canada has lost as many nurses to the United States as it gained from the rest of the world in recent years. All this puts hospitals in a terrible bind, leaving them struggling to keep their heads above water.

Skilled tradespeople, such as tool-and-die makers and industrial electricians, are at the center of an increasingly tight talent market in Canada, largely driven by a decrease in supply. As a greater percentage of young people go on to higher education, the number entering the skilled trades has declined. Even in high school, the number of technical courses has decreased from 20 percent to 5 percent of all courses. At the same time, immigration sources are declining, as entrance requirements have been shifted in favor of

highly educated applicants. Thus, fewer skilled tradespeople are entering the
country. As a result, oil exploration companies, manufacturers, and others are
increasingly worried about the impact that the shortage of skilled tradespeople will have on their businesses.

Some talent markets are experiencing the opposite problem, as they find
themselves with an oversupply of workers. That's the case with masters of library science in Canada. Demand has fallen sharply as technology and the Internet have displaced some of their functions and as educational and public
libraries have gone through tight budget squeezes. Many professional service
firms have downsized or eliminated their research staffs, as consultants are
able to access their own information. Others have offshored their research
staffs to other locations. So while a war of talent may be raging for tradespeople, many newly minted masters of library science are unable to find work in
their field.

The market for IT professionals has gone through the wildest gyrations of
all. In the late 1990s, demand for IT talent soared just as smaller classes of
electrical engineers and computer programmers were finishing the degrees
they had started in the slow early 1990s. Then we saw the whiplash forces roll
in at the turn of the century. Demand nose-dived when the tech sector
crashed just as more supply was pouring into the market. Larger classes were
graduating, lured by the lucrative market of the previous years, and global talent pools were coming online, literally. Thousands of programming jobs
moved to India and Ireland as the Internet facilitated the offshoring of that
work. Within that broad market, however, there are many submarkets with
their own unique dynamics. Years ago, for example, COBOL programmers
were a hot commodity, followed by SAP programmers. Currently, programmers in the Washington, D.C./Virginia areas are hot, since the growing military and intelligence sectors need security-clearable U.S. citizens for that
work. The highly specialized nature of IT work, quickly changing technologies, and the ability to do much of the work at a distance make this a highly
volatile talent market.

Low-Skilled Roles: A Peaceful Front

Workers in low-skilled roles find themselves in a very different situation. Because of the speed with which more people can be trained along with the
small differences in individual performance, there won't be a war for talent in
this part of the workforce. It must be frustrating for people who are in low-
skilled roles or specialized skill roles that are not experiencing a shortage to

read about the war for talent. They are not receiving multiple job offers, and their pay, benefits, and other perks are not going up by leaps and bounds. That's not to suggest that the low-skilled workforce can't be a competitive advantage or that companies don't have to manage this part of the workforce effectively. It can and they do. But it does mean that supply won't run short and the competitive "price" won't be driven up.

Companies need to understand the particular challenges facing each type of worker in their organization so they can tailor their talent management strategies accordingly.

STRATEGIES FOR DIFFERENT TYPES OF WORKERS

Just as there has been confusion about what is meant by talent and whether or not there is a war for talent, there has been confusion about what strategies are most effective for building a strong workforce. Some have gone so far as to say that fighting the war for talent is hazardous to your organization's health. Much of this confusion comes from lack of clarity about what kind of worker each author is talking about.

Many authors, such as Jeffrey Pfeffer, Jon Katzenbach, and Bruce Pfau, are looking at how to get the best performance from the bulk of the workforce.[3] They cite examples of highly performing workforces in companies such as Southwest Airlines, Toyota, Marriott Hotels, The Home Depot, and FedEx where the performance of an army of workers in relatively low-skill jobs is critical to delivering value to customers.

Effectively managing the low-skilled workforce is primarily about engaging and energizing people so they give their best and perform the desired behaviors. Despite the fact that low-skilled workers can be trained and brought up to speed relatively quickly, it's still important to keep turnover low. Recruiting for this workforce is a high-volume operation that should screen for the right attitude and cultural fit. Job security, better-than-average wages, and a supportive, fun environment create a value proposition that engenders commitment and attracts a large pool of applicants. Extensive training in company-specific processes and recognition programs are important, so employees know exactly what behaviors are expected. Most importantly, you need to create a culture that empowers and engages people and to put in place great frontline supervisors who can bring out the best in every person.

Contrast this to the strategies needed for talent-intensive workers, where it is primarily a quality game. To build this talent pool, you have to attract, develop, and retain the very best people. Recruiting talent-intensive workers requires a laserlike focus to identify and assess those with the right innate abilities and seasoned skills. To attract and retain these people, you need to offer exciting jobs, career advancement opportunities, and great colleagues. Once hired, you have to provide them with rich, individualized development throughout their careers, investing the best development opportunities in the highest potential people. You also have to pay the top performers significantly more than the average performers. If you don't recognize and reward them for the disproportionate value they create, some other organization will. Finally, you have to regularly weed out the lower performers to make room for other, more promising people to move up through the organization.

No wonder people argue against applying strategies prescribed for talent-intensive workers to low-skilled workers and vice versa. The primary strategies are so different.

That said, underlying these primary strategies are some universal elements of good people management that are needed for all kinds of talent in all kinds of organizations. Chief among them is a strong culture that fosters teamwork and integrity. Creating an attractive employee value proposition is important for all kinds of roles, and the common company culture will be the foundation for that. The specifics of the value proposition will be different for different types of talent, but as we've discovered, some of the key elements can be quite diverse.

Strategies for managing specialized-skill workers will depend on the demand/supply dynamics for each specific type. If there is a shortage of a specialized skill role—as there is for nurses, pharmacists, and industrial electricians—the fundamental challenge is how to get enough people to fill all the jobs. In this kind of situation, primary strategies include recruiting people from diverse pools, creating an attractive value proposition, tapping foreign labor pools through immigration and offshoring, training and certifying some of your own people, persuading more people to enter this career, and restructuring jobs to reduce the number of the people needed.

Companies need to identify the types of talent in their organization and apply different strategies to the different types. Painting all employees with the same brush will result in watered-down solutions for some and excessively costly solutions for others. When facing an especially tough war for talent, companies need to reach for bold, creative solutions. Everybody is going to be improving compensation and benefits and everyone is going to be recruiting more aggressively. What are you going to do that's different and better?

CONCLUSION

Perhaps the biggest mistake in our original work was to talk about "the *war* for talent." If we had said "the *wars* for talent," it might have been clearer. To tackle the wars for talent effectively, you need to understand the differences between talent-intensive, specialized-skill, and lower-skilled roles. In particular, you need to keep in mind the differences in how they create value and the different dynamics affecting supply and demand.

Navigating the messy wars for talent requires clear thinking, a keen sense of direction, and strategic focus. The biggest success of the original war for talent work is that it got senior managers interested in the issue. By paying heed to the concepts laid out in this chapter, they will be equipped to map out their strategy for tackling this critical task.

CHAPTER 6

STAFFING FOR THE FUTURE

NEXT GENERATION WORKFORCE MANAGEMENT

ROBERT P. GANDOSSY AND TINA KAO

THE NEXT generation of talent poses many new challenges for American companies—not the least of which is an impending shortage of workers. In recent years, we've been alarmed to discover there simply won't be enough workers to fill all the job openings. For decades, organizations have enjoyed a ready supply of talent in the form of baby boomers. Standing tall as the largest generation in U.S. history, boomers make up a whopping 60 percent of the workforce. But with most of their generation scheduled to retire over the next decade—and fewer young people entering the workforce to take their place—experts project a shortfall of 10 million workers by the year 2010.[1] It's not just entry-level positions that are going to be difficult to fill, either, as the number of workers in the "key leader age" range of 35 to 44 years is projected to drop 15 percent.[2]

Not only are these organizations losing bodies, but they are also losing invaluable knowledge and skills that cannot be replicated easily. Unfortunately, says Dave DeLong, author of *Lost Knowledge* (Oxford University Press, 2004), many executives fail to recognize the seriousness of the situation. "A lot of senior executives don't have a clue about the critical knowledge that they are losing in their organizations," he explains.[3] Granted, that doesn't make it any less real. The loss of one single senior research scientist may cost an organization precious days or weeks when bringing a series of new products to market. That's real revenue loss, and it hurts.

According to DeLong, too many organizations continue to embrace antiquated policies that are designed to encourage early retirement. While that may have been a desirable outcome five years ago, it's no longer a wise move in light of the current situation. It's not like they can console themselves, safe in the belief that the impending talent shortage won't touch them. On the contrary, no one is immune to the shortage. It threatens virtually every organization. Of course, those industries that are inherently knowledge-intensive are likely to be disproportionately impacted. Take health care and technology companies, for example. They will surely feel the pain, as the specialized skills of knowledge workers in their respective industries will become harder to find. Likewise, employment in science and engineering fields has grown four times faster than overall employment since 1980. While it's true that we've managed to produce a growing number of engineering and science majors during that time, the problem is that we've produced them at a much slower rate than the demand.

As the workforce shrinks, it's also growing more diverse and varied. From the techno-savvy members of Generation Y to the many older employees who simply aren't ready to retire, more generations are working than ever before. And as society continues to shed long-held notions with regard to so-called women's work, more and more women have entered the workforce. Nearly three-fourths of all adult females are now gainfully employed in paid jobs throughout the developed world.[4] At the same time, the percentage of minorities with either full- or part-time jobs has also grown dramatically.

Along with these demographic trends, we see rapid growth in nontraditional work arrangements, such as telecommuting, job sharing, free agency, and other so-called virtual ways of working. In 1997, 11.6 million employees of U.S. companies worked at home at least some of the time. By 2004, that number had swelled to 23.5 million—fully 16 percent of the nation's workforce.[5] One recent study found that free agents—temporary and contract employees, freelancers, and consultants—make up 28 percent of the U.S. workforce.[6]

If the U.S. government were to institute a system of universal health care, the number of people working for themselves would double, speculates Daniel Pink, author of *Free Agent Nation* (Warner Business Books, 2001) and *A Whole New Mind* (Penguin Group, 2005). Pink believes that it's women, in large part, who are driving the trend toward free agency, primarily out of a desire to "reconcile the demands of work and family, but instead of relying on government or relying on the corporation, they are saying, 'I have to do it my own way.'" Previously, organizations would have avoided hiring anyone who had spent any amount of time working for themselves. Over the past eight years, however, Pink says free agents have become more legitimized. "When you say 'I work for myself' or 'I work out of my house,' that is no longer a euphemism for being unemployed."[7] Consequently, there's much more migration between the worlds of free agency and traditional employment.

RETURN OF THE TALENT WARS

Economists argue that talent is the last competitive advantage and that organizations have no choice but to "bet on people—not technologies, not factories, and certainly not capital."[8] Faced with the combination of a smaller talent pool and a rebounding economy—what some have described as the "perfect storm" of labor markets—the ability to effectively manage the workforce is going to be more important than ever. Add to that Hewitt Associates' studies, demonstrating that one out of every two workers is currently disengaged at work—with an astounding 40 percent expressing interest in being employed elsewhere—and you've got quite a challenge indeed.[9]

By all indications, the talent wars that plagued the closing years of the twentieth century have already returned. Unemployment for 2005 averaged 5.3 percent, down from a high of 6.3 percent just two years earlier. It's not just existing jobs that are being filled, either. According to a recent survey, more than a third of U.S. employers plan on adding jobs to their payrolls, while just 7 percent intend to reduce their payrolls.[10] Recruiters are citing a pickup in requisition loads, along with increases in signing bonuses and costs per hire. Such progress on the employment front hasn't fallen on deaf ears, according to a 2004 online Yahoo! poll, which found that nearly 50 percent of U.S. workers plan to look for a new job over the next year.[11]

Leading companies recognize that the ability to attract and manage intellectual capital is a significant—and necessary—differentiator. They also realize that tough circumstances demand smarter and bolder solutions. To win this next wave of the talent wars, they have abandoned the piecemeal approaches that failed them in previous years. Instead, they are considering workforce challenges in their entirety and taking a forward-looking approach to planning for today and tomorrow. A significant part of the equation lies in getting the right talent in the door, despite a smaller labor pool and a scarcity of critical skills. Perhaps even more critical, though, is the ability to maximize the value of the incumbent workforce through smart staffing and innovative development.

Experts argue that the needs of both workers and organizations are shifting. Workers want more options and freedom in how they work, while businesses seek to treat talent more as a variable cost to ensure scalability and flexibility. Leaders expect loyalty, but they are unwilling or unable to grant it in return. Some companies are shifting their practices to align with this new reality. They accept the fact that the average tenure for an American worker today is only four years and that the notion of the "organization man"—the loyal, lifelong employee—is a relic of a bygone era. The workforce models of tomorrow incorporate the evolving nature of the employment relationship. The result is a new paradigm focused around a truly on-demand workforce of project-driven teams, free agents, and borderless structures.[12]

A WORKFORCE TO MEET CHANGING BUSINESS NEEDS

Imagine what it would be like to work for a company with a precise, real-time understanding of the entire workforce—from full-time employees to contract workers. Laptop at hand, you could sit anywhere in the world and with a mere point-and-click, take the pulse of the workforce. From the comfort of your armchair, you could make critical decisions that ultimately could generate—or squander—millions of dollars.

At a macro level, decisions on whether to develop, buy, or borrow talent are aligned with short-term and long-term business needs. Each employee's individual employment history is carefully tracked and monitored to ensure that business needs are met, skills are utilized, and careers are managed. At the same time, performance data and assessments of future potential are carefully tracked to better match high-performing employees with the best business opportunities. Various employment models are used to contract with full-timers, part-timers, free agents, temporary workers, and SWAT teams. Even forecasts of external factors—the economy, interest rates, the political situation in China, South Korea, or Madras, or Bratislava, or *wherever*—are incorporated into the staffing model to deliver the best "right person, right time, right place" staffing solutions. Could such an idealized scenario actually become a reality or is it merely a pipe dream in the mind of an overly weary executive?

There's no question that workforce management is a top-of-mind business issue. According to one study, chief executives' number one priority moving forward is "speed, flexibility, and adaptability to change."[13] From a staffing perspective, that means finding the perfect combination of employees and work—and a method for sustaining it. Unfortunately, many companies are years away from achieving that degree of precision at a firmwide level. Many just don't have enough time to focus on the issue. This is evidenced in a 2004 Hewitt survey, which found that HR leaders were spending less than 25 percent of their time preparing for the workforce of the future.[14]

STAFFING FOR THE NEXT GENERATION WORKFORCE: MOVING BEYOND HEAD COUNT PLANNING

No longer are a handful of recruiters and HR generalists sufficient for keeping the talent engine humming along. Companies need innovative, holistic workforce solutions that respond to the ever-changing business needs of today and tomorrow. The solution lies in becoming true "talent management organizations," according to Allan Schweyer, author of *Talent Management Systems* (John Wiley & Sons, 2004). He advocates a combined effort in which the senior HR leader shares his or her talent management mind-set with the non-HR leaders of the organization, from hiring managers all the way to the CEO.[15]

Struggling to get their arms around the issue of effective workforce management, companies clearly are pushing the envelope when it comes to traditional areas of workforce planning, sourcing, and development. On the pipeline side, this translates into better sourcing and recruiting to find critical talent. On the inventory side, it means managing the workforce as effectively and efficiently as possible to improve productivity.

For most organizations, the workforce planning process hasn't really changed all that much. Each year, they embark on business planning to review the strategy, growth objectives, and anticipated work for the following year. This data is then fed into a workforce analysis that examines the talent implications—demand for talent, supply of talent, and talent gap—of the business. Finally, a workforce plan is developed with specific actions for meeting the organization's talent needs. It's a logical and straightforward process, and it works—for the most part—assuming an ample supply of qualified talent is available, that is.

As the talent wars heat back up and talent management gets more complicated, the workforce planning process becomes less relevant. As Kevin

Wheeler, an expert on recruitment and development, observes, "The comfortable, stable business world of the twentieth century with its abundant workforce is gone, and with it, the traditional workforce planning tools and concepts."[16] Leading companies are not sitting still. They are redefining the way the workforce is staffed, sourced, and managed through a number of bold practices.

Build Talent Assessment to Identify the Best

While traditional recruitment metrics on process and cost remain relevant, leading organizations are focusing on measuring talent quality. When you consider that it costs between 100 and 200 percent of base salary to replace an employee, you want to make sure a new hire is the right fit. Leading companies know that finding the right talent is a two-way street—they want to assess whether someone is a good fit for them and help candidates assess whether they are right for the company.

Always ahead of the pack when it comes to recruiting and retaining workers, Home Depot is developing a Web-based "smart" technology to drive candidate assessment for their retail stores. Cindy Milburn, senior director of staffing, who leads the effort, describes an assessment process whereby each prospective employee is given a customized evaluation. His or her output feeds directly into recruitment, learning, and other HR needs. "If I'm hiring a master plumber and I pay him that way, then I can pull him out of the plumbing curriculum," explains Milburn. "I'd rather invest and train him in electrical, so that he can develop broader skills."[17]

The company also runs some high-profile pipeline programs targeting older workers, the military, and the Hispanic population through alliances with AARP, the U.S. government, and various Hispanic organizations. In part, this is because these groups reflect its customer base. But there's more to it than just mirroring shoppers. Historically, these demographic groups have shown themselves to be great hires. According to Home Depot's proprietary studies, older workers exhibit better work attendance, longer tenure, and stronger performance. What's more, they bring existing knowledge and skill sets to the job. "The near-retired base [consists of] great associates," says Tim Crow, senior vice president of HR, because they "provide job knowledge to consumers that others can't."[18]

Leading search engine company Google employs a somewhat different approach to assessment, but its assessment process produces a huge flow of applicants nonetheless. The company drew over 14,000 applicants for the Google India Code Jam, a contest designed to find the most brilliant coder in South and Southeast Asia. The winner of the software back-off is offered a coveted job in one of Google's research and development centers.[19]

Companies like SAS Institute and Disney are known for their grueling interview processes. SAS has a "we hire hard and manage easy" reputation. It all begins with a Web-based application and test based on biographical and noncognitive factors—something they call a "managerial situation analysis." Candidates who pass the Web-based testing are scheduled to visit testing centers near their hometowns. Capital One has contracted with Comp USA and other external partners to use their on-site facilities and to conduct and score these tests.

At this stage, only half of the candidates move on to a "power day" at a Capital One facility where four to five business leaders—not HR staff—conduct structural behavioral interviews and one to two business case analyses. At the end of the day, consensus meetings are held with the interviewers and the candidates are scored. The meeting determines whether to end discussions with a candidate, make an offer, or bring the candidate back for further assessment. At this stage, about 20 percent of the candidates receive an offer and over 85 percent of these accept. From the web site application to this point, Capital One's yield is extremely low—only about 4 percent—but the process ensures the company gets the best candidates.[20]

CULTIVATE INNOVATIVE TALENT POOLS

Great companies have always sought great talent. That revelation should come as no surprise to anyone. What has changed, however, is that an organization no longer needs to bring the talent to its existing facilities. Instead, they can go wherever the talent is. The fundamental shift we are seeing today is twofold—the movement of commodity-like jobs toward the location of world-class capability and the ability of individuals to work from anywhere. Where you are matters little.[21]

Naturally, this new reality of talent sourcing hasn't escaped the original giant of the fast-food world, McDonald's. If you were to pull up to the drive-up window at the McDonald's restaurant located just off Interstate 55 near Cape Girardeau in Missouri, you never would suspect that the person taking your order is actually 900 miles away in a call center in Colorado Springs. But that's exactly what's going on. From his or her far-flung location, the order taker is connected to the customer—and to "co-workers" who are preparing the food—via high-speed data lines. He or she zaps the order back to the restaurant as you drive around to the pickup window.

Likewise, if you call JetBlue to book a flight, your reservation agent will be one of hundreds of housewives working from their homes. That's because Jet-Blue has outsourced its entire reservation system to working moms who take reservations between caring for their children and running their households. CEO David Neeleman, who founded the innovative, low-fare airline in 1999, calls it "homesourcing."

Nearly a quarter of a million hardworking Indians earn their livings by manning phone lines for corporations across the globe. In this capacity, they solicit people for credit cards and cell phone bargains or track down over-drawn accounts. Meanwhile, radiologists stationed near Bangalore airport read CAT scans from Massachusetts General Hospital in Boston. And a division of B2K, called Brickwork, provides personal assistants from India to global executives operating anywhere in the world.

From call center operators taking orders for McDonald's drive-throughs hundreds of miles away, to JetBlue reservationists booking tickets from home, to personal assistants, operators, radiologists, and software engineers operating in India or China, these long-distance workers are all part of the same phenomenon: sourcing.

Other companies are building talent pools of internal and external workers as well. Home Depot continuously collects resumes of potential employees to build a rich bank of prospective talent. Explains Cindy Milburn, "In retail hiring, you can't wait to get a vacancy to start recruiting; you need it to be pool driven." Another way to ensure a ready talent supply entails building communities of passive candidates—that is, individuals who may not be ready to join the organization at the moment, but who could be ready in the not-too-distant future. Other companies create positions whenever talented candidates surface. Take Semco, for example. Even when it doesn't have any job openings, the diversified Brazilian company runs ads, asking potential employees to present what they could do for the company. If Semco is impressed, it creates a new position for the applicant.[22]

Another company taking a future-focused approach to talent is Zoom Information Inc. (formerly Eliyon Technologies). Its unique search software combs the Internet 24/7 for information on companies and personnel. A search on an individual can reveal a number of details, including education, work history, e-mail address, and the person's own network of contacts. More than 25 million such profiles currently exist. And when recruitment needs dictate special attention be paid to a particular area, Zoom is able to conduct competitive intelligence for a specific zip code to find potential talent in the vicinity.

Increasingly, companies are establishing internal labor markets through which employees sell their services for short- and long-term engagements. With these internal project-based employment systems, workers from anywhere in the organization match their skills, interest, and capacity to open projects.[23] According to Allan Schweyer, this kind of practice typically results in a better quality of hire and better retention down the road. This understanding of the internal labor markets is different from the standard economic definition, which defines internal labor markets as those governed by a "hire from within" practice wherein wages are determined internally—that is, unaffected by market mechanisms.

Technology giant EDS Corporation built a global skills inventory of its entire employee population, numbering more than 100,000 strong. The company examined both current and future business needs, which it then matched against the skills of the workforce. In doing so, EDS identified shortages and surpluses for technical skills up to three years out. Employees were then sent individualized career planning notes, encouraging them to sign up for training in areas where gaps were projected. According to Tina Sivinski, executive vice president of HR, nearly 10,000 employees signed up for the training.[24]

PricewaterhouseCoopers advertises opportunities for internal movement across professions and fields—as well as geographical boundaries—throughout the company. All job openings are displayed on the company's intranet. Employees also receive regular voice mails and e-mails about job listings, and new-hire orientation includes a section on internal mobility and career opportunities.[25]

Hewlett-Packard (HP) is experimenting with an internal labor market based on project teams for new ideas. Anyone at the company may propose a new project to the VC Café, a team of senior managers who act as a venture capital group by funding those projects they deem viable. Once approval is granted, projects are publicized through the intranet, and any employee can apply to participate on the team. With this efficient application of both skills and interests, HP is able to build pools of talent across the globe on a real-time basis.[26]

CREATE A WORK ENVIRONMENT NOT JUST TO ACCOMMODATE, BUT TO INSPIRE

Leading organizations understand the growing diversity of the future workforce, but they know that accommodating work schedules is simply not enough. Beyond part-time work and telecommuting, they are coming up with truly groundbreaking ways to accommodate employees' diverse needs, while creating an inspirational work environment.

For companies' top performers, this is especially critical. Studies have consistently shown that top performers produce in value at least 100 to 150 percent more than average performers in similar jobs. And today's high-potentials place great importance on having a balance between work and personal life. In a recent study on high-potentials and the factors that motivate them to excel at work, work/life balance ranked fourth in importance out of 20 total factors.[27] According to one high-potential, "Work/life balance ranks up there with eating and breathing for me."

Some companies are building work arrangements for a targeted pool of employees. They cater to a segment with the intensity of a targeted marketing campaign and build a miniculture and support network to sustain it. At Ernst & Young LLP, an accounting, tax, and legal services firm, employees create flexible schedules to accommodate personal and professional needs. Some work full-time part of the year and part-time the rest of the year. Employees using flexible scheduling are not hurt in terms of promotions and rewards, either. Ernst & Young has a philosophy that workers will be more productive and will produce higher-quality work if they're not distracted by work/life balance concerns.[28]

Sun Microsystems' iWork program offers employees across the globe a variety of choices for getting work done—in the office, at home, or at drop-in centers. Employees armed with a "Sun Ray" smart card, introduced more than a decade ago, can access the Internet and Sun's network from anywhere. This type of virtual flexibility has been widely embraced by Sun's employees. Nearly half of Sun's workforce of 15,000 work either from home, at drop-in centers, or in Flex Zones within Sun office buildings. The program enables them to be better able to accommodate their work/life needs and personal work styles. What's more, they have saved the company money on real estate and back-office support.[29]

According to Daniel Pink, the most talented workers are in the driver's seat when it comes to job choices. Pink argues that "today, talented people need organizations a lot less than organizations need talented people."[30] As a result, companies need to pay more attention to what truly drives and engages top talent and work hard to build an inspiring work environment and experience. Pink believes that many companies "overlook how much people draw meaning and purpose and even pleasure, satisfaction, or challenge from their jobs." Similarly, James Ware and Charles Grantham of the Work Design Collaborative write: "For high-performing talent today, lifestyle has become just as important as work style; in many respects, the two are inseparable."[31]

Capital One pushes the notion of work environment one step further. Through the company's "Future of Work" pilot project on the sixth floor of its McLean, Virginia, headquarters, employees get to experience the workplace of the future. Traditional enclosed offices and desks give way to movable workstations, islands of common space to encourage dialogue, and glass-enclosed meeting rooms. There are creative spaces with couches and toys to promote brainstorming and quiet spaces devoted to silent work. Associates have flexibility to work as residents in one location, as mobile workers moving from space to space, or as telecommuters. All are armed with WiFi-enabled laptops, voice-over-IP (Internet protocol) software phones, and portable printers. A leading member of the joint IT, HR, and real estate team behind the initiative, Sallie Larsen says, "Capital One is a culture that obsesses with taking it to the next step. The Future of Work is part of that."

MOVE BEYOND METRICS REPORTING AND USE DATA FOR DECISION MAKING

Leading companies know that the future is a world of increasing data, and they seek to harness this information to help drive their businesses. Just as customer relationship management data can help a company develop detailed sales, marketing, and pricing strategies for its products, human capital data can be analyzed to inform critical workforce strategies. Today, many HR organizations are still bound to traditional workforce metrics and methods of reporting, such as number of hires, attrition rates, and performance ratings. They sit on top of valuable information, but don't have the capabilities or foresight to use the data to inform critical business decisions.

Home Depot tracks literally hundreds of data points from promotions to attrition, cycle times, cost per hire, and time to fill. The company focuses on the quality of hires, speed, cost, and future talent needs. It keeps its finger on the pulse of the future by reviewing workforce demographics, as well as worker attitudes, behaviors, performance, potential, and skills. Every Monday morning, the talent data is reviewed with senior management, including CEO Bob Nardelli. "The biggest dependent factor we have at Home Depot," says Nardelli, "is our associates—and the biggest *variability* is our associates." When you hire 160,000 people per year, you can't afford to get it wrong.

Within the human resources function at Capital One, Shyam Giridharadas, a former McKinsey consultant, heads a team of former consultants and engineers dedicated to helping Capital One's business leaders in making more informed human capital decisions. "Historically," Giridharadas says, "HR looks in the rearview mirror rather than through the windshield. We aim to change that." And this team doesn't stop with simply organizing vast amounts of data on people into the HR dashboard. They conduct analyses on everything from employee engagement and productivity to finding the right mix between insourcing and outsourcing. "Metrics tell you where you are," says Andy Suh, a member of the team. "Analysis tells you where you need to go."[32] Right now the team is working with its business customers to look at the correlation between promotion rates, employee engagement, and attrition. For Giridharadas, this is another example of "moving beyond trivial data, and trying to apply it more strategically."

Gwen Black, who heads recruitment and staffing for Philips Electronics North America, knows the importance of metrics and data. She and her staff are responsible for hiring thousands each year to become the future strategists, designers, and marketers of electric toothbrushes, X-ray machines, and flat-screen televisions. She uses metrics to report on the progress of her organization, but also leverages the valuable data in her talent management and enterprise application software databases to look at broader workforce trends for the organization. Her ability to present a bird's-eye market view of the internal and external labor pool allows her various business unit customers to make critical decisions on whether to build, buy, or borrow talent.

For Home Depot, Capital One, and Philips Electronics, the ability to drive business strategies through workforce data analysis requires new skill sets for their HR teams. No longer will basic spreadsheet skills suffice. The data gurus of the future need to be able to understand fundamental workforce issues and be able to apply information to solve them.

CONCLUSION

We are currently at the beginning of a seismic shift in the workforce. No one is prescient enough to predict how this shift will play out nor to fully understand precisely how organizations should better prepare themselves for the challenges that lie ahead. But one thing is certain—few organizations are ready, and many are just muddling through. In a knowledge economy, with the largest and fastest-growing expense being people, this will be a costly mistake.

The companies described here haven't *solved* the challenge. But they are well ahead of the pack—figuring out how to ensure a steady stream of top talent for the next generation.

CHAPTER 7

HOW AN EVOLVING PSYCHOLOGICAL CONTRACT IS CHANGING WORKFORCE FLEXIBILITY

DAVID E. GUEST

AS ORGANIZATIONS prepare to battle it out in the impending wars for talent, employment flexibility has become a management mantra. And it's not just lip service, either. On the contrary, there is evidence of the increased application of the various forms of employment flexibility in industrial societies in recent years. Although employment flexibility takes on many forms, contract flexibility appears to be the one that holds particular attraction for organizations. The practice entails the use of fixed-term or temporary contract arrangements as a basis on which to employ a portion of the workforce. Depending on how the figures are calculated, 5 to 10 percent of the U.S. workforce is employed on temporary contracts.[1] In some European countries, the figures are considerably higher.

Organizations are employing fixed-term or temporary workers for a variety of reasons. Temporary workers can help the organization cope with fluctuations in demand, for example. They also can fill gaps created by short-term and medium-term absences from work caused by maternity leave or illness, and they can provide the cover and/or distinctive expertise to handle specific projects. What's more, contract staff may require less training and development. In some cases, temporary workers can be cheaper to employ and easier to shed if their performance turns out to be unsatisfactory. On a somewhat different basis, firms may hire workers on a temporary contract as a form of probation or to provide a mutual realistic preview of the likely success of long-term employment.

While seen as good for organizations, temporary employment is often viewed as disadvantageous for workers. The European Union (EU) tapped into this assumption, proposing legislation to improve the employment rights of temporary workers. As the EU's actions attest, fixed-term and temporary contracts are commonly seen to be associated with higher job insecurity, a sense of marginalization or lack of organizational identification, and a loss of opportunities for development. For some temporary workers, this is likely the case. The temporary workforce is heterogeneous, however. As such, it increasingly includes professional workers working side by side with itinerant seasonal workers and those who are on call.

That said, there are some advantages in being a "free" worker: There is no obligation to be a good organizational citizen; it is easy to go home at the end of the official working hours; and it is possible to store up experience and contacts by working in a range of contexts, thereby maintaining employability and minimizing insecurity. Recent research and experience suggest these advantages may be growing, as changes to the psychological contract for permanent workers make temporary work less disadvantaged than it once was.

Here, then, is the wake-up call. A focus on the disadvantages of temporary work has distracted us from what is happening to those in permanent jobs and how it is, in turn, changing the experience of temporary work. Hence, we are about to undertake a review of the concept of the psychological contract, discuss how it is changing for permanent workers, and reveal how these changes are making temporary work more desirable. We will conclude with an overview of best practices for managing the psychological contract for all employees, whether they are working on temporary or permanent employment contracts.

THE CHANGING PSYCHOLOGICAL CONTRACT

While the employment contract covers the formal and legal aspects of employment, the psychological contract is concerned with the more informal and implicit features. It can be defined as the perceptions of both parties to the employment relationship, organization and individual, of the reciprocal promises and obligations implied in that relationship. Employees who say the organization has kept its side of the deal report higher levels of motivation, commitment, and organizational citizenship behavior, and a lower intention to quit. They also report higher work satisfaction, a better work/life balance, and lower levels of stress. While most research has focused on individual employee perceptions of the deal, it is important to bear in mind that employees have obligations to the organization as well—obligations that form part of the equation. In short, the object of the psychological contract is that everyone wins.

Historically, the psychological contract was characterized as offering an upwardly mobile, secure career in return for loyalty, hard work, and good performance—the traditional deal of the "organization man," if you will. Lower down the hierarchy, the focus was more on a fair day's work for a fair day's pay. Today, the changing nature of work and the workforce is making it difficult, if not impossible, for organizations to uphold their side of the traditional psychological contract. Rapid change both outside and inside organizations means that no firm can promise job security. Even highly successful firms suffer employment turbulence and insecurity as they become targets of takeover predators. Changes in technology and service requirements have resulted in constantly changing skill requirements and workloads, while flatter organizations have resulted in the disintegration of the traditional career hierarchy in those workplaces. Meanwhile, changes in values and the feminization of the workforce require that greater attention be given to flexible patterns of work to provide scope to achieve work/life balance.

Not only is there a change in the content of the psychological contract, but there's also a shift from standard deals affecting large sections of the workforce. This trend is resulting in more idiosyncratic deals, tailored to individual circumstances and requirements. Companies are offering many individual deals between employee and boss, replacing those overseen by the human resources department. They often entail medium-term implicit—or what are described as relational—promises. They may include deals on working hours, on travel, on personal development, on future assignments, and on steps toward promotion.

Despite these changes, many organizations are still offering the core elements of the old psychological contract, including the career promise of upward mobility and a long-term career. At the same time, employees are still expecting uniform deals that cover the entire workforce. Problems arise when these promises cannot be delivered and there is a breach of the psychological contract. When this happens, the potential for loss of motivation and commitment among permanent workers is great. Problems also arise when organizations offer one-to-one deals and workers feel that others have achieved a better deal. Trust is implicated when it is uncertain how that deal was struck and whether there was something underhanded about the way in which one person negotiated attendance on a key development program, a fresh assignment, or the opportunity to go home early two days each week. In addition, there are issues when one-on-one deals come to an end due to a manager's departure. At this time, employees may perceive a violation of the psychological contract. Here again, the potential for loss of motivation and commitment is increased.

THE NEW TEMPORARY WORK EXPERIENCE

Permanent workers are becoming increasingly convinced that their psychological contract is being breached, as they experience work intensification, increased monitoring, a reduction in individual autonomy, a culture in which uncertain advancement appears dependent on working long hours and displaying other symbolic acts of commitment, and uncertainty about the ability of the organization to keep its side of the deal. Together, these experiences are making permanent jobs more stressful and less attractive. At the same time, the changing values of permanent workers that give greater emphasis to work/life balance and general well-being are raising the desire for greater flexibility and feeding the feeling that there is a lack of fairness in their deal. In comparison with the "free" temporary workforce, there is a growing band of unhappy workers who do not feel very secure, despite the supposed permanence of their jobs.

While permanent workers have experienced an eroding psychological contract and unmet promises, temporary workers appear to have had a more positive experience. Studies and extensive work in a range of European countries reveal that temporary workers are less likely to report high levels of pressure and stress in work, poor general well-being, and poor work/life balance than are permanent employees. They also report higher fulfillment of their psychological contracts.[2] Although they were more likely to report job insecurity and less likely to be on their employment contract of choice, these factors prove to be less important in shaping the state of their psychological contracts, as well as their general well-being. The more positive experience of temporary workers might be attributed to the fact that temporary workers have narrower and more transactional or transparent contracts, which are easy to monitor and therefore more likely to be kept. It also could be related to the fact that the longer workers stay with an organization, the more implicit and relational their psychological contracts become—and the less likely they are to believe the contracts have been fulfilled.

THE BBC AND THL EXPERIENCES

These changes in the experiences of permanent and temporary workers are illustrated by the experiences of both the British Broadcasting Corporation (BBC) and the UK travel firm THL. When the BBC decided that many of the London-based technical and camera crew were no longer to be employed by the BBC, but should instead become self-employed so that the BBC could hire them back on a short-term basis as required, there was a predictable outcry and strong opposition. Yet the BBC persisted, eager to cut costs and increase efficiency. A year later, few of these technical workers wanted to return to their previous permanent employment status. They had discovered that the BBC's search for flexibility had provided them with similar flexibility. In addition to working for the BBC, they could now offer their services to other TV companies, as well as to organizations such as filmmakers and advertising agencies. This allowed them to broaden their range of experience, thus increasing their employability. In a tight labor market where specialist skills were in high demand, these newly temporary workers flourished. Consequently the BBC lost the flexibility of always having technical and camera crew on call with a sole commitment to them. By contrast, BBC administrative staff who had continued with conventional employment experienced decreased satisfaction, while the satisfaction of the technical employees serving as temporary workers increased.

Despite their strong initial misgivings, the BBC workers moved on to what eventually became their contract of choice. Overall, approximately one-third of temporary workers say they are on their employment contract of choice, while most of the rest would prefer permanent employment. Indeed, many believe that permanent employment offers them something more. This was certainly the view of staff at the UK travel firm THL, which hired many temporary workers at its sales call center, offering permanent employment to a number of them after one year. Morale and satisfaction proved to be highest among those approaching the one-year mark who had been told they had a good chance of permanent jobs. However, six months later, working permanent jobs, their satisfaction had declined. In their view, this was partly because permanent employment had failed to live up to their expectations. In reality, they found it felt little different from temporary employment, except that they were expected to do more for the organization. Previously, they had the prospect of permanent employment as a goal. Now they had nothing attractive to look forward to except for long-term, but not very rewarding work.

MANAGING THE PSYCHOLOGICAL CONTRACT

As these examples illustrate, the balance of advantage appears to be shifting away from permanent workers toward those in temporary employment. Given this change, we must rethink how to manage permanent and temporary workers for the benefit of both the individuals and the organization. We need a new deal that emphasizes a balance of intrinsic and extrinsic rewards. Jobs must provide challenge and autonomy, while experience in the organization should enhance employability and provide sufficient rewards aimed at retaining commitment. Financial rewards must be competitive and related to demonstrated performance; the quality of working life should be high; and there should be scope to manage the relationship between life at work and life outside of work.

Given the growth of individual, idiosyncratic deals, organizations need to

Table 7.1
Managing the Psychological Contract

Organizational Policy	→	The Psychological Contract	→	Outcomes
Progressive human resource practices		Promises and obligations made and fulfilled		*High employee:*
		+		Commitment
Organizational support		Fairness of the deal		
		+		Motivation
Friendly climate		Trust in management		
				Intention to stay
Personal work autonomy				
				Organizational
High employability/ work alternatives				citizenship behavior
				Work satisfaction

place considerable emphasis on developing and maintaining fairness and trust. These deals require much more detailed development, monitoring, and maintenance. They also require that the skills and motivation to manage the psychological contract be dispersed away from the human resources department to local line managers.

Finally, organizations need to learn more about the kinds of people who prefer temporary work and what distinctive personal circumstances are likely to lead to this preference. They also must determine what proportion might be classified as knowledge workers. In the end, organizations that fail to act on this wake-up call run the risk of having to manage an increasingly disaffected and demotivated workforce. Whether managing temporary or permanent workers, there are a number of things that can be done with regard to policies and practices that will likely promote a positive psychological contract. (See Table 7.1.)

- *Having progressive human resource practices in place.* These include provision of training and development opportunities; high involvement practices; good equal opportunities and work/life balance practices; open two-way communication; and promotion from within, rather than from outside, where possible. These practices signal an employer's intent to treat the workforce well. What's more, they create obligations that are relatively easy to monitor. If they have been promised, therefore, there is a good chance that the employer will feel obliged to ensure they are provided.
- *High levels of organizational support.* The importance of a sense of perceived organizational support—reflected in a sense that there is someone you can rely on to provide help when needed and someone you can express concerns to, and that the organization and its senior management team are concerned about your well-being—has consistently been shown to enhance perceptions that the deal is being kept. Support may be dispersed throughout the organization, but is likely to be reflected in the leadership style of the immediate boss.
- *A friendly organizational climate.* It is important not only that the organization provides support, but that it is also a good place to work and that people in it are generally friendly and enjoyable to be with. The opportunity to spend time in a friendly atmosphere and environment alongside people you like can be an important element in the implicit deal. Like so many other things, it can be strongly reinforced by the leadership style of the immediate boss.

- *A degree of work autonomy.* People value their own space to make decisions and to feel that they are in control. A key component of this is the ability to gather resources to manage the pressures of work. Provision of a degree of autonomy can be viewed as a form of organizational respect for and trust in employees, which is likely to be reciprocated.
- *The possibility of alternatives.* Research consistently demonstrates that those who see an attractive future and alternatives should their present employment go bad tend to be more positive about their current deal. When the organization has helped to enhance this mind-set—through development opportunities, as well as through its reputation—this increases perceived employability beyond the organization, while boosting employees' commitment to and identification with the organization.

CHAPTER 8

LEADING THE KNOWLEDGE NOMAD

AN OVERLOOKED SEGMENT OF THE WORKFORCE EXPLODES THE MYTH THAT WORKER MOBILITY COMES AT THE EXPENSE OF WORKER ENGAGEMENT

TODD L. PITTINSKY AND MARGARET J. SHIH

ONE OF the hallmarks of transformational leadership is the ability to inspire high levels of commitment from followers.[1] Extraordinary school superintendents, generals, business executives—indeed, breakthrough leaders in all fields of endeavor—understand that the success of their vision depends on being able to motivate others to go above and beyond what's required. These leaders arouse that extra energy and creativity that come only when followers' hearts and minds are fully engaged in the work at hand.

But knowing the importance of worker commitment and knowing how to secure it are two separate matters. The processes and mechanisms of transformational leadership are just beginning to be explored, and the specific pathways to fostering engagement remain murky.[2] Despite all the uncharted territory in this field, however, management theories almost

Sections of this chapter first appeared in "Knowledge Nomads: Organizational Commitment and Worker Mobility in Positive Perspective," by Pittinsky and Shih, published in 2004 in *American Behavioral Scientist* 47(6), pp. 791–807. In addition, some sections are also drawn from Todd L. Pittinsky's doctoral dissertation. The research reported in this paper was funded by the Harvard Business School and the Center for Public Leadership at the John F. Kennedy School of Government at Harvard University.

universally presume that increased worker mobility and organizational commitment are inversely related. Thus, mobility is seen as coming at the expense of commitment and, by extension, at the expense of the positive outcomes of commitment.

Our analysis challenges this dominant view on two fronts. First, our review of the relevant literature shows that conceptual and methodological biases have exaggerated the degree to which organizational commitment and worker mobility are inversely related. Second, the empirical research we conducted reveals that some of today's highly mobile workers present the potential for fostering organizational commitment *amid* conditions of high worker mobility, not in spite of or instead of it. Such workers, whom we call Knowledge Nomads, are much more mobile than their parents. To better understand their characteristics, it is useful to draw an analogy to the Tuaregs, a nomadic people on the edge of the Sahara desert.

Unlike the sedentary Hausa tribe of the same region, who stay in one village for generations, the Tuaregs carry their belongings from place to place in their search for water and good soil. Once they stop, however, they form a relationship with the land and people around them. They build a settlement and acquaint themselves with their neighbors. They cultivate the land, letting their animals fertilize it. They attend weekly markets, offering their expertise in leatherwork, tailoring, and the making of jewelry, wooden carvings, and colorful straw mats. The settled people in the area are unaccustomed to such goods and are grateful for a visit from the Tuaregs. They try to make the Tuaregs' stay with them as joyful and productive as possible; the Tuaregs, for their part, treat their settlement like home, even though they know that they will eventually move on.

Today's Knowledge Nomads are not unlike the Tuaregs in their movement from job to job as they wend their way through the American employment landscape. The late management expert Peter Drucker defined "knowledge workers" as people who use the greater efficiencies and radically new ways of disseminating knowledge afforded by information technologies to solve problems, generate ideas, and create new products and services.[3] Knowledge workers' value to their employers lies in what and how they think, rather than in what they make or do. Knowledge Nomads are a highly mobile subset of the broad category of knowledge workers. No one organization is their home or life. But like the Tuaregs, they build homes and till the organizational soil wherever they settle. Although they and their co-workers know they will move on, they are motivated, hardworking, and committed during their tenure at any given organization.

The coexistence of strong organizational commitment amid high worker mobility is not just conceptually possible—Knowledge Nomads serve as living proof that the labor pool includes people who exhibit both characteristics. Organizational leaders looking to create a more engaged workforce, therefore, would do well to consider the factors that help Knowledge Nomads thrive.

ATTITUDES TOWARD COMMITMENT IN ORGANIZATIONS AND THE MEDIA—AND THE POSITIVE EFFECTS OF A NEW PERSPECTIVE

Leaders pay attention to workers' level of engagement because it is often associated with desirable outcomes, for organizations and for individual workers.[4] Meyer and Allen (1997) found that, in general, outcomes under an individual worker's control are more likely to be positively affected by his or her commitment to the organization. More specifically, employees with stronger commitment have been found to work harder, perform better, miss work less often, and exhibit increased extra-role or "citizenship" behaviors.[5] Not surprisingly, workplaces are giving employers more freedom to make decisions and manage their day-to-day activities in the hope of creating higher levels of organizational commitment.

Engagement is also associated with desirable outcomes for the workers themselves. There is compelling evidence that individuals want to feel committed. Research shows that attachment is one of the defining experiences of being human, from the cradle to the grave, whereas the opposite of commitment—alienation—is uniformly associated with unhealthy conditions and behaviors.[6]

If leaders paid attention solely to the media, however, they might very well view their efforts to promote organizational commitment as pointless. There has been a great deal of discussion in both the popular press and management literature about supposed declines in commitment—where commitment is defined as the amount of time an employee stays with an organization—because of increased worker mobility. In the United States, for example, Tumulty (2002) claims that job turnover rates have spiked as high as 39 percent. Rice (2002) asserts that 75 percent of workers in Great Britain say they will not stay at a job more than two years. According to the popular press, workers of past generations did not change jobs this frequently.[7]

Whether grounded in fact or trumped up by the media, claims that worker mobility is increasing, and that this increased mobility erodes organizational commitment, can have pernicious consequences. Researchers in psychology and sociology have documented that expectations can trigger self-fulfilling prophecies.[8] Thus, organizations that perceive mobile workers to be less committed often stigmatize these employees as being less ethical, less loyal, more opportunistic, more mercenary, and more likely to abandon the organization in tough times. These negative characterizations can then lead organizations to reduce their commitment to mobile workers. For example, Godinez (2002) cites that mobile workers are more likely to be the first victims of job cuts. Such inequities don't go unnoticed, of course. Just as a jealous lover may eventually drive a faithful beloved into the arms of another, organizations that don't trust mobile workers may bring about the very disloyalty they had suspected.

In our research, we chose not to regard the connection between increased worker mobility and decreased organizational commitment as a fact, but rather as a relationship that sometimes holds and sometimes does not. This approach acknowledges the possibility that highly mobile workers can also be highly committed to organizations.

The reasons for exploring commitment amid mobility are compelling. A demonstration of the coexistence of commitment and mobility would counteract the popularly held belief that mobile workers constitute a "free agent nation" of individuals who forgo commitment, retreating into themselves to create "Me, Inc." Moreover, such a demonstration would help break the unfortunate self-reinforcing cycle in which management's presumption of low commitment among highly mobile workers actually produces low commitment among such employees. Once leaders appreciate the potential for strong commitment among mobile workers, they have good reason to tap that potential, instead of holding these workers at arm's length because they have been unfairly branded as untrustworthy or less committed. This, in turn, could revolutionize organizational policies. When commitment is viewed independently of mobility, a host of new management approaches—designed to elicit commitment rather than simply to reduce mobility—present themselves.

FINDINGS FROM THE LITERATURE

The organizational commitment construct—the inverse association between organizational commitment and worker mobility—runs so deep in the organizational literature that it is often treated as a given. But a thorough review of the literature reveals a systemic overstatement of this inverse relationship. The causes of this overstatement can be traced to three areas of scholarly activity.

Conceptual Definitions of the Organizational Commitment Construct

Researchers' definitions of organizational commitment are sometimes very explicit in the way they make inverse associations between commitment and mobility. This occurs most often when commitment researchers factor "intent to stay" into their definition of commitment (for example, Ben-Bakr, Al-Shammari, Jefri, and Prasad, 1994; Hunt, Chonko, and Wood, 1985). Meyer and Allen (1997) cite a definition of commitment that characterizes a committed worker as one who "stays with the organization through thick and thin." The practical and theoretical limitations that result from such a definition of commitment are obvious. How long does a worker have to stay in one place to demonstrate commitment: two years? ten years? Moreover, does this number depend on the industry, the worker's age, or where the worker is in his or her career? And does it change over generations?

Operationalization of the Construct

Some researchers, such as Mowday, Steers, and Porter (1979), include intent-to-remain questions in their commitment scale. Similarly, scales such as those employed by Porter, Crampon, and Smith (1976) include items measuring withdrawal intentions, but don't expressly reference this factor in their summary definition. When an inverse association between commitment and mobility is not explicitly made in the commitment definition, but intent-to-remain questions are included in the operationalization of the commitment construct, the operationalization of commitment strays from the conceptual definition. This dangerous and unspoken leap from definition to operationalization tempts researchers and practitioners to overstate the degree to which commitment and mobility are inversely related—and to overlook instances in which commitment may actually thrive amid mobility. Our concern here is not that continuance (continuity in a job) is considered a component of commitment, but that it is often considered *the major and defining component* of commitment, and that it is done so surreptitiously, rather than stated outright.[9]

Empirical Research about the Construct

Given that many researchers write continuance into their definition of commitment, and that many of those who do not explicitly write it into their definition include withdrawal questions in their commitment instrument, it should not come as a surprise that a host of studies have found a negative correlation between commitment and turnover.

Most of the existing research on the outcomes of commitment has been devoted to predicting worker turnover. Hulin (1991), for example, writes that "empirical support for the usefulness of the organizational commitment construct comes from empirical studies testing models of organizational turnover." Mowday, Porter, and Steers (1982) argue that the strongest and most predictable behavioral consequence of worker commitment is lower turnover. Similarly, research conducted by Koch and Steers (1978), Mowday, Steers, and Porter (1979), and Mathieu and Zajac (1990) also found evidence supporting this assertion.

In light of the circular state of affairs in which the organizational commitment construct is conceptually defined, operationalized, and researched, perhaps the only surprise is that the evidence for an inverse association is not stronger. But awareness of the bias in the research challenges organizational scholars to disentangle two ideas that have been closely intertwined and to reconceptualize them as independent concepts, thereby opening up the theoretical possibility that workers can be mobile *and* committed to their organizations.

EMPIRICAL STUDY OF KNOWLEDGE NOMADS

In addition to our analysis of the organizational commitment literature, we collected a quantitative data set that allowed us to examine whether workers who move frequently can still be committed to their organizations. We investigated the null hypothesis—that commitment to organization is unrelated to worker mobility.

Seeking to gauge both commitment and mobility, we recruited 115 knowledge workers with similar skill sets and career prospects from two companies.[10] The workers were chosen because they met two important criteria: They were all mobile, moving for both volitional and nonvolitional reasons,[11] and they had been deemed critical to the success of their companies. We administered the survey using a four-step process[12] and collected the survey data anonymously. Our response rate was 54.67 percent. The average age of respondents was 33 years, and the sample was 53 percent male and 47 percent female.[13]

In collecting the data, we used multiple measures. The first of these was Meyer and Allen's (1997) Organizational Commitment Scale, one of the leading instruments for empirical research on organizational commitment, which is weighted toward finding a negative relationship between commitment and mobility.[14] We also measured organizational commitment using a one-item instrument that is employed in many national survey research programs: "I feel very little loyalty to this organization."

We measured worker mobility by using indexes of past mobility and anticipated future mobility. First, we administered Shore and Martin's (1989) Intent-to-Stay Scale. Then, we asked participants for the number of organizational moves they had experienced during their careers.[15] Finally, we asked participants how long they had been at the two companies at which they had most recently worked.

We analyzed these data in multiple ways. A principal way to examine organizational commitment amid mobility is to ask the question, *Do workers who frequently move between organizations tend to be less committed to the organization where they are currently working?* We ran this analysis using two different measures of commitment; in both cases, we found no correlation between a worker's average length of tenure and the magnitude of his or her commitment to the current organization.[16] Workers who move more frequently between organizations felt just as much loyalty to their current employer as those who move less frequently.

Another way to investigate the phenomenon of commitment amid mobility is to examine the question, *Is a worker who is strongly committed to his or her organization less likely to leave the organization in the future?* This question examines the relationship, or lack thereof, between current commitment levels and workers' plans to stay in their organizations; to answer it, we compared workers' scores on Meyer and Allen's (1997) Organizational Commitment Scale with their scores on Shore and Martin's (1989) Intent-to-Stay Scale. Here again, we found no effect: workers' level of commitment had nothing to do with how long they intended to remain at the organization.[17]

Finally, we asked the question, *Are those workers who are the most transient the same as those who are least committed to their organization?* When we focused specifically on workers' ages, we learned that younger workers, who tended to be the most mobile of the people in the sample, were also the most committed to their organizations.[18] This correlation between age and organizational commitment proved highly significant.[19] While younger workers report more commitment to their current organizations, they also report a higher likelihood of leaving them. This demographic matches our description of the Knowledge Nomad: mobile, yet attached and committed to the organization while they are there, participating actively in the organizational community and working toward the organization's goals.

In all our analyses, the quantitative data supported our hypothesis that commitment to organization can thrive amid worker mobility.[20] Our empirical research did not reveal an inverse relationship between mobility and organizational commitment. These findings, together with our analysis of the way that the inverse relationship is overstated in the commitment literature, suggest that the possibility for fostering commitment amid mobility is very real indeed. That said, we do not argue that commitment is *never* inversely associated with mobility—we simply argue that it does not have to be.

Commitment to organization *can* coexist with high mobility. But many leaders still have a deeply ingrained belief that committed workers stay in organizations and do not move. Only by moving beyond this presumption of an inverse relationship can they begin to develop strategies for expanding the sphere in which commitment and mobility coexist and for maximizing the positive outcomes that result.

PARTNERING WITH KNOWLEDGE NOMADS

The frequency with which workers change organizations appears to be a fact of twenty-first-century life. But although Knowledge Nomads move frequently, they *do* form attachments and commitments. In fact, our research indicates that some of the most mobile workers are also those with the greatest commitment to their organizations. To maximize the value of Knowledge Nomads, leaders must invest some of their own time and energy, learning about the conditions that elicit Knowledge Nomads' highest level of commitment.

Consulting projects in which we have worked directly with practitioners to create high-commitment organizations have helped us identify three effective means of increasing the engagement of highly mobile workers.

Don't Retain—Unleash

Leaders who focus solely on retention, seeking a cure for mobility, frequently do their organizations a disservice by engaging in actions that can be unproductive or even dangerous. To demonstrate this phenomenon, we conducted a workshop with managers from a large company. We asked half of the group what steps they would take to *retain* a valued worker; we asked the other half what steps they would take to *elicit commitment* from a valued worker. The two groups produced vastly different action plans. When we replicated this study in a large governmental agency, the results were the same: The goal of eliciting commitment yielded far better management strategies than the goal of merely retaining employees.

The managers who were asked how to *retain* workers made suggestions like "increase salary" and "change his or her title." Such small steps may help keep an employee for a couple of months, but not for the long term—the productivity gains, in other words, will be minimal. By contrast, the managers who were asked how to *elicit commitment* proposed deeper and more individualized action steps. Among them: "find out what challenges make her tick" and "provide opportunities for learning on the job." The benefits, for both the organization and the individual, arising from such steps are obvious.

Granted, the costs associated with turnover can be significant. Nevertheless, concentrating solely on turnover—especially when it's viewed as a uniformly bad thing—can cause organizational leaders to pay attention to the wrong issues. As researchers have observed, some turnover is healthy. It prunes the lower-performing and less motivated workers from the organization. It can also foster innovation, as new employees bring new ideas into the organization. Yet most human resource organizations continue to think more in terms of retaining employees than of eliciting their commitment. This is a sad comment on contemporary workplace culture. The word *retain* makes workers sound like chattel. Who wants to be retained? Most employees seek to be valued; they want to be engaged.

So which organizational arrangements and management practices will have the retention cart following the commitment horse, and not the other way around? Deb Casados, founder of 3's Consulting and a veteran leader of many high-commitment work organizations, proposes that employers spend less time trying to retain employees through shallow incentives like salary bumps and more time wooing them over and over to the job and the organization by offering interesting challenges, greater latitude, and stimulating learning opportunities.

Employee commitment will not be fostered by any one management practice, Casados emphasizes, but rather by the diversity of the organization's efforts to develop commitment. Imagine the organizational mantra changing from "attract and retain the best employees" to "attract the best employees and keep attracting them for as long as they are here." By continually rere-cruiting their employees, organizations unleash them, as it were, to throw themselves into the work for as long as they stay at the organization.

Create Mechanisms to Align Workers' Commitments

Length of time in an organization is certainly the most common way of mea-suring employee commitment, but it is hardly the most interesting or helpful approach for leaders. Far more important than the duration of a worker's stay in an organization is the quality and quantity of the work he or she does while there.

Instead of gauging worker commitment based on the amount of time spent with any one organization, we define commitment as the degree of an employee's psychological attachment to an organization and the intensity (quality and quantity) of physical and mental effort the employee expends on behalf of the organization.[21] This definition has the benefit of being general enough to be compatible with the many different bases or forms of commit-ment—including those of the Knowledge Nomads, who are committed to companies while still mobile.

A common belief about transient knowledge workers is that other com-mitments replace their commitment to the organization. Some argue that mobile high-tech professionals identify more strongly with a project or with their industry than they do with the organization for which they work. Oth-ers claim that a parent's commitment to family necessarily supersedes his or her commitment to work. These commitments are not mutually exclusive, however.[22] Employees can be actively committed to themselves, their fami-lies, their careers, their projects, *and* their organizations. In fact, the most pow-erful and synergistic combination occurs when all these commitments are aligned.

The goal of the organization, and the organization's leader, therefore, should be to have an employee's multiple commitments reinforce one an-other. Harvard Business School professor Rosabeth Moss Kanter (1968) first sparked research into commitment mechanisms in a groundbreaking study that focused on the means through which the social systems of communes elicited commitment from their members. Working with a wide array of or-ganizations, we have refined the commitment mechanisms approach by ex-amining organizational arrangements in which commitment to organization thrives alongside commitment to career, rather than at the expense of it. Fur-thermore, we have developed a method of assessing employees' commitment by examining commitment to personal goals in the context of commitment to the organization.

In our work, we have identified several practical mechanisms by which companies can elicit organizational commitment while strengthening their alignment with employees' other commitments. These include:

- *Opportunities for formal and informal learning at work.* When workers are learning, their long-term career prospects improve. In other words, the organization's current needs become better aligned with the individual's long-term career need to continually develop new skills that enable him or her to remain at the cutting edge of the profession.
- *Small work groups.* Employees feel more attached to their companies when they feel more attached to such groups. But to prevent work group commitments from being antithetical to the organization—for example, a work group's commitment to devoting extra time to a group project that is not aligned with the overall strategic plan—it is crucial for the work group's mission and purpose to have the organization's stamp of approval.[23] When this is the case, workers' commitments to their work group and the organization become mutually reinforcing.

Workplaces that elicit high commitment from mobile workers tend to focus less on traditional rewards and compensation and more on aligning their workers' various commitments. They create jobs in which a worker's commitment to his or her career or family is aligned to his or her commitment to the organization. As a result, workers are not forced to choose one commitment over another.

Establish Alumni Networks

Workers move on for a variety of reasons. Sometimes, they want an adventure or simply a change. In other cases, a worker may move because he or she has been laid off in an organization-wide downsizing. In some instances, workers change jobs to follow their partners. For whatever reason, Knowledge Nomads will eventually move on to their next sites. This transition can and should be viewed as the next step in a continuing and positive relationship.

Ideally, the move should not contain any traces of "good riddance," as if the worker's departure represented a failed retention effort. Nor should a manager let the worker depart without saying good-bye in a way that indicates a desire to work with him or her again. The transition should feel like a release for the organization and the individual, both of who have given and received the best during their time together.

This is not to suggest that all interaction must cease once an individual has left the organization. On the contrary, relationships may continue for years, via e-mail or other forms of communication. Alumni networks have proven to be a particularly beneficial strategy: By staying in touch with the Knowledge Nomad who has gone off to another job, companies are often able to gain new contacts, valuable information about different market sectors, and new prospects.

Today's departing employee can mean tomorrow's deal. In large consulting firms, which often report an annual turnover of up to 20 percent, many workers perfectly match the Knowledge Nomad profile: young, committed, and mobile. After a few years, these employees tend to leave the firm for other commercial venues. Logically, however, the organization still has a lot to gain from these former employees. Julian Critchlow, a partner at Bain & Company, explains that former employees continue helping the organization by sending business their way: "We hope we hired the best in the first place, and then they go off and do something entrepreneurial and introduce us to clients. A lot of our new business comes from [our] alumni."[24]

Alumni are able to offer an honest "third opinion" to their former organization, often from another field. For example, former employees who are now working in financial, governmental, or other sectors can offer their former organizations frank advice on issues, trends, and the market's perception of the organization. Saj-nicole Joni (2004) finds this unbiased perspective crucial to an organization's leadership.

An additional benefit of alumni networks is the opportunity they provide for information sharing. As John Lindquist, vice president at Boston Consulting Group's London office, explains, "We share a lot of information with our alumni, such as new ways of addressing old problems, management developments, and so on. In return, we can use our alumni to help develop our own intellectual capital. If we have a new idea, we can go to one of our alumni and try it out. They speak the same language as us and can function as a real-world lab, a friendly external research and development department."[25]

While organizations obviously have much to gain from alumni networks, they also have a lot to contribute to the alumni: social opportunities, career development opportunities, and possibly even future employment opportunities. Many firms help their Knowledge Nomads with career advice even after they have moved on. Some alumni network web sites list not only job opportunities that are available within the organization, but also openings at outside organizations that have been sent in by alumni scattered around the world. A few firms even have a small professional staff on hand to give career advice.

Other leaders feel that nurturing their former workers is a worthwhile end in itself. "You are the organization that gave them their knowledge, their values, and their standards, and that they carry with them in later life," says Gerry Acher, senior partner at KPMG's London office. "Continuing and preserving that culture is very important to us at KPMG."[26] When both Knowledge Nomad and employer commit to a symbiotic bond, the mutual benefits can continue even after the Knowledge Nomad has left the organization.

Some Knowledge Nomads who leave an organization end up purposefully migrating back. Jill Ward, a marketing manager at Ernst & Young, calls such people "boomerangs."[27] Employees who return for a second tour of duty offer a wealth of understanding and background that other job applicants typically do not have. After all, who is more valuable than someone who already understands your organization?

CONCLUSION

Knowledge Nomads challenge the prevailing view of today's worker as someone who will move from organization to organization to advance his or her own career, showing little commitment to organizations. In fact, Knowledge Nomads *do* commit to organizations, and they do it while maintaining their commitments to their own careers, professions, and families. They move on, and they carry with them the beliefs, methods, and attachments they learned in your organization. Sometimes they even come back.

Rerecruiting (rather than simply retaining) such workers, finding ways to align these workers' various commitments, and building alumni networks all help increase worker engagement. But they also force leaders to articulate why the organization is a good place to work in the first place—a very good wake-up call, indeed.

ACKNOWLEDGMENTS

Laura Bacon (Center for Public Leadership, John F. Kennedy School of Government), Loren Gary (Center for Public Leadership, John F. Kennedy School of Government), Michelle Wu (Harvard College), and John Elder provided very helpful feedback on this manuscript. Deb Casados has been an invaluable collaborator, pushing our thinking and informing our arguments at many critical junctures.

REFERENCES

Ainsworth, M. D. S., M. C. Blehar, E. Waters, and S. Wall. 1978. *Patterns of attachment: A psychological study of the strange situation.* Hillsdale, NJ: Erlbaum.

Auer, P., and S. Cazes. 2000. The resilience of the long-term employment relationship: Evidence from the industrialized countries. *International Labour Review* 139:379–408.

Baker, D. 2001. Best of luck and keep in touch. *Financial Times* (August 22).

Barling, J., T. Weber, and E. K. Kelloway. 1996. Effects of transformational leadership training on attitudinal and financial outcomes: A field experiment. *Journal of Applied Psychology* 81:827–832.

Bashaw, E. R., and S. E. Grant. 1994. Exploring the distinctive nature of work commitments: Their relationships with personal characteristics, job performance, and propensity to leave. *Journal of Personal Selling and Sales Management* 14:41–56.

Bass, B. M. 1999. Two decades of research in transformational leadership. *European Journal of Work and Organizational Psychology* 8 (1): 9–32.

Bass, B. M., and B. J. Avolio, eds. 1994. *Improving organizational effectiveness through transformational leadership.* Thousand Oaks, CA: Sage.

Ben-Bakr, K. A., I. S. Al-Shammari, O. A. Jefri, and J. N. Prasad. 1994. Organizational commitment, satisfaction, and turnover in Saudi organizations: A predictive study. *Journal of Socio-Economics* 23 (4): 449–456.

Bowlby, J. 1982. *Attachment and loss.* 2nd ed. New York: Basic Books.

Burns, J. M. 1978. *Leadership.* New York: Harper & Row.

Drucker, P. 1959. *Landmarks of Tomorrow.* New York: HarperCollins.

Godinez, V. 2002. Job-hoppers find going tough in lean market. *Dallas Morning News* (February 24): 9L.

Hackett, R. D., P. Bycio, and P. A. Hausdorf. 1994. Further assessment of Meyer and Allen's (1991) three-component model of organizational commitment. *Journal of Applied Psychology* 79:15–23.

Hackman, J. R. 2002. *Leading teams: Setting the stage for Great performances.* Boston: Harvard Business School Publishing.

Hulin, C. 1991. Adaptation, persistence, and commitment in organizations. In *Handbook of industrial and organizational psychology,* (ed. M. D. Dunnette and L. M. Hough, 445–505). Palo Alto, CA: Consulting Psychologists Press.

Hunt, S. D., L. B. Chonko, and V. R. Wood. 1985. Organizational commitment and marketing. *Journal of Marketing* 49 (1): 112–127.

Jaeger, D. A., and A. H. Stevens. 1998. Is job stability in the US falling? Reconciling trends in current population survey and panel study of income dynamics. NBER Working Paper 6650, National Bureau of Economic Research, Cambridge, MA.

Joni, S. 2004. *The third opinion: How successful leaders use outside insight to create superior results*. New York: Portfolio, Penguin Group (USA).

Kanter, R. M. 1968. Commitment and social organization: A study of commitment mechanisms in utopian communities. *American Sociological Review* 33:499–517.

Koch, J. L., and R. M. Steers. 1978. Job attachment, satisfaction, and turnover among public sector employees. *Journal of Vocational Behavior* 12:119–128.

Levine, J., and T. Pittinsky. 1997. *Working fathers: New strategies for balancing work and family*. Reading, MA: Addison Wesley.

Marcotte, D. E. 1999. Has job stability declined? Evidence from the panel study of income dynamics. *American Journal of Economics and Sociology* 58:197–216.

Mathieu, J. E., and D. Zajac. 1990. A review and meta-analysis of the antecedents, correlates, and consequences of organizational commitment. *Psychological Bulletin* 108:171–194.

Merton, R. 1948. The self-fulfilling prophecy. *Antioch Review* 8:193–210.

Meyer, J. P., and N. J. Allen. 1991. A three-component conceptualization of organizational commitment. *Human Resource Management Review* 1:61–89.

Meyer, J. P., and N. J. Allen. 1997. *Commitment in the workplace: Theory, research, and application*. Thousand Oaks, CA: Sage.

Meyer, J. P., N. J. Allen, and C. A. Smith. 1993. Commitment to organizations and occupations: Extension and test of a three-component conceptualization. *Journal of Applied Psychology* 78:538–551.

Mowday, R. T., L. W. Porter, and R. M. Steers. 1982. *Employee-organization linkages: The psychology of commitment, absenteeism, and turnover*. New York: Academic Press.

Mowday, R. T., R. M. Steers, and L. W. Porter. 1979. The measurement of organizational commitment. *Journal of Vocational Behavior* 14:224–247.

Munene, J. C. 1995. "Not on seat": An investigation of some correlates of organizational citizenship behavior in Nigeria. *Applied Psychology: An International Review* 44:111–222.

Neumark, D., D. Polsky, and D. Hansen. 1997. Has job stability declined yet? New evidence for the 1990's. NBER Working Paper 6330, National Bureau of Economic Research, Cambridge, MA.

Pearce, J. L. 1993. Towards an organizational behavior of contract laborers: Their psychological involvement and effects on employee coworkers. *Academy of Management Journal* 36:1082–1096.

Pfeffer, J. 1998. Understanding organizations: Concepts and controversies. In *The handbook of social psychology,* Vol. 2, 4th ed., ed. D. T. Gilbert, S. T. Fiske, and G. Lindzey. New York: McGraw-Hill.

Pittinsky, T. L. 2001. *Knowledge nomads: Commitment at work.* Unpublished dissertation, Harvard University, Cambridge, MA.

Pittinsky, T. L. and M. J. Shih. 2004. Knowledge Nomads: Organizational commitment and worker mobility in positive perspective. *American Behavioral Scientist* 47 (6): 791–807.

Porter, L. W., W. J. Crampon, and F. J. Smith. 1976. Organizational commitment and managerial turnover: A longitudinal study. *Organizational Behavior and Human Performance* 15:87–98.

Randall, D. M. 1987. Commitment and the organization: The organization man revisited. *Academy of Management Review* 12 (3): 460–471.

Rice, D. 2002. Two-year itch to change jobs. *The Express* (October 5): 8.

Rosenthal, R., and L. F. Jacobson. 1992. *Pygmalion in the classroom: Teacher expectations and pupils' intellectual development.* New York: Holt, Rinehart & Winston.

Shea, G. F. 1987. *Organizational loyalty: Earning it, keeping it.* New York: AMACOM.

Shore, L. M., and H. J. Martin. 1989. Job satisfaction and organizational commitment in relation to work performance and turnover intentions. *Human Relations* 42:625–638.

Somers, M. J. 1995. Organizational commitment, turnover, and absenteeism: An examination of direct and interaction effects. *Journal of Organizational Behavior* 16:49–58.

Tumulty, B. 2002. Job churning estimated at more than 52 million annually. Gannet News Service (July 30).

Whyte, W. H. 1956. *The organization man.* New York: Simon & Schuster.

Yukl, G. A. 1989. *Leadership in organizations.* 2nd ed. Englewood Cliffs, NJ: Prentice Hall.

CHAPTER 9

WHAT HAPPENED TO THE "NEW DEAL" WITH EMPLOYEES?

PETER CAPPELLI AND ROCIO BONET

MOST OBSERVERS have a strong sense that jobs and especially careers are different now than in previous decades. The traditional measures that we use to describe jobs—long-term versus short-term, high wages and benefits versus low benefits, managerial versus production work—come from an earlier era with different concerns, making it hard to describe what has changed. Many things are fundamentally different about contemporary employment compared to earlier periods, though. It is a story about the rising importance of labor markets in shaping jobs and careers and the associated decline in the ability of employers to manage employment and careers inside their organizations, a development described previously as "the new deal at work."[1] Although employment relationships began to change with the downsizing waves of the 1980s, recognition of the changes became widespread only with the tight labor market of the late 1990s as employers experienced the breakdown in employee loyalty associated with job hopping. As

---

Many of the arguments presented here are developed in greater detail in Peter Cappelli, *The New Deal at Work: Managing the Market-Driven Workforce* (Boston: Harvard Business School Press, 1999) and in Peter Cappelli, "Career Jobs Are Dead," *California Management Review* 42, no. 1 (Fall 1999): 146–167.

the economy softened with the 2001 recession, some observers wondered whether the employment relationship would change again. Has it swung back in the direction of the previous model or moved in a different direction? The evidence presented in this chapter suggests that it has continued to move in the direction of an open market relationship.

HISTORICAL BACKGROUND

As a starting point, it is worth asking what the "good old days" associated with lifetime employment were really like. What led to expectations of secure, stable jobs and protections from the market in the past? Were they the result of a deep employer commitment, perhaps rooted in some deeper value system like a social contract, or were they mainly the result of a stable economic system that made stable employment reasonably costless? Before the 1920s, employment relationships were even more like a free market than now. The "inside contractor" model was the dominant system for manufacturing, essentially a model of virtual organizations where owners outsourced even production operations to contractors operating inside the owner's facility. Professional agents handled the marketing, sales, and distribution of companies on a fee or contingent contract basis. Employees in some industries, such as tapestries, moved routinely from company to company, facilitating knowledge transfer in the process. The turnover of key talent was managed carefully, but turnover of other employees was often remarkably high.[2]

Following the period of early industrialization, there were serious efforts by at least some employers to protect employees.[3] While the intellectual roots of this interest go back to the 1800s, the first arrangements that were reasonably widespread and that had any claim to be concerned explicitly with employee welfare can be seen in the system of welfare capitalism beginning in the 1920s. The motivation for protecting employees was always the self-interest of company performance. Assembly line production systems that benefited from reduced turnover had already driven efforts to stabilize employment, such as Henry Ford's famous five-dollar-a-day program. And union avoidance was far and away the most important objective. The companies most dedicated to stabilizing employment and job security were those whose stable product markets made this outcome relatively easy to achieve. Nor were these arrangements necessarily widespread. Welfare capitalism was primarily a movement of the largest companies and it was not clear how many other employers were influenced by its principles.

Most observers see welfare capitalism fading from the scene, either completely or in large measure, by the Great Depression and eventually being replaced by management's pragmatic acceptance of collective bargaining as the primary mechanism for protecting employee welfare. The main arrangements for protecting employees from economic insecurity and instability, such as seniority-based layoffs and promotions, supplemental unemployment insurance, and severance pay, were collective bargaining outcomes initiated by unions that nonunion firms adopted to buy off employee interest in unionization.[4] It is important to remember that even in this golden age of employee protections, from World War II through to the 1981–1983 recession, workers were constantly being laid off with the business cycle. They had stable jobs in the sense that they would return to the same employer, but layoffs were typical. Employer support for collective bargaining never meant any widespread acceptance of unions, and it may never really have been very deep. By the 1970s, for example, sophisticated union avoidance campaigns were common, and many employers—perhaps a majority—were taking actions to undermine their unions, some of which involved violations of labor law.[5]

The story for white-collar workers was always different. There the model for managing employees was not welfare capitalism, which was directed at production workers, but managerial capitalism, where the managers of the company acted to pursue their own goals as distinct from those of the owners. White-collar and managerial employees *were* the organization, at least in the eyes of the executives.[6] What most people think of as career jobs—good prospects for steady, predictable advancement, lifetime security subject to minimum performance levels, as well as good wages and benefits—was more or less in place with the formation of large, multidivisional corporations, expanding in scope and scale as the management structures expanded. In this model, employees were hired based on general skills and attributes, received elaborate initial training, and had a career that was internal to the firm. The systems for managing employees, such as wage and benefit policies, training and development systems, promotion ladders, and other practices of internal labor markets, were part of the elaborate internal administration of the firm.

What it is easy to forget now is the rather obvious dark side of these arrangements, especially for managers. Internal labor markets with outside hiring only at the entry level and all promotions internal to the company meant that employees were stuck with their current employer. If they did not fit, they had no choice but to suffer or adapt, and fitting in had as much to do with altering one's politics, social attitudes, and values as it did with performance. William H. Whyte's classic, *The Organization Man* (Simon & Schuster, 1956), is perhaps the best-known critique of this system, but other observers like C. Wright Mills, and two decades later, Rosabeth Moss Kanter, helped document the often coercive effects it had on employees.[7] It is difficult to see these provisions as a manifestation of employer concern about the need to protect employees. Elaborate programs for job security and career planning were structured to meet company needs, especially the need for a predictable supply of managerial talent with skills unique to the company. They were not primarily gestures of moral obligation even though they may have been presented and interpreted as such.

Both the operating environment and the nature of companies were different in that period in ways that made it substantially easier to provide stable employment and career paths. Especially for large companies, product markets were stable and much more predictable, in many industries explicitly regulated by the government to ensure stability. Foreign competition was very limited, and domestic competition often operated as an oligopoly where unions effectively took labor costs out of competition with standardized union contracts. Large companies had long-term business plans that made it sensible and realistic to lay out equivalent human resource plans and to say to individual employees, "This is our career plan for you until you retire. And here is how we are going to manage you to ensure that it happens." The economic instability that these large companies experienced was mainly the temporary kind associated with business cycles. They did bear the cost of protecting at least white-collar and managerial employees from recessions and from modest restructuring efforts. IBM in particular argued, with some justification, that the employment security it offered employees facilitated what by contemporary standards was low-level restructuring of operations brought on by unforeseen market changes.[8] But there was relatively little pressure to maximize shareholder value, at least by contemporary standards, and executives had much greater discretion to devote resources to such goals.

WHAT WENT WRONG?

The best way to examine the question as to whether the employee protections put in place by companies represented something other than a pragmatic response to the business environment is to see what happened when employers faced more serious pressures for change. In that situation, almost all of them abandoned virtually everything about the old system, even the rhetoric about their responsibility to employees. The world began to change for employers with the 1981–1983 recession, the worst economic period since the Great Depression, which brought with it structural changes that went well beyond the usual cyclical downturn in product demand. A number of important changes in the economy and in the way business was conducted got under way in that period. They include the following:

- *Pressures to increase shareholder value.* The rising influence of institutional investors and legal decisions that made maximizing shareholder value not only the singular goal for directors of public companies and the executives they managed but made shareholders the only stakeholder to whom companies were legally accountable. New financial institutions such as junk bonds made possible hostile takeovers of companies that were not maximizing shareholder value. Investors and analysts seem to be persuaded that cutting jobs raises shareholder value even though the hard evidence on that point is decidedly mixed. New accounting techniques such as economic value added that sought to maximize shareholder value punish fixed costs, including the fixed investments in employees.[9]
- *Changes in the boundaries of the firm.* Companies were persuaded that divesting unrelated businesses and acquiring new ones with appropriate synergies could raise shareholder value, and mergers and acquisitions rose to record levels year after year. Companies concerned about focusing on their core competencies learned to outsource functions that were not central to their capabilities and to pursue joint ventures as an alternative to internal development of capabilities. The consequence for employment was to disrupt long-term career paths and, more fundamentally, to make the security of all functions and jobs uncertain. Any operation could be divested if changing markets and changing patterns of competition align themselves, and all functions could be outsourced if a low-cost vendor comes along. One might say that the number of good jobs stays the same in this model and just moves around from company to company, but such movement and the constant uncertainty about movement undermines job security and any attempt to develop long-term careers.
- *Changes in the nature of competition.* Shorter production cycles and more rapid change in business strategies associated with faster-paced competition make skills obsolete more quickly. The examples here are like the change from physical chemistry to biotechnology in pharmaceuticals or

from one market segment in insurance to another, where the skills needed are completely different. Employers simply do not have time to develop the new skills they need internally where dramatic changes in products and strategies happen quickly. So they turn to outside hiring to obtain those new skills. They also turn to outside hiring to get the managerial skills and experience to facilitate changes in their administrative operations. One way to think about these developments is that product life cycles have now become shorter than the expected career of an employee (see later discussion).

- *Changes in the management of organizations.* Work systems that empower employees, such as cross-functional teams, break down traditional job ladders, eliminate supervisory positions, and widen spans of control. Information systems eliminate many of the internal control functions of middle management positions, and decentralizing operations through the creation of profit centers and similar arrangements further reduce the need for central administration. Flatter hierarchies and the sharp reduction in central administration reduce promotion prospects.

- *Policy decisions.* Public policy in the 1980s contributed to the pressures to unbundle employee protection provisions inside firms. The Reagan administration explicitly argued for increasing employer discretion in employment decisions in an attempt to link economic competitiveness to the ability to shed redundant employees, a position that arguably had more influence on management than the decision to fire the striking PATCO workers (PATCO originally stood for the Professional Air Traffic Controllers Organization, Inc.). Various reports gave guidance as to the best ways to cut workforces. Even under a Democratic administration, the U.S. Department of Labor had by 1995 accepted that companies would continue to restructure their operations in ways that cut jobs. It argued not for preventing such changes but for minimizing the damage to employees.[10] Peer pressures from leaders in the employer community also reversed direction. IBM's announcement of its decision to abandon employment security and lay off employees, for example, was followed shortly thereafter by a wave of layoffs among other large employers. The business community organized itself to press for greater flexibility in employment. For example, the Labor Policy Association, an employer group concerned with public policy, produced a widely circulated study arguing that the key to improved corporate performance is greater management discretion in employment decisions—in other words, the end of administrative practices to protect jobs.

- *The requirements of employment legislation.* Employment legislation also created incentives to unravel the internalized employment structure, incentives that built as regulations increased. The vast array of federal legislation directed at employment has largely been tied to the traditional, internalized model of employment. Alternative arrangements, such as contracting out or contingent work, can mean that employers are no longer covered by the legislation, freeing them from its obligations.
- *Market alternatives.* An enormous market has developed to outsource and now offshore functions that were previously performed inside companies. Further, staffing agencies will lease employees with any set of skills, even CEOs, so that labor costs can be transformed from fixed to variable costs. And, as noted later, corporate recruiters now offer a rich menu of available applicants to any employer willing to pursue outside hiring.

The protections against temporary, business-cycle layoffs for blue-collar workers proved largely useless against plant closings and other sources of displacement brought on by these changes. In an effort to reduce fixed costs, employers also shift more of their tasks to vendors and contingent workers. And the terms and conditions of employment in these facilities are now governed less by internal considerations, such as equity, and much more by conditions in the outside market. White-collar and managerial employees have experienced the most fundamental changes because they were the ones with the most protections to lose. First, they now face much the same increased insecurity and instability as production workers, a profound change as it undermines what had been the very basis of the distinction between white collar and blue collar. That distinction stems from the New Deal–era Fair Labor Standards Act, which is based on the assumption that production workers needed legislative protections that white-collar workers did not because the latter were already protected by the firm. Second, white-collar employees who kept their jobs also saw internal careers evaporating as job ladders shrank, restructuring disrupted the promotion tracks that remained, and external hiring blocked advancement by filling senior positions.

EVIDENCE OF A CHANGING RELATIONSHIP

Attempts to measure changes in the employment relationship are confounded by the fact that there were few parsimonious ways to define, let alone measure, employment relationships. The U.S. government, for example, did not attempt to measure permanent (as distinct from recession-based and temporary) job losses until after 1984. Some large percentage of the workforce never had anything like job security and organization-based careers. Perhaps only as many as 10 percent experienced the real "organization man" system.[11] So a finding that there is only a modest decline in some outcome for the workforce as a whole might mask a considerable breakdown in relationships for that segment of the economy that truly had career jobs, such as managers.

The place to begin a review of the evidence is to acknowledge the sharp rise in unemployment for white-collar employees relative to other groups,[12] which is certainly among the strongest evidence that whatever special protection this employee group had in the past is gone. In Europe, the trend toward longer-term unemployment began even earlier.[13] There is no evidence of a reversal in these trends since the late 1990s. Indeed, the evidence suggests that during the 2001 recession, U.S. employers cut back on workers harder and sooner than in any equivalent downturn. The level of "contingent work," defined by the Bureau of Labor Statistics as jobs that are expected to end, was not even measured before the 1990s. It remained roughly constant at about 4.3 percent of the employed workforce through the late 1990s, even as the overall unemployment rate fell and the labor market tightened.[14]

It is difficult to measure job security directly except through changes in employer policies. As late as the end of the 1970s, survey evidence from The Conference Board indicated that management's priorities in setting employment practices were to build a loyal, stable workforce. But a decade later, by the end of the 1980s, that priority had clearly shifted to increasing organizational performance and reducing costs.[15] The most powerful evidence in this regard is another Conference Board survey, which finds more than two-thirds of the large employers in the sample reporting that they have changed their practices and no longer offer employment security; only 3 percent said that they still offered job security to employees.[16]

Employer decisions to end job security through downsizing and permanent job loss are another lens into the world of changing employment relationships. Cutting workers to reduce costs and improve financial performance, not just to respond to declines in business, is the essence of downsizing. It is a new phenomenon that begins in the 1980s. The American Management Association (AMA) surveyed its member companies about downsizing from 1990. They found that the incidence of downsizing increased virtually every year through 1996, despite the economic expansion. Roughly half the companies reported downsizing, and 40 percent had downsizing in two or more separate years over the previous six.[17] Other surveys report roughly similar rates of downsizing. The scale of these job cuts was unprecedented in a period of economic expansion.

The causes of downsizing have also changed with a growing number of companies reporting that they now result from internal management decisions—restructuring (66 percent) and outsourcing (23 percent). Virtually none now cite overall economic conditions as an explanation, and most of the companies that cut are now profitable in the year they are cutting. Further, downsizing is no longer necessarily about shrinking the size of the workforce. Thirty-one percent of those firms in the AMA surveys were actually adding and cutting workers at the same time in 1996, and the average firm that had a downsizing was in fact growing by 6 percent.[18] This development suggests that firms are relying on the outside labor market to restructure, dropping skills that are no longer needed, and bringing in new ones. Further, the risk of job loss since the 1980s actually increased for older workers, those who otherwise find it more difficult to locate new jobs, even as the improved economic picture saw the job loss risk decline for other workers.[19]

Data on workers who have been permanently displaced from their jobs confirms the fact that job security is declining and is now no longer dependent on business cycles. The overall rate at which workers have been permanently displaced backed down a bit in the late 1980s from the peak of the recession period, 1981–1983, but then rose again—despite the economic recovery—and jumped sharply through 1995. The rate at which workers were thrown out of their jobs was about the same in 1993–1995, a period of significant economic expansion and prosperity in the economy as a whole, as compared to the 1981–1983 recession.[20] It is difficult to think of more compelling evidence that the nature of the employment relationship has changed than this. About 15 percent of the workforce saw their jobs go forever during 1993–1995. The cause of the job losses reported in these surveys mirrors the developments in the firm surveys—shifting away from economy or company-wide reasons such as downturns in business or plant closings toward eliminating particular positions associated with restructuring.

Other manifestations of declining job security include the fact that job losses now are much more likely than in previous decades to be permanent; that dismissals for cause, such as poor performance, have increased along with downsizing; and that the employees who were once largely immune from business-cycle-related layoffs—not only white-collar but also older and more educated workers—have seen their rate of job loss rise in comparison to other groups. Again, these reductions in security occurred in a period of economic *expansion*.

EMPLOYEE TENURE

Much of the argument suggesting that little has changed in employee relationships turns on research about tenure, how long an employee stays with an employer. While it is a mistake to confuse stable jobs with secure jobs—it is possible to keep a job for quite a while and be concerned the entire time that it could disappear—unstable jobs and hire turnover are clearly signs of a different employment relationship. Steven Allen, Robert Clark, and Sylvester Schieber found, for example, that tenure rose in large, stable firms during the 1990s at the same time that 16 percent of the jobs in those firms were cut.[21]

Tenure is a confusing concept to interpret because it is driven by two quite distinct components: voluntary quits and terminations. From the perspective of employees, only terminations, not quits, drive job insecurity. We also know that these two components move in opposite directions with the business cycle. Quits fall and dismissals rise during downturns, vice versa during expansions. Because the two components move in opposite directions, stability is built into the overall tenure measure over time, which makes any changes in tenure meaningful. The more important findings concern trends in quits and in terminations examined separately. Here the results suggest, based on three different sets of data, that permanent dismissals rose through the 1980s and early 1990s while quit rates were falling. One study in particular finds that the rate of dismissals increased sharply for older workers with more tenure, doubling for workers age 45 to 54.[22]

Not all workers had long-term, stable relationships even in earlier periods. For example, now as in the past, roughly 40 percent of the workforce has been with their current employer less than two years. And, as noted earlier, average stability can mask considerable variance for subgroups in the workforce. While studies found reasonable stability comparing the 1980s with earlier periods, more recent results using data from the mid-1990s find declines in average tenure, especially for managerial employees but even for the workforce as a whole. These include studies that compare cohorts over time, which seem to find the biggest changes, such as a 10 percent increase in the rate of job changes for younger workers now as compared to earlier decades.[23] They also find large declines in tenure for older white men in particular, the group most protected by internal labor markets. For example, for men approaching retirement age (58 to 63) only 29 percent had been with the same employer for 10 years or more, compared to a figure of 47 percent in 1969.[24] The percentage of the workforce with long-tenure jobs, 10 years or more, declined slightly from the late 1970s through 1993 and then fell sharply through the mid-1990s to the lowest level in 20 years.[25] The finding that tenure declined for managerial jobs is especially supportive of the arguments for the erosion of internal career systems.[26] The declines in overall tenure for the workforce as a whole come despite the fact that tenure for women has been rising because they are now less likely to quit their jobs when they get married or have children.[27] The most recent data, through 2004, suggests that tenure for women continued to increase since 2000 and to decline for men, especially older men.[28] Figure 9.1 suggests how dramatic the declines in tenure have been for older men.

The declines in tenure with the most impact are those that have appeared in the executive ranks, especially for CEOs. A 2002 study finds that CEO tenure has been declining steadily around the world.[29] More generally, the percentage of lifetime employees among top executives has fallen sharply in the past 20 years, as has average organizational tenure.[30] As compared to their counterparts in a previous generation, contemporary executives have shorter and more fractured job ladders—they hold fewer jobs before getting to the executive suite, get there faster, and do so by moving more often across companies.

Figure 9.1
Decline in Tenure for Older Men

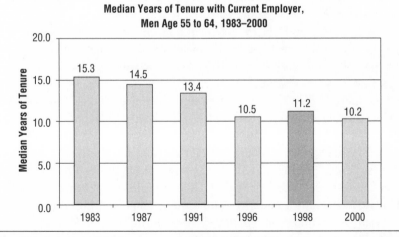

Source: "Median Tenure Declines among Older Men," *Monthly Labor Review*, September 1, 2000, www.bls.gov/opub/ted/2000/aug/wk4/art05.htm.

WAGES

Employee compensation has changed in ways that also suggest a fractured employment relationship. The most important effect is earnings instability, variation in earnings that cannot be accounted for by the usual characteristics of jobs.[31] The instability of unemployment, specifically the growing incidence of job loss, contributes in important ways to an overall instability of earnings, especially for older workers.[32]

One of the main functions of internal labor markets is to create distinctive wage profiles that differ from market rates in order to serve the internal goals of the organization. Job mobility within the same organization tended to produce greater benefits in the form of higher wages. This was seen in part as the result of a better match between the attributes of the employees and the requirements of the jobs as compared to job changes in the outside labor market and was a testament to the advantages of the internal labor market in allocating labor. But by the early 1990s, there was no longer any advantage to the inside moves compared to those across employers.[33] The steady progression of wages based on seniority or tenure was one of the hallmarks of internal systems. The apparent decline in the return to tenure with the same employer is perhaps the most compelling evidence of the decline of more traditional pay and employment relationships. Researchers studying the semiconductor industry, for example, found a decline in the wage premium paid to more experienced workers. Among the explanations are that new technical skills are becoming more important, and those skills are learned not inside the firm but outside, typically in higher education.[34] In aggregate data, the returns to seniority—that is, tenure with the same employer—have collapsed in recent years.[35] Other studies find a sharp decline in returns to seniority of about $3,000 annually between the 1970s and 1980s for workers with 10 years of seniority.

Another way to describe this effect is that the costs of job changing dropped dramatically. Workers who changed jobs every other year saw almost the same earnings rise in the late 1980s as did those who kept the same job for 10 years.[36] Further, the probability that employees who quit would find a job that offers a large pay raise has increased by 5 percent, whereas the probability that those who are dismissed will suffer a large decline in their pay has risen by 17 percent over the previous decade.[37] These results suggest that a good lifetime match between an employee and a single employer is becoming less important in determining an employee's long-term success. By default, what must be becoming more important are factors outside of the relationship with an individual employer, factors associated with the outside market.

A hallmark of internal labor markets was that pay was assigned to jobs rather than to individuals and that differences in pay were associated with differences in jobs. Some part of the greater variance may be because of a much stronger relationship between individual performance and pay. Hay Associates, the compensation firm, collects data from clients on the pay increases associated with different levels of individual performance as measured by performance evaluation plans. In 1989, the increase associated with the highest level of performance was 2.5 times larger than the increase associated with the lowest level. By 1993, that ratio had risen to a factor of four.[38] A 1996 Towers Perrin survey found that 61 percent of responding firms were using variable pay and that 27 percent of firms were considering the elimination of base pay increases altogether so that the only increases in compensation would result from performance-contingent pay.[39] Data from the Bureau of Labor Statistics finds that the percentage of employees eligible for bonuses rose from 29 percent in 1989 to 39 percent in medium and large firms and to 49 percent in small firms by the end of the 1990s.[40]

The change in contingent compensation has been especially great for executives.[41] Bonuses as a share of total compensation rose more than 20 percent from 1986 to 1992.[42] Contingent pay erodes the importance of internal, administrative pay systems by placing greater weight on factors that vary, such as business and individual performance. Stock options are now much more common than they were a generation ago and have expanded in recent years to include employees farther down the organizational hierarchy. In 2000, 10 million employees received stock options in the United States.[43] Stock options per se would be a net benefit to employees if they were an addition to compensation. Instead, they are a substitute for more stable forms of pay.

BENEFITS

Employee benefits are an important part of compensation, especially the fixed costs component of compensation. They have been seen as one of the important factors making employment an expensive option as compared to temp work, independent contractors, and other nonstandard work for which benefits are typically not paid. One function of the insurance-related aspects of benefits is that they help protect workers against risk. The decline of many employee benefits has been part of the systematic shifting of business risk onto employees that accompanied the restructuring of companies.[44]

Pension plans have been the employee benefit with the most important

Figure 9.2
Decline in Pension Coverage in United States

Full-Time Employees

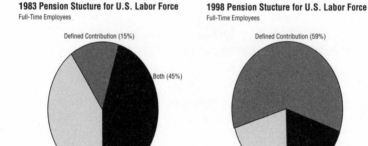

NOTE: Includes only those individuals that specified pension type.

Source: Leora Friedberg and Michael T. Owyang, "Not Your Father's Pension Plan: The Rise of 401(k) and Other Defined Contribution Plans," *Review, Federal Reserve Bank of St. Louis* 84, 1 (January/February 2002): 23.

implications for the employment relationship as they represent a continuing obligation to employees even if employment ends (at least for vested employees) and, as such, are an indication of a more permanent obligation by employers. Even more important than the decline in pension coverage has been the shift in the nature of pensions from defined benefit plans, where workers earn the right to predetermined benefit levels according to their years of service, toward defined contribution plans, where employers make fixed contributions to a retirement fund for each employee, especially 401(k) programs whereby employees contribute directly to their retirement funds.[45] With this shift, the employer no longer bears the risk of guaranteeing a stream of benefits. Now the employee does. Employees no longer have an incentive to stay with the company long enough to gain access to those pension contributions. The employer's obligations to the employee end with employment, signaling a move away from long-term obligations and relationships. Figure 9.2 outlines the overall decline in pension coverage in the United States over time as well as the change in the composition of pensions, from defined benefit to defined contribution plans like 401(k)s.[46]

NONSTANDARD WORK

Another aspect of changes in employment is the rise of temporary help, part-time, and self-employed, collectively known as nonstandard work because the common characteristic is something other than full-time employment. The rise of nonstandard work suggests something about the growing employer preference for variable as opposed to fixed employment costs. Whether nonstandard work continues to grow is an empirical question. In 2003–2004, temporary jobs accounted for almost one-third of new jobs in the economy, although sharp increases like this are usually associated with periods of economic recovery. It is worth recognizing, however, that most estimates indicate that nonstandard work already accounts for just under one-third of United States jobs, with part-time and self-employment constituting the lion's share.[47] It might be reasonable to include contracting out and vendors in this category, at least from the perspective of the original firm, because they represent the movement of work that had been inside the firm at fixed cost to work that is now done outside the firm at variable cost. The outsourced jobs may still be good jobs, of course, although they often represent significantly reduced career opportunities.[48]

OUTSIDE HIRING

Arguably the main factor pushing employment relations away from the old model is the greater use of outside hiring by employers as it pulls employees out of existing relationships and disrupts career advancement in others. It is difficult to assess the extent of outside hiring, but one study that did so in 1997 found a sizable increase in the proportion of employers that sought experienced workers for entry-level jobs.[49] An examination of proprietary surveys of employers finds them reporting a greater interest in outside hiring to meet skill needs.[50] One interesting proxy for the growth of outside hiring is the fact that the revenues from corporate recruiting firms that perform outside searchers for companies *tripled* just during the mid-1990s.[51] In a sample of 120 U.S. industrial corporations that are reasonably representative of publicly held companies, the prevalence of outsider selection, a rarity in earlier generations, was approximately 25 percent.[52] Another study reports that outsider CEOs represented 30 percent of all CEOs in the late 1990s. At least one argument suggests that the rise of outside hiring for CEOs as well as the sharp increase in CEO pay are related to the rising demand for general managerial skills, as opposed to company-specific skills, in those positions.[53] Outside hiring of CEOs and executives is particularly important because the new hires often bring with them their own team of managers, causing extensive disruption to existing career paths.

When employers switch from internal promotions to outside hires, they effectively shut down their own internal labor market by eliminating promotion prospects. They also eviscerate the internal labor markets of competitors because the investments made in that employee leave. Outside hiring shifts the attention of employers from inside the firm to the network of potential employers outside the firm where more—and quite likely better—career opportunities lie. There is no evidence that employers are making investments in their new hires, and the evidence that we have suggests that they are making substantially fewer investments in new hires now than in the past, particularly in the extent of training to learn new jobs.[54]

How are employees reacting to these changes? Some suggest that the economic decline associated with the 2001 recession has made employees

Figure 9.3
Results of Conjoint Analysis

I would change jobs for . . . ?

I would leave for . . .	25% of Workers		50% of Workers		75% of Workers	
	Units	Dollars	Units	Dollars	Units	Dollars
Stock grant face value	50 shares	$500	100 shares	$1,000	1,000 shares	$10,000
Vacation days	7 days	$652	10 days	$1,400	15 days	$2,769
Bonus opportunity	$1,000	$1,000	$5,000	$5,000	$10k	$10,000
Salary increase	10%	$3,750	20%	$7,500	35%	$15,000
Potential salary in five years	$6,000	$6,000	$15k	$15,000	$35k	$35,000
One-time retirement contribution	$5,000	$5,000	$20k	$20,000	$50k	$50,000

Source: Sibson & Company, 2003.

more interested in job security and less interested in hopping from job to job. A national probability survey of employees conducted in 2003, when the job market was at a low point, asked what would be required in terms of compensation to get them to leave their current job and take an equivalent position elsewhere. The results of conjoint analysis, reported in Figure 9.3, suggest that even in 2003 large proportions of employees were willing to leave for small amounts of additional compensation. For example, 25 percent of workers would change jobs for additional vacation days worth $652 per year.

A simple comparison of annual quit rates over time (Figure 9.4) shows a strong relationship between the tightness of the job market, as measured by the unemployment rate, and annual quit rates: As jobs become plentiful, workers quit; as jobs become scarce, workers stay put. There is nothing in the past 20 years to suggest that this relationship will change in the future.

Figure 9.4
Comparison of Annual Quit Rates

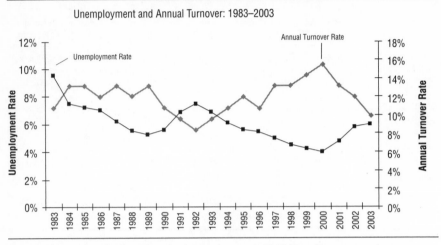

Unemployment and Annual Turnover: 1983–2003

Source: U.S. Bureau of Labor Statistics (unemployment): BNA, Inc. (turnover rate).

CONCLUSIONS

The evidence does not suggest that all employers are necessarily headed toward open market relationships. But the set of industries that are moving well toward that model is more than just at the margins of the economy. Silicon Valley is often held up as the example of open labor markets with high levels of mobility across firms and little planned internal development. Silicon Valley is not just a geographic location, though. It is a metaphor for much of the entire high-tech sector across the country. Something like free agency now dominates creative industries like movies and television, much of the investment industry, and professional service firms (accounting, consulting, and law firms in particular), where promotion to partner previously meant a lifetime career at that firm. Now movement across firms is common even for partners. Outside hiring may be more common for higher-skilled employees because their higher value added makes search and recruiting costs easier to recoup. But poaching (hiring away employees from competitors) is now a phenomenon for all jobs where labor is in short supply. Call centers, for example, have been particularly subject to retention problems from outside hiring. Even state beaches on the East Coast have engaged in poaching lifeguards from each other.

During the period of tight labor markets in the late 1990s, bargaining power in the labor market shifted to employees, and they secured many important gains, especially in terms of compensation. There is no evidence whatsoever, though, that employees were using their newfound bargaining power to demand anything like a return to the older model of employment relations. Unless the changes in the business environment outlined in this chapter are rolled back, it is difficult to believe that any promises of a return to a model of protected careers would be credible even if employees were to ask for it. And in tight labor markets, the last thing employees want is an arrangement that would buffer them from those markets and their benefits. Ninety-four percent of employees in a recent survey reported that they believed that they, and not their employer, were responsible for their own job security. When asked what they wanted from employers in a different survey, the top places went to development opportunities. Job security came out in the middle of the list. Surveys of MBA students find greater willingness to take risks and little interest in the large corporations that may still offer the best internal career paths.[55]

When the market cooled off after 2001, power shifted back to employers as job seekers outnumbered openings. Employers used their power to reduce compensation, cut back on many of the perks that employees had previously received, and increase work time and effort. There is no evidence that employers used their power to revert to anything like the traditional model of employment relationships. There are some companies that continue to offer some security to employees, or at least to talk about it. Often these are privately held companies, not subject to the financial pressures of the investment community, and making products with some protection from fast-changing competition. Finding continuing examples of the old arrangements is no evidence of a *return* to those arrangements, though. New work systems like team-based arrangements might be expected to require greater investments in employees and in continuity, but there is no evidence that employers are making those investments.[56]

Further, it is not within the power of an individual employer to return to the older arrangements. Consider an employer who decides to return to more traditional arrangements with long-term investments in employees, internal promotions, and lifetime careers. Even if such a model made sense for the employer's current context, it will work only if competitors agree not to poach away valuable talent and employees agree not to leave for what, at some point, could be better offers than they have internally. Neither is likely. And where commitment by workers is needed, it does not seem to require secure careers or even permanent jobs as indicated by the studies showing that contingent workers are just as committed to their jobs as full-time employees.[57]

These new arrangements do create new sets of winners and losers. While traditional arrangements sheltered employment from market pressures, the new arrangements make the market the arbiter of labor market outcomes. As noted, in slack labor markets, employers are able to push even more costs onto employees, whereas in tight labor markets, employees are able to extract more rents from employers. Within the labor market, those with marketable skills and the ability to manage their own careers have made out very well; those without skills, with constraints on their mobility, and lacking career management skills have suffered even more than in the past. These developments may help account for rising inequality in outcomes, and they no doubt will exacerbate that trend.

There clearly is and should be concern about the increasing insecurity and instability that workers, and in turn their families, face under these new arrangements. It is not obvious what interventions would help them, though, and even less obvious whether they would be actionable. The approach of prohibiting undesirable outcomes, such as prohibiting layoffs along the lines of some European employment regulations, does not seem feasible in an environment where business flexibility is seen as driving the overall performance of the economy. Reducing the burdens associated with transitions between employers might help, such as making employee benefits more portable so that employees do not lose health care coverage or pensions when they switch employers; reforming unemployment insurance, a program designed to accommodate temporary layoffs, to help assist employees who face permanent job loss (California, for example, allows companies to draw on unemployment insurance funds to retrain workers who are at risk of layoff); providing much more substantive assistance for retraining employees who are displaced from jobs, including greater access to education; moving away from economic assistance tied to employment, such as the minimum wage, and toward other forms of assistance such as earned income tax credits. The most important factor, however, may be the labor market itself. Employees have always made out better when the economy is running hot. The difference now is that they make out *much* better when it is hot and suffer much more when it is cool. Finding ways to keep the economy running hot should therefore be a bigger priority for labor. In practice, it may require that the economy run a greater risk of inflation than policy makers have been willing to take in the past in order to improve the conditions of employees.

The rising power of markets is one of the most important developments of our generation. Given that, it should be no surprise that the power of labor markets is rising as well. The effects are unfolding now and are likely to be profound. No doubt we will be visiting them for decades to come.

CHAPTER 10

HUMAN CAPITAL RELATIONSHIP MANAGEMENT

USING CUSTOMER RELATIONSHIP MANAGEMENT TO CUSTOMIZE EMPLOYEE RELATIONSHIPS

CARYN ROWE AND ELISSA TUCKER

SIGNIFICANT CHANGES are anticipated in the workforce over the next decade: demographic shifts, talent shortages, skill deficits, and an emergence of a more virtual, global, diverse, and demanding workforce. As a result, organizations will require dramatically different approaches to managing employee relationships to ensure that their high-value, business-critical employees remain motivated and engaged over the long haul. Targeting specific benefits to the employees who will value them is more important than ever. To attract and retain the new generation workforce, companies will have to replace one-size-fits-all employment relationships with more customized and fluid employee relationships. In this chapter, we discuss why the current employment relationships—generic and one-way in nature—are losing their effectiveness as the workforce changes. Then, we present a potentially powerful solution for building stronger and longer-lasting employment relationships— a solution we call Human Capital Relationship Management (HCRM).

At present, this approach is in its evolutionary stages. While many organizations are aware of changing employee preferences and the need to tailor employment relationships, only a handful of corporations have taken appropriate actions. We anticipate that these concepts will become more necessary and more doable as the workforce changes, technology advances, human resources (HR) outsourcing grows, and legal and privacy issues are ironed out. We hope that by presenting the fundamental principles of HCRM and providing examples of actions taken by pioneering companies, we will help you find some strategies for implementation in the near term. And, although many of the bigger-picture concepts that we present may seem difficult, expensive, or even risky to implement right now, we hope our discussion of them will encourage you to think about the future. That said, let's begin by taking a look at how today's ways of relating to employees are losing their effectiveness.

TRADITIONAL EMPLOYMENT RELATIONSHIPS LOSING GROUND

Today's one-size-fits-all static employment relationships no longer meet the needs of employees or employers. A workforce that is now highly diverse, accustomed to customization in the consumer marketplace, gaining power in the job market, and increasingly expensive to employ is rendering these once pragmatic employment strategies inadequate for reaping the returns required by today's employers. Some of the workforce trends impacting traditional employment relationships are explained in this section.

Diverse Workforce

The days of the middle-aged American, white male, married with children, full-time worker—a description that fit most employees of U.S. corporations—are gone. The workforce in the United States and in many other industrialized nations is highly diverse in terms of demographic characteristics such as gender, age, race, lifestyle, nationality, location of employment, type of employment, skill level, and income level.

The workforce is also growing more diverse in terms of employee needs. Generally, in the past, people needed the same things from employers because they lived relatively uniform lives doing relatively uniform jobs. Today, loosened societal norms and globalization allow workers to pursue a broader array of life paths and lifestyles. As they do so, their requirements from employers are becoming more varied.

Ironically, at a time when employees' needs from employers are growing highly individualized, companies are finding greater challenges to being anything but impersonal. The emergence of multinational corporations, the globalization of business operations, the advent of virtual work, and the replacement of relationship-based employment with results-focused work have all contributed to making impersonal, cookie-cutter employee relationships the norm. While the lack of a personal touch in the employment experience may have worked well for a time, it will soon become problematic. A workforce with heightened diversity will respond less and less to these impersonal, one-size-fits-all employment engagements that do not have relevance to them personally.

Mass Customization in the Consumer Realm

The mass customization of products and the personalization of the customer experience have created exceedingly high expectations among individuals who expect to get exactly what they want without sacrifice. Amazon.com's approach to the delivery of services, where users are greeted by a personalized home page with product recommendations tailored to their individual needs, is getting people accustomed to personalization. Competition from global and niche markets, spurred by the rise of the Internet, is conditioning people to shop around for the purchasing options that most closely meet their unique needs and wants. As a result, employers will find their employees, who are increasingly used to their personalized consumer experiences, no longer respond to, let alone settle for, mass management practices and one-size-fits-all employment offers and communications.

Employee-Favorable Job Market and Rising Workforce Costs

The balance of power between corporations and employees will shift. Worker and skill shortages have begun in some areas and are expected to spread and intensify. Once again, workers will have the upper hand in the job market, especially the workers that companies need most—those with hot skills and those with high-performer or high-potential status. In addition, there will be a growing group of highly skilled older workers with the financial resources to work their way or not work at all.

A more global and transparent labor market, coupled with the portability of knowledge and benefits, is virtually doing away with the practice of lifetime employment. Not only is it becoming easier for employees to leave employers for better opportunities, but it is also becoming easier for the competition to poach talent. Advances in technology and globalization mean the threat of poaching will eventually come from all reaches of the globe.

Making matters worse is an increasingly strained relationship between employers and employees as organizations work to reduce their labor costs (cutting back on training and benefits, automating, sourcing globally, etc.) in response to economic pressures.

Given this talent landscape, it would be beneficial if companies could increase their efforts and investments in attracting and retaining employees. Unfortunately, the money HR leaders spend on the workforce is under mounting scrutiny. In most companies, employees represent the greatest expense. Therefore, in times of severe cost constraints HR leaders are required to do more with less. Making this especially difficult are rising employment costs related to key employee benefits such as health care and retirement. In this environment, it is essential that HR leaders develop insight and strategies for optimum allocation of scarce, yet desperately needed, workforce dollars. And once allocated communicate the value of these human capital investments to employees on a personal level with a personal message.

THE HUMAN CAPITAL RELATIONSHIP MANAGEMENT SOLUTION

Convinced of the need to develop more customized and fluid employee relationships, how can your organization make the transformation? It is our belief that the Customer Relationship Management (CRM) principles, which have been used successfully by marketing professionals to customize the customer experience, and provide a blueprint for developing a more customized approach to managing and interacting with human capital. We call this approach Human Capital Relationship Management (HCRM) and see it as a major innovation in the way organizations will interact with their workforces in the decade to come. Let's take a look at CRM and how it lends itself to the development of an HCRM strategy.

A Brief Look at CRM

Whether you realize it or not, chances are you come into contact with CRM nearly every day. When you visit Amazon.com and are greeted with a personalized home page including product recommendations tailored to your unique interests and needs; stop at Starbucks and the barista knows how to

"Make It Your Drink"—a half café, nonfat mocha, hold the foam; or turn on your TV to find Tivo has automatically recorded a multitude of programs it thinks you would like, you are experiencing CRM. At its core, CRM is about enhancing understanding of customers, anticipating customer needs, and proactively addressing them with customized and personalized products and services. CRM is about targeting marketing efforts to get the most out of these investments. CRM looks to identify and prioritize the highest-potential-value customers, targets them to get the most out of marketing efforts, and focuses on increasing share of these customers rather than increasing share of the total market.

With CRM, companies are better able to meet the challenges of a changing consumer landscape—more diverse customer base, frequently changing consumer needs, less brand loyalty, and more competitive pressures—by abolishing the impersonal customer legacy of mass production, messaging, and marketing; closing the distance between company and customer; and returning to the intimacy of the corner store. CRM has helped companies increase the value of existing customer bases, strengthen competitive advantage, and enhance customer satisfaction. It has allowed companies to better use existing resources, make more informed decisions, and even predict and drive customer behavior.

Moving from CRM to HCRM

Just as CRM has enabled companies like Amazon.com to revolutionize the customer experience, HCRM will allow employers to dramatically alter the employment experience, taking it from one characterized by impersonality to one typified by new levels of intimacy. HCRM is about identifying and targeting the employees with high value and future potential. In its true form, HCRM involves acquiring superior knowledge of employee aspirations and preferences, planning and forecasting employee needs, and proactively satisfying them with personalized employment offers.

To companies willing to try this new approach, HCRM will bring many benefits, including increased contributions from the existing workforce, strengthened competitive advantage in the talent market, and enhanced employee satisfaction and engagement. It will aid organizations in better using existing resources earmarked for the workforce, in making more informed workforce decisions, and even in predicting and driving employee behavior.

PUTTING HCRM INTO ACTION

So, how do you put HCRM into action at your organization? You can start by looking to your production and marketing departments and learning the CRM techniques these areas have mastered. In doing so, you will likely uncover what research on CRM best practices has shown us—five key steps to effective Human Capital Relationship Management: (1) determining the aim and scope of your HCRM initiative, (2) improving awareness of your employees, (3) documenting information about your employees, (4) turning information about employees into understanding of your workforce, and (5) taking action on your newfound workforce knowledge.

Step One: Determine the Aim and Scope of Your HCRM Initiative

There are a number of ways to determine where in your organization HCRM is needed most and can have the greatest impact. First, uncover areas where your employment contract, explicit or implicit, is not living up to expectations—yours, your employees', or both. For example, is your current employment deal failing to surmount a highly competitive talent environment or providing less than adequate returns on workforce investments? Is it leaving you with skill or labor shortages or failing to keep key employees from joining your competition? Are employees wasting employment dollars because they are not savvy health care consumers? Are they dissatisfied due to misunderstandings about pay for performance? Or are they facing financial stress due to lack of preparation for retirement?

Next, consider how much the value of individual employees varies within your organization. Areas of significant employee value differentiation highlight the importance certain employees have to your organization's success. They point to individuals your organization will want to single out for strengthening of the employment offer, regardless of whether it is living up to expectations.

Finally, review your organization's business strategy and ascertain what it requires from employees. Articulate specifically what HCRM efforts aim to achieve for your organization in both the short and the long term. Then, coordinate all stakeholders needed to implement HCRM. Communicate the stated objective of HCRM and the stakeholders' roles in achieving the desired employment experience. Highlight how HCRM will benefit them and not just the organization. Track and publicly recognize and reward their efforts.

Step Two: Improve Awareness of Your Employees

Once the aim and scope of your HCRM initiative are determined, you will want to turn your focus toward boosting your organization's awareness of its employees. Only with ample and accurate employee information will your organization meet the basic objectives of HCRM: to anticipate employee needs, create customized employment offers, target workforce spending, and even predict future employee behavior.

Begin by making it an organization mission to consider every employee interaction as a listening and observation opportunity. Encourage employees to speak up, listen to them without judgment, and show them how sharing information can improve their employment experience. In doing this, leverage both technology and humans as listening tools and make use of traditional listening approaches such as annual or quarterly engagement studies, focus groups, town hall meetings, and quick polls, as well as more innovative approaches such as corporate ethnography, employee advisory boards, and internal employee Web logs (blogs). One company that has taken an especially innovative approach to gathering information on employees is Capital One in the United Kingdom. When faced with low employee morale and high turnover in the Nottingham call center, Capital One asked employees to keep stress diaries. The diaries not only revealed specific causes of stress, but also showed a strong correlation between stress and turnover. As a result, Capital One knew what actions to take to remove stressors and combat turnover.[1]

Continue by assigning frontline managers, the predominant contact point between the organization and individual employees, a key role in your listening efforts. Train them in observation and listening techniques. Make it a requirement for them to have ongoing conversations with individual employees about unfulfilled needs and to identify ways to meet these needs that will also benefit the organization.

As you will see later in this chapter, the uses for this information will be many. For example, it will allow you to more closely match skills and interests with projects, institute development programs to remedy skill gaps, design and redesign customizable total rewards menus, and educate employees on strategies for getting the greatest value from their benefits.

Step Three: Document Information about Your Employees

To fully realize the value of increased employee awareness efforts, you will need organization-wide information management systems. Here, you can let technology be your organization's memory, leveraging existing investments in human resource information systems (HRIS) and self-service HR technologies. Begin by giving employees, managers, and HR the ability to record employee information in HRIS systems and making it mandatory for them to do so. Encourage employees, managers, and HR to use HRIS for maintaining sophisticated employee information such as work histories, skill assessments, career aspirations, reward preferences, performance data, development plans, compensation and reward histories, job and project openings, and so forth.

In addition to actively recording employee information, consider leveraging any employee self-service technologies that are already used. Take the information that these systems passively collect for administrative purposes and integrate it with your other employee data. Consider storing all employee information in one HR data warehouse for easy retrieval. HR outsourcing providers can be of great benefit here. Hewitt Associates, for example, builds and maintains data warehouses for its large Fortune 1000 outsourcing clients.

Step Four: Turn Information about Your Employees into Understanding of Your Workforce

With employee information collected and documented, you can turn your attention to generating human capital intelligence. This involves moving the organization away from making decisions based on intuition or imitation toward taking action based on scientific workforce analyses. To achieve this, data mining techniques such as segmenting, answering questions, and making predictions can be leveraged.

Segmentation Analytics

This technique groups employees according to classes that either management defines or analysis of the workforce uncovers. For example, grocer Tesco segmented its workforce into five groups: want it all, work/life balancers, pleasure seekers, live-to-workers, and work-to-livers, and tailored benefits to the needs of each.[2] University Healthcare System of Augusta, Georgia segmented its workforce into three categories: the healthy, the at-risk, and the ill, targeting the at-risk with wellness coaches and assigning wellness case managers to the ill.[3]

Answering Questions

HR data warehouses and analytics software can also be used to answer a myriad of human capital questions that in the past would have been unanswerable at least in a reasonable time frame and from a factual standpoint. For example, they can offer empirical answers to questions such as: What rewards are generating the highest and lowest return on investment? Do we have health care coverage gaps by race and ethnicity? Are employees able to move throughout the organization? For example, International Finance Corporation (IFC), part of the World Bank Group, used data mining to answer the question, "Why are our MBAs, hired out of college, leaving before reaching five-years tenure when they are just becoming highly productive?" IFC isolated the problem: a failure to differentiate high and low performers in compensation and a lack of career paths.

Predictive Workforce Analytics

This is perhaps the most useful and revolutionary data mining technique. It leverages the history of warehoused data to predict how a particular change in workforce management will impact employee behavior. Predictive analytics can reveal how an increase in compensation will impact employee productivity or how an increase in health benefit cost sharing will impact voluntary turnover. Capital One has been a pioneer at predicting workforce behavior. Using its HR data warehouse and predictive analytic techniques, Capital One can indicate which potential job candidates are most likely to be successful at the company. The key to making this prediction is having a history of data on the traits of its most successful employees to which it can compare the traits of potential hires.[4] What stands to be one of the more revolutionary uses of predictive workforce analytics is Hewitt's Human Capital Foresight (HCF) methodology, which, drawing from years of Hewitt's outsourcing client data, can help predict the impact specific human capital management changes would have on turnover and the bottom line.[5]

To get the most out of these powerful data mining techniques, consider assembling a dedicated workforce analytics team. At the same time, build an interface for your HR database and analytics software and give leaders and managers user-friendly access to the results of data mining efforts, as well as some access to raw data to do their own analyses. The U.S. Census Bureau has such an interface through which managers generate customized reports on everything from training to salary, diversity programs, benefits, alternative work patterns, and retirement. Information that used to take them days to assemble or was impossible to assemble can now be instantly retrieved. And managers, those best equipped to make many workforce decisions, have the information they need to do so.[6]

Step Five: Take Action on Your Newfound Knowledge about Your Workforce

The final step in launching your HCRM approach involves taking action on your newfound employee knowledge. One way you can put human capital intelligence to use is by personalizing employee communications. A relatively simple and inexpensive approach is to customize the information you deliver to employees without actually altering the workforce product that the information addresses. Halliburton, for example, customized its deferred compensation plan communications by sending nonparticipating employees Hewitt's Quick Enrollment communication—a postcard where the employee only has to check "yes" to be enrolled in the plan. The targeted communication received nearly a 25 percent response rate and no changes had to be made to the 401(k) plan, just a change in the communications to a specific group of employees.[7] Using its employee Web portal called MySource, Qualcomm delivers customized messages to employee desktops about generic workforce programs, such as performance, management training and development, benefits, and pay.[8]

A slightly more involved yet potentially more beneficial approach is to use interactive recommendation systems to provide employees with customized recommendations based on their self-expressed attitudes and behaviors, with or without changing the actual workforce deliverable. For example, Hewitt's Focus on My Future web site allows employees to modify a set of financial assumptions ranging from future pay increases to retirement income targets and then receive a personalized action plan for reaching their unique retirement goals. In addition, Hewitt employees can take a personal engagement survey anytime and receive a customized action plan detailing steps they could take to enhance their engagement.

Another highly fruitful application for your human capital knowledge is to customize employee rewards. Here the most cost-effective routes involve modularizing rewards—offering a standard menu of options within a single reward category such as health care or offering a standard menu of total rewards options from which managers or individual employees can choose based on individual needs. With Hewitt's assistance, Dell implemented a Build Your Own (BYO) health plan. Based on personal factors such as risk tolerance, need for care, and the prior year's health expenses, employees receive guidance on choosing from a menu of benefit levels, network options, and contribution rates. To date, 60 percent of Dell employees have built and enrolled in a customized health plan, resulting in a reduced total health care cost trend of 14 percent and $6 million in savings.[9]

Finally, but still very important, your newfound human capital intelligence can be used to guide managers in personalizing the employment experience or, in other words, managing by exception. Here, managers stop spending time trying to change or fix employee differences or weaknesses. They move away from managing with the aim of employee conformity to an organizational notion of the ideal worker toward managing to accentuate and leverage individual talents.

Managers use employee knowledge to be champions of individual employee abilities, manage according to the way each employee wants or needs to be managed, and work to closely match assignments with the skills and aspirations of individual employees. Hewitt's Talent Match is one tool that helps managers match employee skills and interests to project needs. Employees create and maintain profiles with basic personal data, skill and knowledge profiles, work preferences, and current assignment information. Managers and leaders query these profiles to identify associates whose skills, knowledge, availability, and preferences best match open projects.

A more controversial but potentially more beneficial approach to managing by exception involves asking managers to strategically select employees they can invest greater time and money on. Similar to providing differential pay based on performance, managers can offer varying levels of support based on individual employee performance. This could mean significant focus on strong contributors and lesser focus on the lowest performers. SAS, for example, encourages managers to dismiss their lowest performers and their problem employees so they are not distracted from the management of the most valuable employees.[10] To become comfortable with management by exception, performance managers will need guidance from their legal departments regarding cases where it is not ethically or legally appropriate to provide differential treatment.

FROM TESTING THE WATERS TO PLUNGING IN

We predict that many companies will begin HCRM efforts by testing the waters with more narrow or isolated initiatives such as those being used by the companies profiled in this chapter. As they gain comfort with these techniques, we predict companies will begin building more holistic, company-wide HCRM strategies. If your company is looking to be a first mover in the HCRM realm, there are some actions that you can take to accelerate your organization's adoption of this new and powerful strategy. You can build marketing skills within your HR department, hiring employees with marketing and CRM experience or developing these skills within your current HR staff. You can view HCRM as a cultural transformation, treating it like any other culture change initiative where you must work to change mind-sets, re-place old habits, launch new systems, spread new skills, and foster new relationships. Finally, you could explore the HCRM capabilities offered through HR outsourcing relationships, relying on an HR outsourcing provider for data warehousing, workforce data analytics and reporting, and human capital decision support and program implementation. Companies that use these tips to become HCRM pioneers will reap the significant benefits of having stronger, more fruitful relationships with the employees that make up this new, emerging workforce.

CHAPTER 11

GETTING THE "NEW" NEWCOMER CONNECTED AND PRODUCTIVE QUICKLY

ROB CROSS, SALVATORE PARISE, AND KEITH ROLLAG

NEWCOMERS TODAY face a very different set of challenges than their predecessors did 25 years ago, demanding a new approach to employee orientation. Rapid and effective "onboarding" is becoming more about relationship building than training and information transfer. Savvy managers help their newcomers build a diverse, strategic network of relationships that gets them up to speed quickly and makes them feel like an accepted, valued part of the organization.

THE "NEW" NEWCOMER

Not long ago, the typical newcomer was a recent high school or college graduate, arriving en masse with other recruits in early June. The entering new hire would attend a classroom-styled orientation session presented by the HR department and then be escorted to a new desk or workstation, located among seasoned company veterans.

In those days, supervisors didn't expect much from their newcomers for several months. Usually, managers would start by giving newcomers relatively low-priority work, ensuring that they had plenty of time to watch, listen, and learn from more experienced co-workers sitting nearby. Thus, the knowledge needed to complete their first assignment was often only a few feet away, either in the heads of fellow teammates or in file cabinets lining the office walls. As the newcomers slowly absorbed the company culture and started to fit in, they were given more important assignments. After several years, the recruits lost their newcomer status and became regular employees, greeting and training the next batch of June graduates.

Those days are gone forever. Beginning in the 1970s, newcomers stopped being just another set of "new boys" in the "old boys network." Instead, they represented a diverse mix of gender and ethnicity with radically different backgrounds and behavioral styles. The rise of the matrix organization and cross-functional project teams in the 1980s further complicated the onboarding of newcomers, since much of the information they needed to be successful shifted from their nearby co-workers to teammates located on different floors and in nearby buildings. Finally, the explosion of information technology (IT) and globalization in the 1990s shattered the traditional world of the newcomer and created an entirely new set of challenges for newcomers and managers alike.

Today, the "new" newcomer arrives at any time of the year, often with only a few days' notice. Most "new" newcomers aren't recent graduates joining the lowest rung of the organization, but a complex mix of age, educational background, and management experience entering all levels of the firm. Their desks may be 10 feet or 10 time zones away from managers and key resources. The "new" newcomer may be a permanent addition to the group or temporary help that is quickly replaced by yet another new arrival. He or she may be a member of the same organization or work for a supplier, joint-venture partner, or an outsourcing firm. In booming economies, the newcomer may be one of many recent hires eager to share in the company's success. In shrinking economies, the newcomer may be a weary, transferred survivor of a major corporate downsizing.

These days, newcomers account for a significant portion of the American workforce, as a great many workers are new to their organization, department, or work group. According to the U.S. Department of Labor, 25 percent of all workers in the United States have been with their company less than a year, and more than 33 percent have tenure of less than two years. Incredibly, American workers will change jobs an average of 10 times between the ages of 18 and 37.[1] Competitive success is now measured by not only how fast companies can transfer new ideas and best practices across geographic and functional boundaries, but also how fast they can transfer knowledge from veterans to new arrivals. A 2003 study by Mellon Financial Corporation found lost productivity due to the learning curve for new hires and transfers to be between 1 percent and 2.5 percent of total revenues. On average, the time for new hires to achieve full productivity ranged from eight weeks for clerical jobs to 20 weeks for professionals and to more than 26 weeks for executives.[2]

Work Relationships: Now More Important but Harder to Establish

Over the past 10 years, we have used a mix of interviews and surveys across more than 40 companies to understand the challenges faced by the "new" newcomer. We have compared the behaviors of newcomers who have quickly become productive with those who were not as successful. Overall, we found that the key to rapid onboarding in today's complex work environment is *relationship building*—but not just indiscriminate networking as is so often popularized by self-help books that advise people to build large networks. Rather, we have found that those newcomers who quickly build a strategic network of targeted relationships are more often seen as better performers, and they also feel more connected to the organization and more satisfied with their new job.

We use a technique called *social network analysis* to explore the pattern of information flows inside organizations. By asking employees whom they turn to for information and advice, we create a map detailing the degree to which each employee is connected to every other worker in the group. The social network diagram in Figure 11.1 is from a department in a large U.S. multinational company. Those who are connected to many others are in the center of the network, and those who are less connected are on the periphery. Note that most of the newcomers (represented by circles) are on the periphery of the social network, but a few have quickly become central to the firm's set of information flows. Through our research we've found that these highly connected newcomers tend not only to be better performers, but also to be more satisfied with their new positions.

Why have relationships become more important for newcomer productivity? First, the work of all employees, including newcomers, has become embedded in highly complex, cross-functional, matrix-based work processes that are largely built on relationships. Newcomers cannot contribute to these work flows until they have established a minimum number of relationships

Figure 11.1
Rapid Onboarding Is All about Relationship Building

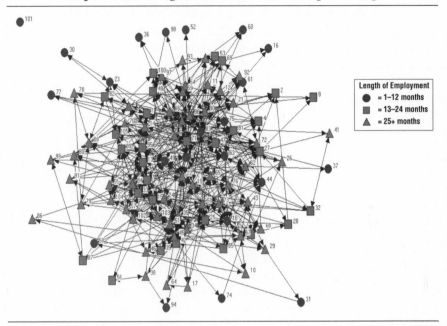

with key managers, project team members, and experts. Despite the dramatic rise and sophistication of computing power and storage, most of the knowledge a newcomer needs to be truly productive resides not in company databases, but in the heads of fellow employees. Even if information does reside in IT systems, newcomers often need help to locate, filter, and make sense of the massive amount of information found there. In the words of one manager, "Only people who have been here awhile know what is important or necessary to know. A new guy wouldn't know that."

The need for relationships becomes even more important as more newcomers enter the organization at higher levels. For middle managers and executives, their overall effectiveness is largely based on their ability to establish, nurture, and leverage relationships across the entire organization.

However, modern work arrangements and technologies have conspired to make it more challenging for the "new" newcomer to establish these critical relationships. In the old days, newcomers typically entered organizations that looked and talked a lot like they did. What's more, most of their initial relationships were with nearby co-workers. Today, newcomers must establish relationships with a wide variety of people located all around the world. Even if newcomers and their key contacts all have the best of intentions, language and culture differences make network building more difficult, thus decreasing the probability that a relationship will be established. Geographic and time zone differences only make things worse. Not only do time and space decrease the chance that a newcomer will actually become aware of a key resource, but research has shown that it also dramatically reduces the probability that a relationship will occur.[3]

Though the rise of e-mail and instant-messaging technologies has given newcomers access to a larger number of distant co-workers, the communication medium itself often hinders relationship development. Busy managers and experts find it easier to ignore e-mail requests from unknown newcomers, and after a failed attempt, newcomers are less likely to reapproach that person for information or advice. Electronic communication technologies are often better at nurturing and facilitating existing relationships than they are at creating new ones.

The rising pace of work and the pressure to build professional credibility also conspires against newcomer relationship building, causing newcomers to feel they don't have time to build and maintain work relationships, especially if those relationships don't seem to have immediate value. As a result, in their rush to get work done, newcomers often avoid meetings, off-sites, and other events that would actually help them network and get up to speed more quickly. One newcomer expressed regret at having exhibited this kind of initial behavior. When asked if he had any advice for future newcomers, he suggested that they should "try to establish as many contacts and as wide as possible," adding, "I suffered from not spreading out as fast as I could have. In a sense, I had my head in the sand. I got on with my work and did it. I should have taken the time to spread my wings a bit."

Finally, when it comes to relationship building, newcomers are often their own worst enemies. In their desire to quickly prove themselves, they are reluctant to introduce themselves to busy, high-status managers and experts. Often, they fear they might "look stupid" by asking for information they feel they should already know. Or they fear bothering already overworked teammates. In the words of one newcomer, "I was terrified to ask people questions there just for fear of seeming dumb. I don't think that was a good approach, because I would spend a lot of time trying to learn something that someone could tell me in a few minutes."

Still, introductions and question asking are the critical first steps to any relationship. Reluctance to ask questions emerged as a pervasive problem for newcomers in almost every company we studied. At one software company, we interviewed almost all of the firm's newcomers and then asked managers to classify their newcomers into two groups—those who quickly became productive, connected contributors and those who lagged in their ability to get up to speed. The primary difference between the two groups was that all the slow onboarders said they preferred to figure things out by themselves before asking questions.

A Network Approach to Rapid Onboarding

If relationships are so important, how can you get newcomers connected and productive quickly? Based on our research, here are some best practices.

Map Out the Newcomer's Ideal Network

Before the newcomer arrives, take some time to draw the network of relationships you would like to see the newcomer develop within a few weeks or months of arrival. Include not only the immediate work group but also other key resources throughout the company and beyond. Don't forget important resources both above and below the newcomer's managerial level.

If you discover that your newcomer's first assignment requires interaction with only a few co-workers, ask yourself whether this is a good idea. While newcomers might be able to complete their project quickly and easily, they won't build the network of relationships or the visibility that will help them succeed in future projects. Through our research we've discovered that newcomers' ultimate connectedness to the company's social network is partly a function of how much their first assignment requires them to build relationships to get their work done.

When they arrive, spend some time describing their ideal network and go over a list of key resources with them. Clearly set the expectation that you want them to take the time required to establish these relationships, even if the information value of each resource is not immediately obvious.

Make Strategic Introductions

Most managers introduce newcomers to only a few nearby co-workers, often as part of the obligatory office tour on their first day. In our research, only about one-third of all newcomers are really satisfied with the number and quality of introductions they receive. Through introductions, newcomers learn something about their co-workers (and vice versa), reducing the awkwardness of future interactions. In the words of one newcomer, "It's who you know that counts, and you have so much more mileage if you have already been introduced."

While some newcomers are proactive about introducing themselves, many are reluctant to "bother" busy co-workers. Savvy managers often set up brief introductory meetings with key resources in advance, saving the newcomer the awkwardness and uncertainty of cold-calling strangers. In particular, long distance virtual relationships are far more likely to be productive if they begin with face-to-face introductions. Thus, several managers have told us that spending travel money up front to connect newcomers with dispersed teammates quickly pays off in increased productivity.

Leverage Information Technology but Don't Rely on It for Onboarding

Information technology can be very useful in helping get newcomers connected to key resources. Many companies use online employee directories and "expert locators" to help newcomers identify and build important relationships. Ensuring that newcomers are enrolled in the right mailing lists, discussion boards, and instant-messaging groups can also help newcomers determine where to go for information and advice. Some companies even have special online "newcomer forums," so that newcomers can support each other as they learn about the organization.

That said, it's important not to assume newcomers can leverage IT in the same way that experienced veterans can. Just because an expert is identified in a web site or a database doesn't mean that (1) the newcomer will feel comfortable contacting the expert and (2) the expert will respond promptly and enthusiastically. The size and disorganization of most IT systems also tend to overwhelm newcomers, requiring them to sift through hundreds of documents before they find something useful. This is only going to get worse as information systems become bigger and more complex.

One newcomer summed this matter up succinctly:

> So far, the most helpful part of orientation is having someone whom I can openly approach and ask any questions I have. . . . The least useful would probably be the first day in which I was left alone to learn

about [the company's product] on the intranet. I did not really know anybody at the company and I would have appreciated being connected with the people first before reading copious amounts of material on the web.

Find Them a Buddy

Besides building connections with key experts and managers, newcomers need to build relationships with those they can comfortably ask "newbie questions," like the location of office supplies, lunch routines, and norms for office behavior. Through our research, we found that newcomers who got up to speed quickly tended to have a formal or informal buddy who provided orientation and advice as needed, reducing the amount of time and frustration spent trying to figure things out on their own. One company described their buddy system this way:

> Buddies are people within the project team, but not their manager. They take care of the new person on the first day, things like showing them how to log in to e-mail—we use Outlook—accessing the Internet, mailing lists, public and user file folders, how backups work. Then they possibly get into training on what they will do in the afternoon. The buddies take the new person to lunch, sometimes with their manager. We make sure they get something to eat, take a break, get to know their buddy better. The buddy is their first friend in the company, and usually they end up being good friends. If we had managers do it with each new hire, that's all they would do. The buddy is more like a confidant, someone you can always talk to. They form an alliance and work closely together.

Invite Them to Lunch and Key Meetings

Not all relationship-building needs to be formal and planned. One of the best ways to get newcomers connected is to invite them to lunch with a variety of co-workers. Lunch is a valuable but often underutilized time for newcomers to meet other managers and experts, get the inside scoop on office politics and issues, and start to make sense of organizational hierarchies and decision-making processes. Inviting newcomers to key meetings can also help them understand the existing network of relationships between individuals and departments, as well as the mix of personalities, priorities, and values within the organization.

Periodically Do a Network Checkup

When you meet with your newcomers to discuss progress on their initial projects, take time to review and discuss their progress on relationship building. Ask them to draw their current network of relationships and compare it to what you initially envisioned they would need to be productive. Identify any gaps in their network and look for ways to get them introduced and connected to the right people. In other words, instead of only asking, "What have you accomplished?" or "What have you learned?" take time to ask, "Who do you know?" and "Whom do you want to meet?"

CONCLUSION

The complexities of modern business require a new breed of newcomer who can quickly develop a diverse set of work relationships. Not only will network building help increase their initial productivity, but a wide variety of relationships also makes newcomers feel connected and valued by the organization, thereby increasing job satisfaction and reducing turnover. A well-developed information network also reduces the need for newcomers to approach their managers for help and advice, thus reducing the amount of supervision required.

Training and orientation programs are important, but they are poor substitutes for careful, strategic relationship building. The more quickly newcomers are connected to the rest of the firm's knowledge network, the more efficiently they can locate and leverage information—and the better they can help the company innovate and compete in a global economy.

PART III

TREAT TALENT WELL

AS ORGANIZATIONS search for a true competitive differentiator, they are increasingly recognizing it is the talent, skills, and knowledge of the workforce that will ultimately determine whether a business succeeds or fails. Ironically, this recognition surfaced just as employers found themselves confronting perhaps the most trying times in the history of talent management. With the mammoth baby boomer generation reaching retirement age, taking their immense knowledge and skills base with them, organizations face a shrinking labor pool and a severe shortage of leadership talent. Recognizing the need to adopt new strategies for attracting, nurturing, and engaging talent, companies are challenging traditional people management practices, building more rewarding environments, and allowing employees to shape the world in which they work.

In this section, the authors not only examine the challenges that lie ahead, but also offer tangible guidance for organizations seeking to harness the full potential of their people and inspire them to do their best. Included is an inside look at one of India's most successful information technology (IT) firms, Infosys Technologies, which advocates a system of lifelong learning and skills development. Also included are unique insights into one of the world's most unusual workplaces, Semco, where employees are encouraged to follow their instincts and find their bliss. In both instances, senior management credits the talent and ingenuity of the workforce for their immense success.

CHAPTER 12

CREATING A VIRTUOUS SPIRAL ORGANIZATION

EDWARD E. LAWLER III

TODAY'S BUSINESS environment is difficult and challenging. Organizations are struggling to be competitive and individuals are struggling to develop meaningful careers. To provide people with meaningful work and rewards, organizations must be successful; to be successful, organizations need high-performing individuals. The solution, therefore, is to create a win-win relationship. While this is certainly easier said than done, it most definitely *is* possible to achieve.

The elements needed to create a win-win situation involve a complex set of actions on the part of both organizations and people. Organizations must develop ways to treat their employees so they are motivated and satisfied, while employees must behave in ways that help their organizations become effective and high-performing. The challenge is to design organizations that perform at high levels and treat people in ways that are rewarding and satisfying. In order to accomplish this, organization designs and practices that are good for *both* individuals and organizations need to be developed and implemented.

Based on Edward E. Lawler, *Treat People Right* (San Francisco, Jossey-Bass, 2003).

A FALSE CONFLICT

At the core of many people's thinking is the belief that there is an irreconcilable conflict between what is good for business and what is good for employees. Although it would be foolish for me to argue that there is never or seldom a conflict between these two outcomes, the fact is that the right organization design and human capital management practices can produce substantial positive long-term payoffs for both organizations and people. For organizations, the payoffs come in the form of being able to attract better people, retain them longer, obtain high productivity from them, and create excellence in performance. The payoffs for people come in the form of satisfying careers, more interesting and meaningful work, and increased rewards. Particularly in the chaotic business world of the early twenty-first century, such payoffs can make the difference in the survival of an organization faced with changing markets, fickle customers, and a volatile stock market.

For individuals and organizations to succeed, they must both understand how the other operates and they must make informed decisions. Simply put, they need to actively manage their relationship (no matter how short or long), based on mutual understanding and shared information. This can only happen if organizations commit themselves to practices that are good for both their performance and their employees.

Just as the organization must adopt new attitudes and programs that respect its people, individuals must also recognize that they too have a responsibility in this new world of organizational high performance. They have to take greater responsibility for their knowledge, skills, and ultimately their careers. That is, they must effectively manage their development and performance to enjoy success.

TALENTED PEOPLE AND
WELL-DESIGNED ORGANIZATIONS

I am not suggesting that having the right people alone can save organizations from the ravages of change. On the contrary, organizational effectiveness is not just about talented people; it also requires strategies, practices, organization designs, and policies that make companies the kind of place where people *want* to work and *can* work effectively. Extraordinary results can be obtained only by having talented people and well-designed organizations with the best management systems.

Some academics, such as Charles O'Reilly and Jeffrey Pfeffer, argue that companies can gain competitive advantage and achieve extraordinary results with ordinary people. In their view, if you have the right systems, you don't have to worry about having the best people. Others have argued that people are all that count. In many of his speeches on leadership, former Secretary of State Colin Powell has argued, "Organization does not really accomplish anything. Only by attracting the best people will you accomplish great deeds."

My position is that both these views are wrong. Achieving competitive advantage requires both great people and great organizational practices. It is misleading to claim that organizations can get extraordinary results with ordinary people, just as it is misleading to argue that organizations can get extraordinary results with ordinary designs and practices. The most effective organizations have both outstanding people and outstanding management systems because that is what produces world-class results for both individuals and organizations.

Outstanding individuals and organizational practices tend to reinforce each other and seek each other out because of the momentum they create. Effective organizational practices attract outstanding people, and outstanding people create effective structures and practices. The key is to identify and implement designs and practices that create virtuous spirals that are good for organizational performance and individuals.

THE ULTIMATE GOAL: A VIRTUOUS SPIRAL

Virtuous spirals occur when an organization takes intelligent, conscious actions to attract, retain, motivate, develop, and effectively organize committed, high-performance individuals. This generates a high-performance organization that generates increased rewards for employees, which in turn increases their motivation and commitment. The more challenging and rewarding environment further reinforces the organization's ability to attract, retain, and develop effective employees, who further positively impact performance. Thus, a virtuous spiral forms and expands, carrying the organization and its members to greater heights. (See Figure 12.1.)

To successfully develop a virtuous spiral, organizations need to emphasize ever-increasing levels of performance, higher rewards for individuals, and increasingly competent employees. As they achieve them, a positive performance momentum develops that feeds on itself.

Figure 12.1
Virtuous Spiral

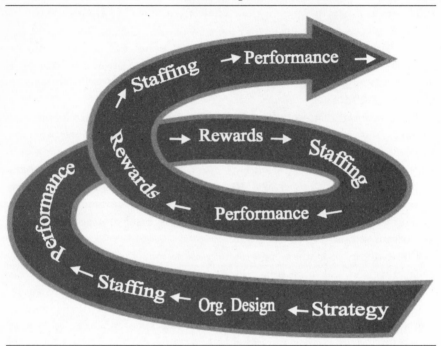

EXAMPLES OF VIRTUOUS SPIRALS

Microsoft stands tall as one of the most impressive examples of a company that has profited from a virtuous spiral relationship with its people. Since the early 1980s, the company has had an environment in which its employees have done well and the company has done well. The employees have had challenging work and, of course, one of the most highly rewarding stock plans around. Microsoft has been an enormously attractive place to work, especially for high performers. As a result it has attracted some of the country's top talent among software engineers and marketing geniuses.

Because of its relationship with its human capital, Microsoft has been able to generate a powerful dynamic in which success begets success, which begets more success. The company's seemingly unstoppable growth only began to slow in the late 1990s, when it faced a rapidly changing competitive environment along with government challenges to its growing power. But even in the market downturn of the early years of the new century, Microsoft has largely continued on a virtuous spiral of increasing growth and success.

General Electric has also clearly enjoyed a virtuous spiral of success for decades. Even before Jack Welch became CEO in the early 1980s, GE had already established an environment where highly talented individuals wanted to work because of the opportunities the company offered for career development and financial rewards. Able to attract and retain highly talented individuals, GE has enjoyed decades of enviable growth in profits, and as a result, attracted more talented individuals. Fortunately, GE's virtuous spiral did not end with Welch's departure. On the contrary, the company has continued its virtuous spiral under new CEO Jeffrey Immelt. It is a clear example of a cycle of successful performance leading to successful recruitment, development, and motivation of individuals, which, in turn, produced more successful performance.

Southwest Airlines is yet another example of an organization that has managed to maintain a virtuous spiral for decades. From its very beginning, Southwest was a human capital–focused organization that sought a high-quality relationship with its employees. From day one, founder Herb Kelleher stressed that the company's competitive advantage was its people. The result has been excellent customer service and an absence of the hostile labor relationship characteristic of every other major airline. Despite being highly unionized, Southwest has never had a strike and is frequently cited as one of the best places to work.

Like many organizations that have created virtuous spirals, there is no one secret to Southwest's success. The company has emphasized the careful selection of employees, building an employee-friendly work environment, and giving employees freedom to control their own jobs, in addition to the overall work environment, profit sharing and stock ownership for all employees, and the opportunity to grow and develop with advances in the company.

The list continues with Procter & Gamble. Though well over 100 years old, the last 40 years of P&G's existence have been marked by many forward-thinking efforts to establish a virtuous spiral relationship with its employees, based on employee involvement and the development of leaders throughout the company. An early adopter of employee involvement practices in its manufacturing plants, P&G also has a stock ownership plan that has placed more than 30 percent of its stock into the hands of its employees.

DEATH SPIRALS

Organizations that do not initiate a virtuous spiral are susceptible to the opposite result: the death spiral. Lasting as long as several decades or as briefly as just a few days, death spirals occur when organizations mistreat their human capital. As a result, their performance declines, causing repercussions that lead to further declines and in most cases death. When organizations develop downward momentum, they are perceived to be in trouble. They cannot attract the right human capital to fix their situation nor the financial assets or customers needed to reverse the decline. They soon find that no one wants to be associated with them. They become less and less of a competitor and ultimately die.

Perhaps the most recent dramatic example of a death spiral is the complete collapse of Arthur Andersen. In a very short period of time, it went from being one of the world's five premier accounting firms to oblivion. In essence, it lost the reputation of its brand and its attractiveness as an employer, as a result of the way it managed its people and business. Both customers and employees began leaving the company, and in just a matter of months, its ability to function was over.

The collapse of Arthur Andersen illustrates an important point about death spirals. Organizations whose market worth lies in intangible assets, such as reputation, brand, and human capital, are extremely vulnerable to sudden death spirals. Many knowledge worker firms, like consulting firms and publishers, have intangible assets that represent more than 75 percent of their market value. Only a small portion of their assets is in their plant and equipment. When such organizations lose their attractiveness as an employer or their reputation as a good place to do business, they can plunge, much like an airplane that has lost its forward momentum. Their assets decrease so quickly that they simply go out of business.

Rapid death spirals rarely happen to old economy companies in industries like steel, automobile manufacturing, and transportation because they have more tangible assets. As a result, it usually takes longer for them to fail. They can even defy gravity and exist in a zero-momentum condition if they have significant tangible assets and operate in a forgiving environment. For example, most public utilities have been able to maintain a steady-state existence because of their monopoly power. But when they have been deregulated they rarely do well: Witness the decline of AT&T, Nortel, and Lucent.

Without exception, those organizations that are in death spirals have failed to fully recognize and respond to the compelling forces of change in the world today. None has adequately altered its strategy and management practices to fit the new world nor changed their relationship with employees in ways that can reverse their death spirals. They are no longer seen as good places to work and have increasing difficulty attracting the kind of human talent they need to be effective.

SEVEN KEYS TO CREATING VIRTUOUS SPIRALS

By now, hopefully, the rationale for creating a virtuous spiral is crystal clear. Fortunately, it's something most organizations can do. The only question that remains is how to do it. What steps do organizations need to take to launch a virtuous spiral? Through my research and study of many leading organizations, I have identified seven "must do's."

Value Proposition

Organizations must create a value proposition that defines the type of workplace they want to provide so they can attract and retain the right people.
   Illustrative practices:

- Create an employment contract based on employability.
- Commit to rewarding performance.

Hiring Practices

Organizations must hire people who create the best fit with their values, core competencies, and strategic goals.
   Illustrative practices:

- Use realistic job previews.
- Have multiple potential co-workers interview job candidates.

Training and Development

Organizations must continuously train employees to do their jobs and offer them opportunities to grow and develop.

Illustrative practices:

- Provide targeted development opportunities that give company-wide exposure.
- Post job openings on the intranet.

Work Design

Organizations must design work so that it is meaningful for people and provides them with feedback, responsibility, and autonomy.
Illustrative practices:

- Use self-managing work teams.
- Provide employees with customer contact.

Mission, Strategies, and Goals

Organizations must develop and adhere to a specific organizational mission with strategies, goals, and values that employees can understand, support, and believe in.
Illustrative practices:

- Involve all employees in developing a mission statement.
- Include corporate values in the performance management system.

Reward Systems

Organizations must devise and implement reward systems that reinforce their design, core values, strategy, and commitment to shared success.
Illustrative practices:

- Pay for skills, knowledge, and performance.
- Offer broad-based stock ownership and profit sharing plans.

Leadership

Organizations must hire and develop managers and leaders who can create commitment, trust, success, and a motivating work environment.

Illustrative practices:

- Evaluate and reward managers on how they lead.
- Have senior managers model effective leadership.

Virtuous spiral organizations develop only when all seven of these "must do's" are supported by multiple organization practices. Thus, they should be used as a guide for selecting and developing the right practices. As organizations devise new and exciting designs and practices, they must be tested against these "must do's" both individually and in totality.

CHAPTER 13

MANAGING WORKFORCE CHALLENGES IN INDIA'S IT INDUSTRY

N. R. NARAYANA MURTHY

INFOSYS TECHNOLOGIES was founded in July 1981 by seven people who shared the dream of building India's first company *of the professional, by the professional, and for the professional.* Our aim was to build a globally respected corporation that was dedicated to creating sustainable wealth, legally *and* ethically.

The odds were against us—we didn't have an office, and money was in short supply. We were neither rich nor politically connected; we lacked both infrastructure and a recognized brand name. We had given up safe and promising corporate careers to launch the company, and our families and friends viewed us as risk-taking mavericks. We borrowed the initial seed capital of $250 from our wives, and our first office was my 700-square-foot apartment. (All dollar amounts are U.S. dollars.)

From the beginning, we faced significant hurdles to our growth. Our effort to build a professionally owned and managed company was a rarity in India at the time. In 1981, India's economic environment was closed and highly bureaucratic, and high levels of protection to domestic, state-dominated industries prevented competition. A system of financial repression and complex licensing discouraged entrepreneurship; venture capital was nonexistent; and businesses faced difficulties in accessing even basic infrastructure, such as phones or data communication lines.

Yet our team had lots of confidence, commitment, passion, and hope, not to mention an enthusiasm for hard work and a sense of sacrifice. We believed, as the writer Frank Baum did, that "things have to be dreamed of before they can become realities."

Our team boasted a mutually exclusive and collectively exhaustive set of skills, expertise, and experience. In addition to their vast software expertise, some of our people had experience in human resources, finance, strategy, technology, sales, and marketing. Together, we worked hard and built the organization, step by step. Infosys grew from $130 thousand in revenues and 12 employees in 1982 to $3.89 million and 300 employees by 1992.

As Charles Darwin rightly said, "It is not the strongest of the species that survive, or the most intelligent, but the ones most responsive to change." Thus, it was critical that Infosys seize upon the opportunity to grow when the economic reforms of 1991 reduced the friction for conducting business in India and improved the velocity of decision making in organizations. We took the opportunity to globalize our operations. We focused on exports, conceptualized and implemented the Global Delivery Model (GDM), built world-class infrastructure, and became the first Indian company to be listed on the NASDAQ.

Over two decades, Infosys has grown into a corporation with a market capitalization greater than $13 billion. The company boasts over 37,000 employees and revenues of more than $1.6 billion, as of March 2005. We have in excess of 30 overseas offices and over 400 satisfied clients and have witnessed a consistent increase in revenues and net income 49 quarters in a row.

From day one, the growth of Infosys has been supported and driven by an ambitious, relentless team. Whether it was seven people in 1981 or 37,000 people today, our business has always been centered around the talent our employees have brought to our business. As Lee Iacocca once said, "In the end, all business operations can be reduced to three words: people, product, and profits. People come first. Unless you've got a good team, you can't do much with the other two."[1]

Infosys is a people business, and how we manage our industry's emerging workforce challenges will be central to our future success. To get a real understanding of the challenges we face today, however, we must first view the growth of Infosys and the Indian information technology (IT) industry through the wider lens of globalization and the rise of the knowledge economy.

GLOBALIZATION AND THE RISE OF THE KNOWLEDGE ECONOMY

The forces of globalization and technology are continuously reshaping our world. Falling geographical constraints, technological advancements, and new-economy communications have integrated the world's economies, made business capabilities more portable, and led to the creation of a highly competitive, global marketplace. As *The Wall Street Journal* puts it, "Businesses across countries that could hardly get a dial tone a decade ago can now link into the world."[2]

The new global dynamic has revolutionized the competitive structures of individual industries. Businesses today are making their value chains more elastic and flexible. The "anytime, anywhere" paradigm of the Internet has enabled remote delivery. Consequently, factor costs and skill availability have become important determinants of where business processes are undertaken. The convergence and pervasiveness of information and communications technologies have thus given rise to a new type of economy—a knowledge economy in which global economies can trade what has long been untradable: the education and skills of their workforces.

The dictates of the new economy have propelled intellectual capital to the front line of a nation's competitive advantage. Global revenues from the licensing of patent rights alone have increased from $15 billion in 1990 to more than $110 billion. Over 50 percent of gross domestic product (GDP) in the major Organization for Economic Cooperation and Development (OECD) economies is now based on the production and distribution of knowledge.

Clearly, India has a significant advantage when it comes to competing in the global, knowledge-based economy: its vast pool of low-cost, English-speaking, analytically strong talent. Of the total potential talent in developing countries—which exceeds 6.4 million people—India accounts for more than 30 percent, while China and Russia comprise 11 percent and 10 percent, respectively, according to estimates by the McKinsey Global Institute. Every year, educational institutions across the country train over 2.5 million university graduates, 280,000 engineers, and 165,000 IT professionals. India's pool of university graduates alone is 1.5 times the size of China's and twice as large as that of the United States.

In a knowledge-based industry like IT, India's talent pool is a valuable asset. The Indian IT industry plays to the country's strengths—a well-educated workforce with strong IT competencies and English language proficiency.

Today, India has emerged as the most preferred offshoring destination in the world for IT software and services. Over the past decade, the industry has grown by leaps and bounds, from revenues of $150 million in 1991–1992 to revenues of over $17.6 billion in 2003–2004; from an employee base of 6,800 professionals in 1985 to over 450,000 professionals, second in number only to the United States.

The rapid growth of the industry has also led to new challenges and concerns. Despite India's vast labor pool, for example, Indian IT companies are faced with a shrinking base of experienced talent. The level of employability of Indian graduates is in large part to blame. McKinsey estimates that 25 percent of engineering graduates and just 10 percent of graduates with general degrees in India are of employable standards. Varying higher education standards across India are a key factor for this low rate of employability. While leading Indian educational institutions such as the Indian Institutes of Technology, Indian Institutes of Management, and National Institutes of Technology are renowned for high standards in education, there has been a significant decline in the quality of education offered across the rest of India's universities and colleges.

Consequently, the Indian IT industry is facing an aggressive labor market while experiencing a talent squeeze in the supply of engineers and managers. The demand for qualified labor in the industry is expected to exceed supply by over 200,000 professionals by 2008. This increasing scarcity has led to rising wages and high turnover within the sector. Over the past four years, for instance, it is estimated that annual wages for project managers have increased by 23 percent annually. Meanwhile, the salaries of entry-level programmers have risen by 13 percent.

Clearly, growth in talent availability has failed to keep up with the growth of IT industry clusters in India. The Indian IT industry faces critical challenges in terms of hiring, talent management, and workforce retention. And as these constraints develop, countries such as China, Russia, and the Philippines are emerging as strong competitors to India's IT industry, challenging India's lead in the sector.

MANAGING WORKFORCE CHALLENGES AT INFOSYS

In the face of fierce competition for talent within the IT industry, the management of human resources plays a key role in determining Infosys' competitiveness. The success of Infosys' business model depends on our ability not only to attract the best, but to then nurture and engage outstanding individuals once they are in the organization. This tenet is enshrined in our vision for Infosys: "We will be a globally respected corporation that provides best-of-breed business solutions, leveraging technology, delivered by best-in-class people."

To attract and motivate the best and the brightest, an organization must empower its employees. At Infosys, we have focused on nurturing leaders across the organization. Employees need leaders who will not only inspire them, but also act as change agents in achieving progress. Toward this end, the Infosys Leadership System (ILS) was set up to groom leaders across all levels of the corporation and pass on the skills of leadership from one generation to the next.

The first Indian company to establish a formalized leadership institute, Infosys developed a three-tier leadership model, based on the belief that "the company is the campus, the business is the curriculum, and leaders shall teach." Senior members of Infosys management conduct select courses at the institute, drawing from their real-life experiences. Tier 1 leaders are mentored by the board members, Tier 2 leaders by Tier 1, and Tier 3 leaders by Tier 2. We have also instituted 360-degree leadership assessment to provide well-rounded feedback and development plans to potential leaders.

At Infosys, every senior leader is given the mandate to recruit people better than himself/herself. The uncompromising quality of our hiring system ensures the excellence of the people who join Infosys. Through our highly selective processes, less than 1 percent of job applicants are selected to the company every year.

To institute a culture of high performance, we have embraced meritocracy and pushed it relentlessly through the organization. Growth and reward mechanisms are aligned to performance, both of the company and of the individual. Our performance appraisal is based on clearly identified objectives and measures, and we establish stretch targets to constantly raise the performance bar for our employees. In addition, events such as the Annual Awards for Excellence help showcase achievers to the larger Infoscion community. Infosys has also introduced the Quarterly Rewards and Recognition program, a key agenda for every unit to reward excellence and acknowledge key contributions.

Infosys recently moved to a role-based structure. Out of a desire to maintain a high-performance work ethic, all roles within the company have been mapped to different jobs and personal bands. Career planning, growth, compensation, incentives, and training requirements are based on these bands. The

role-based structure provides an equitable framework for people-related decision making based on contribution to business and value addition. This emphasis on merit and data orientation has helped enhance the confidence of
employees in the fairness of the corporation.

As the shelf life of knowledge gets shorter and the knowledge turnover
across industries increases, lifelong learning and skills development become
even more critical for keeping employees relevant and agile. In the words of
Alvin Toffler: "The illiterate of this century will not be those who cannot
read and write, but those who cannot learn, unlearn, and relearn."[3]

Consequently, training is a critical aspect of our employee retention strategy. Over the years, Infosys has grown from offering a few hundred training
and competency development programs to offering several thousand. They
span everything from competency building in technology, domain, quality
process, and personal effectiveness to managerial training and leadership development. All Infoscions have a responsibility to leverage training opportunities to enhance their skills and knowledge, and they must complete a
minimum of 10 days of training every year. Continuous learning is emphasized, and regular assessments and certifications are mandatory to keep the
competency index healthy within the organization.

One of Infosys' most important people-related initiatives has been to recruit engineers who do not necessarily have a background in computer science. We then equip them to take on roles in the software industry, thus
expanding the talent pool available to us in India. We have managed this successfully through the culture of learnability within our organization. Investments in skills acquisition and competency enablement are linked to project
needs and market trends. Our focus on assertive talent engagement and the
cultivation of cross-disciplinary competencies have thus enabled our employees to remain engaged and flexible in a changing environment.

To help our employees adapt to a workforce that is distributed across geographies and time zones, we have focused on creating a learning system that is
flexible, decentralized, and technology-driven. Among the learning methods
employed are e-learning and distance learning, as well as blended learning,
which combines e-learning with the traditional classroom setting. The company has also built K-Shop, a collaborative knowledge management system,
which utilizes reusable objects and learning platforms for both technology
and business domains. It awards KCU units, which are convertible to money,
to contributors, based on the number of times the knowledge unit is used.
Accessible via intranet and extranet, this multimedia, self-learning system
runs on the 40,000-node Infosys network spanning six continents. Such

knowledge management practices have won us the Most Admired Knowledge Enterprise (MAKE) award twice globally and three times in Asia.

Greater specialization requirements across the IT industry, coupled with a challenging labor market, are magnifying the role of IT employers in India's education systems and their infrastructures. It has become critical that the private sector play a key role in reforming India's higher education system, addressing the lack of industry and resource focus. To nurture talent pools across the country, Infosys has focused on deepening the industry-academia relationship through our "Campus Connect" initiative, aimed at aligning college curricula in engineering colleges with industry requirements. Infosys freely shares technical knowledge gained over the years with participating students and faculty members at engineering colleges across India. In addition, it provides engineering faculty with sabbatical opportunities at Infosys in order to enable an industry perspective. With project assignments, we also enable students to bridge academic learning to corporate realities.

CREATING A POSITIVE WORK CULTURE

We realize that to attract, retain, and motivate professionals at Infosys, we must encourage a culture that upholds respect for and the dignity of the individual. From the very beginning, we eschewed any transaction that created asymmetry of benefits between the founder-employees and other employees. In fact, Infosys was the first Indian company to conceive and implement employee stock option plans (ESOPs) on a widespread basis. This has also enabled us to institute a culture of strong employee ownership within the organization.

We strive toward a culture where participation of employees is encouraged, feedback is valued, and action is never delayed. To that end, Infosys provides a variety of forums through which employees can impact company policy and future direction. The Policy Council at Infosys, for example, is a forum that represents the voice of the employee during the designing of corporate policies. STRAP—the annual strategy retreat—is a forum of Infosys leaders across the globe, focused on strategy formulation and action planning. The Voice of Youth allows young minds to influence overall corporate strategy, while IWIN, a forum for our female employees, functions as an advisory body to ensure inclusive management policies and decisions. Additionally, Infoscions across levels and geographies are part of our InfyPlus change management initiative.

We believe that creating a quality, collegial work environment enhances performance and helps attract and retain the best talent. Therefore, the company has invested significant resources in creating a campuslike environment with world-class facilities. Employees can even bring their families on-campus for a weekend excursion. Initiatives such as the Petit Infoscion Day provide an opportunity for kids of employees to have a day out at Infosys locations and experience where their parents work.

The company also emphasizes the culture of the "Infoscion family." Line managers are available on a 24/7 basis to help employees with personal issues for which they may need advice and guidance. Initiatives such as Health and Life Enrichment (HALE) and Infosys' hotline counseling help employees deal with health issues and emotional distress. Concurrently, the family of the concerned employee is provided with emotional, logistical, and financial support.

Regardless of how large we have grown, our core people principles have stayed the same: a drive toward commitment, innovation, self-motivation, ownership, and pride. From the beginning, our team was unique in our commitment to a strong value system. We have espoused our five core values in C-LIFE—Customer delight, Leadership by example, Integrity and transparency, Fairness, and the pursuit of Excellence. Today, our employees share a sense of pride in belonging to an organization with a strong foundation of ethics and values. We constantly reinforce these values and the vision of Infosys through messages from senior leaders.

Today's Indian IT industry faces important challenges. We are competing in a global, rapidly changing environment, where the fight for talent, resources, and market share has never been greater. As an industry, however, we have significant advantages. We have a young, highly motivated workforce; and our entrepreneurial organizations have, time and again, proved our ability to compete in a changing marketplace.

As Jim Collins says, "Fundamentally, the world is uncertain. Decisions are about the future and your place in the future when that future is uncertain. So what is the key thing you can do to prepare for that uncertainty? You can have the right people with you."[4] It is our ability to harness the potential of our people and inspire them to meet emerging challenges that will ensure our future growth and success.

CHAPTER 14

UNLEASHING THE POWER OF A HIGH PERFORMANCE WORKFORCE

BOB CAMPBELL, BETSY SCHEFFEL, AND NIDHI VERMA

IN THE book *The Perfect Storm* by Sebastian Junger, the once-a-century maelstrom at the center of the story was the result of three powerful storm systems converging at a single point in the North Atlantic. In much the same way, organizations in every industry face turbulent times ahead for managing talent because of three simultaneous forces:

1. Growing pressure on business performance requiring greater productivity.
2. Ever-tightening talent pool with a changing demographic mix and global reach.
3. Shrinking leadership pool as baby boomers retire, along with increased accountability and pressure on senior leaders brought on by ethics spotlight and new regulations.

These are rough seas indeed, with much at stake in responding effectively to these forces—and not just to weather these challenges, but to emerge stronger and better positioned for inevitable shifts in the future competitive climate.

Increasingly, organizations look for practical solutions for managing these issues—a more connected, coherent approach to the central human resources issue faced by many organizations today—Building a High Performance Workforce. Corporations able to build and sustain a High Performance Workforce master the management of each of these forces and ensure that their organization and people are equipped to adapt, to thrive, and to excel in the fast-moving business environment.

This chapter is a by-product of our pioneering work in building and enhancing human performance in organizations. It emphasizes the daunting need for managing people effectively to deliver enduring and extraordinary business results and presents an innovative framework to attract, select, deploy, and develop an organization's human capital.

REALIZING THE RETURN ON HUMAN PERFORMANCE

A High Performance Workforce is not just a productive workforce, but it is a *competitive differentiator*—people at every level in every function focused on the right priorities, feeling accountable to deliver great results, energized and engaged and positioned to give their best, and building skills important for growing the business (or for fulfilling the organization's mission).

So, is there a tested technique for building a High Performance Workforce? As we sharpened our focus on what this takes, we drew chiefly from two data sources—our experience in working with leading organizations that are tackling the tough talent issues, and Hewitt's proprietary Double-Digit Growth (DDG) Companies research conducted in association with Michael Treacy and his book, *Double-Digit Growth: How Great Companies Achieve It No Matter What* (New York: Portfolio, 2003), which spotlights how the strongest companies attack talent issues differently from lower-growth businesses. This data showed us a very clear and consistent pattern: Organizations that are achieving great results pay particular attention to three talent activities and issues—the ones most critical to Building a High Performance Workforce:

- *Building accountability everywhere, for the right results.* Everyone is working on what's important, hitting targets, and playing by the rules.
- *Making sure the people we depend on are convinced we value them.* Those who perform feel recognized, appreciated, and ready to give their best.
- *Managing opportunity for impact and growth.* The strongest performers are in our key jobs, and every job provides the chance to grow.

These aren't abstract concepts; they're the fundamentals that build spirit, energy, alignment, and an achievement mind-set—all critical to a High Performance Workforce.

As we explored further, it became clear that each of these three high performance fundamentals has two or three building blocks, which are some of the specifics we can act on to deliver these three core factors for the organizations we support. Figure 14.1 illustrates these building blocks of a high performance culture.

The strongest organizations approach these building blocks of high performance differently than other companies do. Unlike most other organizations, the strongest companies are not satisfied with implementing new or modified programs and processes supported by training modules. They understand that while such practices are a good foundation, it takes a very different level of focus to get these *right* and realize their potential return on investment (ROI)—a High Performance Workforce—for the business. For these strong organizations, there is also an extraordinary focus on execution—investing in and committing to strengthening their manager capability for leading people. They don't just execute them; *they execute them well enough to be a competitive advantage.*

Figure 14.1
Building Blocks of a High Performance Culture

High Performance Workforce—Creating the Conditions for People to Excel

Accountability for the Right Results	• High-Achievement Goal Setting • Performance Coaching

People Who Perform Know They're Valued	• Reviews and Rewards That Build Winners • A Culture of Earned Respect

Opportunity Managed for Impact and Growth	• Key Talent Deployed for Impact • People Directed toward Future-Critical Skills • Growth Built into Every Job

ROAD MAP FOR BUILDING A HIGH PERFORMANCE WORKFORCE

While there are other things that are critical to creating and sustaining a High Performance Workforce—such as work and organization design—these seven elements make a critical difference and underpin the three high performance fundamentals we've outlined. Let's examine, then, the progressive ways strong organizations are tackling them, and uncover how they address the three talent forces we discussed earlier in the chapter.

High-Achievement Goal Setting—First Building Block of a High Performance Culture

A high performance culture must be grounded in a clear definition of desired outcomes and business results. Aligning the entire workforce behind a common direction requires effective goal setting. This is one of those areas in which leaders in most organizations will proclaim, "We're doing that—we have things like goal cascading, SMART goal setting (specific, measurable, attainable, etc.)."

But it's clear that organizations with best-in-class goal-setting processes do more. Approximately 15 percent more employees in DDG companies than in low-growth ones report that they are clear about the organization's direction and how their goals fit into the mission. Notably, employees in DDG companies consistently reported being asked to "reach high," indicating that managers at all levels are more comfortable with setting tough targets. In contrast, employees in roughly 50 percent of organizations reported that their company doesn't set high standards. Further, a DDG company puts its money where its mouth is—30 percent more DDG organizations reported withholding short-term incentives for underperformance.

While most organizations focus on ensuring that all employees have goals in place and that those goals are defined in a specific format, the real challenge is in the content of the goals—the degree of stretch and the alignment with desired business outcomes. When this challenge is met, then organizations can move to real high achievement.

Lack of stretch goals tends to have its roots in the culture of the organization and spreads across the organization. One global financial services firm sent a strong signal about accountability and result focus at a very early stage in an employee's career. Starting at new-hire orientation, the message people received was "What counts here is achieving your goals, hitting your targets!"

This meant a high degree of personal accountability, but the unintended consequence was that nobody took big risks and no employee stepped forward for that tough project nobody else had cracked. All the approval and reward signposts signaled that it was far worse to miss a goal—even if it was something important to try for the good of the business—than to shy away from such risks and aim low, ensuring you hit your targets.

Figure 14.2 illustrates how performance is rewarded in most organizations—the highest rewards go to those best at predicting what they can achieve rather than to those who achieve the greatest performance. The chart shows that the highest rewards go to those who did the best job relative to their performance goals—regardless of the degree of stretch or challenge in those goals. So the performer who sets tough targets and misses some but still achieves great results is, in effect, penalized for those tough goals. High performance organizations need to move to a model where courage is rewarded over caution.

In a $6 billion manufacturing organization with 30,000 employees, tougher competition demanded more aggressive thinking and action to drive desired business results. To meet these demands the organization needed to change behaviors across levels and functions and particularly needed top managers to modify their behaviors and show the way. But the senior managers themselves had become conditioned to avoid the types of behaviors

Figure 14.2
How Performance Is Rewarded

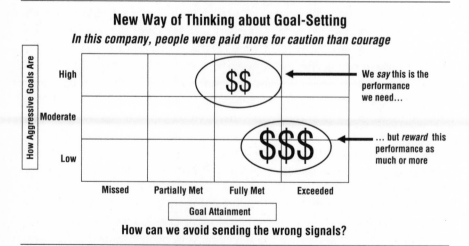

New Way of Thinking about Goal-Setting

In this company, people were paid more for caution than courage

How Aggressive Goals Are: High / Moderate / Low

$$ — We *say* this is the performance we need...

$$$ — ... but *reward* this performance as much or more

Goal Attainment: Missed / Partially Met / Fully Met / Exceeded

How can we avoid sending the wrong signals?

needed because of what was measured and rewarded in the past. When we drew the graph in Figure 14.2 for the executive team to show what was happening, they acknowledged, "We're rewarding comfort-zone effort as much as the ability to take risks needed by the business! We're telling people to play it safe and if you're smart, there's no premium for reaching higher and, in fact, you might lose if you do!"

By using this chart with each employee and group, managers can communicate a powerful message about goal attainment. By changing the size of the rewards at different points on the chart, managers can depict how coming close on a really tough goal is valued as much or more (that is, gets the bigger dollar signs on this graph) than meeting or exceeding an easy one. This, of course, needs to be backed up with appraisal and pay actions, especially during this period of change. The task ahead was clear to the senior team: Managers would need to understand and act on a new set of rules. First, they needed to topple the sacred cow of goal completion as the ultimate criterion. Second, managers needed to buy into a broader way of looking at performance that not only stressed completing goals, but also included the courage to take risks and tackle the toughest things.

In both of these examples, what was actually tracked and rewarded inadvertently prevented actions that could have contributed significantly to the business. But not just that—many employees had become confused and cynical hearing that competencies such as risk taking and initiative were essential for their roles while seeing a different performance yardstick actually used.

Creating a new norm of aiming for tough targets is central to high-achievement goal setting, but to achieve it, managers need new capabilities and new tools. This means clear goal alignment and getting comfortable measuring what's tough to measure, establishing simultaneous team and individual ownership, and generating commitment to nonnegotiable (that is, preset) goals. This must start at the very top of the organization and effective execution must be demanded throughout.

Equipping managers with concrete tactics and the capability to handle these issues is what makes the difference between simply having a goal-setting process and making high-achievement goal setting a competitive advantage.

Performance Coaching—Helping People Give Their Best

"I need to make my dancers stretch a little more than they believe possible—in terms of their performance, their energy, the amplitude of their movements," says Twyla Tharp, world-renowned dancer and choreographer. It is no different for managers. High performance organizations build a capability in their managers that goes far beyond managing for compliance, to managing for performance. These managers help their teams to focus on priorities amid potential distractions, ensuring that targets are met. What really differentiates them is that a coaching capability is built deep into the organization, guiding every employee to continually learn, to grow, and to contribute their best.

What's striking is that the best-in-class companies are not creating lofty academic programs steeped in theory and concepts but instead deploying practical, real-world tools and strategies to build strong coaching skills. These organizations provide managers—from executives to team leaders—with concrete, usable job aids and techniques that translate sound coaching methods to the language and level that can be easily understood by stretched and always rushed "manager-doers." These managers need simple ways to have effective performance discussions that tell it like it is and are constructive and motivating.

For example, one simple coaching tool valued by managers is a 2×2 "window pane" with each cell containing one of these four words: Stop, Start, More, Less. It is a simple but effective device that helps managers prepare their thoughts and comments before giving feedback to their employees. It allows them to determine what specifically they want to ask the employee to stop doing, start doing, do more of, or do less of (or continue to do as is). From senior officers to new team leaders, managers instantly understand how valuable this simple tool is—though very rarely used—to get to the level of clarity and confidence that's essential to effective coaching. It provides a guide to clarify for employees what the manager and the business expects from them—that is, more contribution, different contribution, new behaviors, and so forth. Employees can also use the tool during the discussion to help managers see how to make the new expectations doable. What's important is that it is not another form or process, but rather a quick back-of-the-envelope guide that managers and employees can use when headed into a coaching discussion to ensure that an accurate message is conveyed and desired changes are understood.

A central group of leaders or functional HR professionals cannot create clarity and high performance expectations for every employee. To achieve the goal of clear accountability for results, every manager must engage in the process and execute against the business objectives required to drive competitive advantage. Without this clear accountability, remaining building blocks are nearly impossible to achieve. With it, great organizations are able to respond to the first storm front we identified—growing pressure on business performance that requires greater productivity.

Reviews and Rewards That Build Winners—
Conveying the Messages That Matter Most

From the back offices of business process operations to the front lines of customer service, once clear accountability is set, employees want to be valued and acknowledged for delivering outstanding results. The challenge is effective measurement and reward of consistent superior performance. In many organizations, at the end of the performance year half or more employees leave their performance review discussion deflated, if not cynical. Most are resigned to having been processed in a bureaucratic labeling and salary budget allocation exercise.

Leaders intending to foster accountability do things like "suggest" (that is, impose) rating and ranking distributions that don't work at the small team level, but must be applied there so the broader unit and organization achieve the budget when ratings are rolled up. In addition, the 5-point scales used by about half of all organizations, as reported in our latest performance management practices research, typically result in 50 to 60 percent of employees getting what they perceive to be a C grade.

What's going on? In the quest to develop and apply talent management systems consistently and prudently across a large enterprise, it's easy to lose sight of how these practices affect people at the team and individual level— and to lose sight of the fundamental goals of delighting the highest achievers, putting underperformers on notice to improve or leave, while at the same time—and here's the most elusive part—making solid contributors feel successful, not like also-rans.

One biotech firm in the U.S. Northeast wanted to crack this problem to recapture the energy and spirit that filled the labs and offices in its start-up years. Conservatism and cynicism were starting to creep in as more formal appraisal and reward processes were introduced and had the effects just described. It was time for action. So the firm rebuilt performance ratings to eliminate the "C syndrome" by redefining the scale and giving solid contributors—those under the dome of the bell curve in a high performance organization—the new message that they're doing great work that's highly appreciated and valued. For this organization, that meant moving to a smaller set of ratings, and renaming them to better describe the intent of the ratings: Leading Performance—for the employees who make a breakaway contribution; Strong Performance—for those who are solid contributors; and Building Consistency—for those employees who show potential and need to contribute at the necessary levels. Those whose performance fell far below expectations receive a rating of Not Building Consistency. Using these labels, the organization communicates to the majority of employees, those falling into the second rating, that their performance is contributing to the success of the business and making a difference. The key, as Chemtura Corporation has recently demonstrated, is to match these new labels with the richer goal-setting process described earlier, so that managers are working with employees to set aggressive goals and adding stretch to the process—not stretch for stretch's sake—but the kind of stretch needed to ensure that each person in each job is doing what it takes to help the organization win in the market.

At the same time, high-impact recognition and reward methods geared to convince stars throughout the year that they're treasured were identified. This eliminates the pressure to have multiple "exceptional/outstanding" scale points for them at review time, which had inadvertently made strong-but-not-stellar employees feel discounted.

Other organizations across industries have taken a similar approach. Changing a name can feel like window dressing—but when coupled with the right messages, with reward systems that complement the message of success for reaching high, managers and employees can feel that the performance management process is making a difference in what they achieve both individually and as an organization.

A related challenge is faced by other organizations, where ratings are inflated to combat the demotivation that occurs when being told that one is average. A leading insurance company recently described it this way: "Making solid performers feel like winners is great, but our problem is we have *too many* winners—people whose managers give them higher ratings than they've earned instead of giving them straightforward feedback about increased effort and results needed. They need to feel more accountability, not be told they're terrific!" Addressing *this* issue almost always requires an initial focus on high-achievement goal setting and performance coaching, the building blocks that get managers capable and comfortable to set the bar high. With a clear definition of the desired outcomes, it is easier for managers to then have direct discussions about gaps and provide guidance on how to close the gaps. This lays the solid foundation of results accountability needed for a High Performance Workforce.

A Culture of Earned Respect—Creating an Affirming Climate Based on Performance

The year-end performance and rewards discussion is just one element of a culture of earned respect. The manager mind-set and actions needed to create this kind of culture are related to reviews and rewards that build winners, but distinct in important ways. They require a sharp and constant focus in the following areas:

- Providing the recognition it takes to build real momentum.
- Sharing enough information so performers feel like insiders.
- Involving people in decisions that impact their job or work group to the extent possible and practical, and when not possible explaining why and how the decisions were made.

Many new *and* experienced managers either aren't aware of or—given the pace of the business—don't have time to remember how motivational these are. And elaborate programs or processes won't help here. These managers need practical guidance, reminders, and job aids that build their comfort and capability to do these things easily and effectively within the rushed flow of work. Many managers even allow negative myths about recognition to stop them from recognizing employees at all.

For example, for a major department store company, we worked with managers to identify the biggest roadblocks about recognition. A few roadblocks commonly identified by managers include:

- Praise or rewards counter the message that giving our best every time is what's expected.
- In giving special recognition we run the risk of alienating those who don't receive it (but who may have played a part in the results delivered).
- "I had a boss who rarely gave out praise, so the rare times she did, it made it that much more meaningful." That has more impact in the long run.
- Giving out rewards *now* just ups the ante—escalating peoples' expectations for next time.
- Praise won't sound earnest or be welcome in our hard-driving culture. That's worse than saying nothing.

These roadblocks are really myths based on managers' misinformed but very human and typical assumptions. Practical tips and simple genuine scripts then provide the how-to tools they can start using—and we can start reinforcing—right away. One step that has been extremely valuable for many organizations is to openly discuss each of these roadblocks, allowing for managers to share and learn from each other about how to work around them and realize the benefits of recognition.

Sharing business information, as with recognition, creates complexities for managers who are trying to balance distracting employees from daily priorities, revealing confidential information, and making employees feel like partners in the business. Managers should be trained on how to quickly decide whether and how much information to share with employees in any situation and to gauge when and to what extent people should be involved in a particular decision without sacrificing speed for the sake of consensus. There are practical measures to give managers what they need to be accountable for, and good at, thereby creating a culture of earned respect.

With these building blocks of a high performance environment in place, we're creating a magnet for strong performers because cultures that value *and* validate those who perform attract and keep great people. And that creates a buzz in the talent market. Having a high-energy climate and being a great place to work powerfully address the second challenge we teed up at the outset, operating in a tightening talent pool while retaining key talent and attracting great people.

Key Talent Deployed for Impact—Right People, Right Roles, Right Time

The third storm front we identified at the outset—a shrinking leadership pool—requires that organizations are focused on growing tomorrow's leaders at all levels. Great organizations are simultaneously positioning the right people in mission-critical roles while building opportunity to grow into every assignment and job.

This requires that key talent is deployed to the places where they can have the highest impact—something we call "opportunity management." To make this work well, we need an effective workforce planning or process that identifies who the key people are and the skills they require to drive the business forward. But beyond workforce and talent planning—processes in place in some form within most organizations—managers need the skills to carry out the thinking, discuss, and take decisions to match open assignments with the people the organization especially wants to invest in: high potentials, high performers, and those with scarce in-demand skills.

One leading aviation business has found that there are a number of critical success factors in deploying talent effectively. These factors spell the difference between "we've got a process for that" and the fluid deployments and prudent stewardship that grow the best people and position them to contribute their best. Examples of these critical success factors include:

- Hinge the key talent deployment process and each deployment decision on a solid business rationale.
- Make sure someone in a leadership role is talking to all key people to understand their personal goals and explain the organization's commitment to them.
- Plan two moves out to help key employees build career continuity and see the trajectory.
- Use efficient practical templates and tools to accelerate and quality-check data gathering, discussions, and decisions.
- Base all deployment assignment decisions on fact-based judgment—not assumptions. One way to do this is to require peer discussions among managers to defend and challenge these assignments.

With the available leadership talent pool shrinking, making sure the skills and systems are in place to deploy the right people to the right roles throughout the organization is essential. This allows the organization to identify, motivate, and affirm a commitment to potential leaders at all levels, in addition to ensuring strong players are in each key role.

In equally powerful ways, each of the other high performance building blocks—for example, high-achievement goal setting, performance coaching, growth built into every job—also drives leader development, each contributing an essential part to a climate conducive to challenging and growing strong people. That's why organizations are increasingly determined to build a High Performance Workforce as their core leadership development approach.

People Directed toward Future-Critical Skills— Real Opportunity, Real Plans

High performance organizations are better than their competitors at defining and explaining where the real opportunities for growth are, and this helps them channel talent to both current and future mission-critical areas in the business. A leading financial services organization has mapped 11 experiences (for example, listening to and serving customers, managing a profit and loss (P&L), mastering a critical skill area) they see as essential for building readiness for certain key leadership roles. This shows employees the route to increased impact, defined by increased ability to make an impact on business performance. It also allows managers to plan developmental opportunities for high performers to ensure they are gaining the necessary experiences to be ready for those key roles. Another organization has developed online career/growth planning tools that include diagrams clearly charting how the business model and strategy will require particular skills in pivotal roles, for example, engineers in certain disciplines. This is providing employees with a picture of the key capabilities so they can focus on building the skills critical to the enterprise.

Importantly, organizations that are building these types of "opportunity route maps" are finding them to be not only essential for providing current employees with a picture of their prospects and potential, but also excellent recruitment tools—they're attracting more of the best candidates who are drawn to and encouraged by this tangible evidence of the organization's commitment to being clear about routes to success. To do this effectively, though, requires a real assessment of what *will be* required to drive future business success, instead of a summary of how current leaders achieved success or what was required of those current leaders to progress through the organization. This future focus is another example of applying stretch to expectations throughout the organizations—a key component we described earlier in effective goal setting.

Double-digit growth companies are much better at focusing their people on activities that drive competitive advantage, and they are more likely to outsource noncore activities to gain access to scale and expertise while reducing costs. At least half of the DDG respondents report that their companies are currently engaged in outsourcing relationships. Moreover, the results indicate that while 50 percent of the DDG companies are currently involved in outsourcing relationships, an additional 25 percent are proactively preparing to manage and coordinate future relationships. Seventy-five percent of the DDG companies have a department or person responsible for strategic sourcing and/or vendor management, compared to 66 percent at single-digit growth (SDG) companies. This frees up internal resources to drive the core business and focus on the activities where the organization can be best in class.

Growth Built into Every Job—Progress Not Tied to Promotions

Hewitt's employee engagement research clearly shows that perceived opportunity is the most prevalent issue affecting employees' commitment to giving their best efforts—a crucial element driving superior business results. At the same time, as organizations have delayered to drive out bureaucracy and to lower costs, opportunities for growth through the traditional promotion route have disappeared.

Therefore, it's not surprising that one of the ways high-growth companies are significantly different from slow-growth organizations is that they have learned to focus on managing opportunity in role, helping employees develop and build critical business skills that don't rely on promotions. These organizations are equipping managers with realistic, practical techniques and tool kits to help people grow in place. One very effective example is a "development dashboard." As illustrated in Figure 14.3, the dashboard provides a road map of the best high-impact, low-budget strategies and the steps to offer people learning opportunities that kindle a feeling of growth, not stagnation.

Because they know the business payback of creating a performance *and* growth culture, these organizations hold managers accountable for having the discussions, making the decisions, and taking the actions to help every employee to keep improving and learning.

At the same time these companies are communicating broadly about the skills the business requires to reach and exceed established business goals. They then equip employees to take charge of their own in-job development by providing practical self-guided assessment and development resources, all

Figure 14.3
Development Dashboard

Development Dashboard

Cross-Business Assignments
• Cross-Function
• Cross-Department

Action Learning Teams

Self-Assessment and Awareness Tools

Internal and External Training

Eight Ways to Build Business-Critical Skills

Multisource Feedback

Individualized Resources
• Personal Learning Accounts
• Mentors

Real-World Coaching

Job Engineering

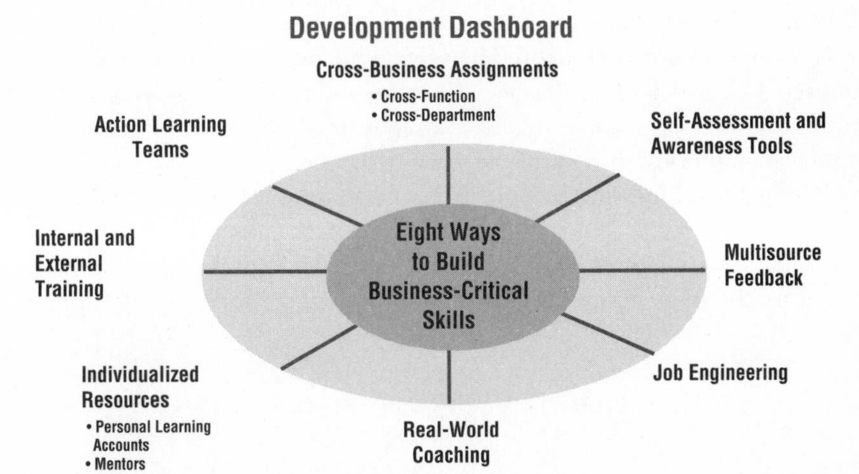

synchronized to the probable opportunities the business will present going forward. When mapped with the effective talent deployment process defined earlier, real growth is demonstrated across the organization—providing all employees with real-life models of career progression, high-impact contribution, and exciting opportunity—all within the organization.

IN CLOSING

The corporate landscape is littered with change initiatives marketed as cure-alls for lackluster business performance and low engagement. Sadly, the overwhelming majority of such initiatives fail to meet the lofty goals they set, and some fade into obscurity as quickly and dramatically as they were launched. Many organizations attempt quick-fix initiatives to achieve growth, and such initiatives often fail. These initiatives tend to only scratch the surface—they aren't cognizant of an organization's values or a manager's capabilities or take into account the type of work environment necessary to drive high performance.

Building a High Performance Workforce is a full contact sport. As we've described here, it requires not just elegant programs and practices but skills used by all managers to ensure that expectations are clear, great contributors feel cherished by the organization, and ambitious, high-energy people can't imagine a place with more opportunity for them to grow and contribute. The seven high performance building blocks we've defined here, alongside effective organization and job structures, culminate in the conditions that define a High Performance Workforce.

With the three forces we defined at the outset on the horizon, no organization can afford to stand still. They represent urgent business challenges—not just HR or talent challenges. The strategies defined here define the path to engaging our people in becoming our competitive differentiators, equipped and ready to achieve the strategic mission.

The potential for what people can contribute, and how they and the enterprise can thrive, is dramatically underrealized in most organizations. These fundamentals strengthen and support the manager capability that is crucial—to realize the tremendous ROI in Building a High Performance Workforce.

CHAPTER 15

OUT OF THIS WORLD

DOING THINGS THE SEMCO WAY

RICARDO SEMLER

"MR. SEMLER . . . can you please tell us what planet you're from?" I had just finished giving a speech at a conference in the far north of Brazil and was preparing to field questions from the hundreds of people in attendance when a man seated in the front row posed this provocative question. Before I could open my mouth to reply, the crowd erupted in gales of good-natured laughter, and it took several minutes for the room to quiet down enough for the Q&A portion of the session to continue.

Who would have the audacity to pose such an inflammatory—albeit, humorous—question? Believe it or not, it was the man who invited me to speak at the conference—Senator Jose Macedo, a prominent Brazilian politician and wonderful self-made man. Senator Macedo began his working life as a soap salesman before branching out into the flour, biscuit, beer, and car dealership businesses. When we first met he was already a billionaire, and by the time I was invited to speak at the conference in question, he had earned my utmost respect.

Most people would allow themselves to be insulted by such an exchange. At first blush, you too might think I should have considered Senator Macedo's question an affront. After all, I had just finished giving an hourlong presentation in a hot, humid auditorium and deserved to be afforded the respect of an honored guest. Surely, I didn't deserve to be laughed at for being different.

The thing is, though, my company, Semco, *is* different. We have no official structure, no organizational chart, no business plan or company strategy, no two- or five-year plan, no goal or mission statement, and no long-term budget. And while many journalists and commentators brand me "CEO" when describing the company, the fact is that Semco doesn't *have* a fixed CEO. We also have no vice presidents and no chief officers for information technology or operations. There are no standards or practices, no human resources department, no career plans, no job descriptions or employer contracts. No one approves reports or expense accounts, and supervision or monitoring of employees is a rarity.

Semco's history can be traced back to my father, Antonio Curt Semler, a Viennese immigrant. Shortly after moving to Brazil from Argentina in the mid-1950s, he patented a centrifuge for separating oils. Building on his invention, my father founded a small machine shop, which quickly became a $2-million-a-year business. In the late 1960s, he grew the business exponentially when he formed a partnership with two British marine pump manufacturers, making Semco a major supplier to the Brazilian shipbuilding industry. Over the next quarter-century, Semco built marine pumps and its name became synonymous with the shipping industry.

As far back as I can remember, my father assumed I would accept responsibility for managing Semco when I got old enough. As for me, I wasn't so sure I wanted to take the reins of a company I considered too rigid and steeped in tradition. After all, I was having too much fun playing in a rock band to contemplate spending my life doing what I considered babysitting people just to make sure they clocked in on time.

After much debate and negotiation, I agreed to take over Semco and my father agreed to step back and allow me to make over the company as I deemed fit. Within just days of accepting the reins, I had fired two-thirds of my father's most senior managers. Sure, it was a risky move, but one I felt was necessary to quickly implement reforms without having to endure the inevitable foot-dragging of long-entrenched executives. My reinvention of dear old Dad's company didn't end there. I spent the next two decades questioning, challenging, and dismantling the traditional business practices my father had spent the previous three decades instilling at Semco.

Starting to think Senator Macedo was justified in asking me what planet I'm from? It's okay if you do. You wouldn't be the first and you most certainly won't be the last. I guess you could say I come from the planet

Semco because life sure is a lot different here than it is just about any other place on Earth.

THE SEVEN-DAY WEEKEND

I'll be the first to admit that Semco is one of the world's most unusual work-places. Many of our basic tenets fly in the face of even the most progressive owners or managers. For starters, we don't do the standard Monday to Friday workweek. Instead, we operate in a fashion that I like to call the "seven-day weekend." Operating under the conviction that people are the best judges of where and when they can best get the job done, we give our employees the freedom to customize their workdays. For Semco employees, the hours they work are determined by their own self-interest, rather than by company mandates.

Don't get me wrong. The seven-day weekend isn't about giving employees permission to play hooky. It's about creating an atmosphere and culture in which employees have permission to be whole people seven days a week. We humans are complex creatures with many facets, interests, talents, and person-alities. If forced to shut off any portion of ourselves from Monday morning till Friday night, we are not living truly fulfilling lives. No one should feel they have to leave half of themselves in the parking lot each and every day. It's a lousy way to live and a lousy way to work.

At Semco, we not only allow, but actively encourage our employees to pursue their interests, leaving it to them to perform their work duties where and when they feel they are likely to deliver the best results. If a Wednesday morning rock-climbing expedition is more inviting than a budget planning meeting, then by all means, break out the rope and pitons! If lighter traffic on a Saturday afternoon makes the commute to the office more bearable, then feel free to spend a few hours at work. We don't care when you get your work done, just as long as you get it done. It's up to employees to decide when they will best be able to perform their duties.

One of the best examples of living the seven-day workweek can be found in Jose Carlos Reis de Magalhaes (known as Zeca to his friends and colleagues), who came to work at Semco at the age of 23. A recent gradu-ate of one of Brazil's top business schools, Zeca had been employed by an important, aggressive investment bank, where he managed its Internet ventures in the construction industry. When I first met Zeca, I quickly re-alized that he reminded me of myself at his age. Immediately recognizing his passion for work, I asked him to help launch Semco Ventures, our new high-tech unit.

As luck would have it, shortly after Zeca started working at Semco, Brazilian tennis champion Gustavo Kuerten reached the finals of the French Open—France's Wimbledon, if you will. An avid tennis fan, Zeca made it clear he'd be home watching Kuerten's televised matches during the day and performing his work for Semco at night. He didn't agonize over the decision, and he didn't ask permission. "Only because I work at Semco," he says. "Nowhere else could I do that without feeling guilty."

When Zeca tendered his resignation at the investment bank to accept my job offer, his infuriated bosses couldn't understand why he would leave an established, venerable organization for a start-up. In spite of his youth, Zeca already possessed one priceless piece of knowledge that the older executives obviously had yet to learn—that status, power, and even money are sometimes not enough to make a job fulfilling.

As the French Open drew to a close that year, Zeca hadn't missed a match. He also hadn't missed an opportunity to impress me, performing all his duties in an exemplary fashion. You see, Zeca brings the same passion to Semco that he feels for his beloved tennis. It's not at all unusual to find him working 12-hour days. No one tracks when he puts in those 12 hours, mind you, and they are often in the middle of the night.

The fact that Zeca tailors his work schedule around tennis tournaments or long lunches with his girlfriend (another favorite pursuit) doesn't make him any less effective of an employee. In actuality, granting him permission to be a whole person 24/7 makes him a better employee—not a lesser one. The freedom to pursue his hobbies and spend time with his girlfriend allows him to create balance in his life.

The pursuit of personal interests isn't the only reason to allow for elastic work schedules. If an employee, by nature, regularly sleeps until 9:00 A.M. and I demand she reports to work by 8:00, then all I've accomplished is securing myself a couple of hours of her least productive time. At the other end of the spectrum, if I insist on closing down operations at 6:00 P.M., I'm forcing her to leave work just as she may be hitting her stride. By insisting upon standard work hours, I end up sacrificing a certain amount of employee potential each and every day. The trade-off for uniformity is lost productivity. Who in their right mind could make a justifiable case for that?

Naturally, there are those who argue that such freedom only leads to disaster. They assume that chaos will ensue if people are given some latitude when it comes to designing their own work schedules. To them, I say: nonsense. I simply cannot believe that responsible adults would simply fail to show up when they are needed—that a journalist who undoubtedly understands the urgency of deadlines would go to the movies rather than putting the finishing touches on a critical story . . . that an anesthesiologist would pull up the covers and roll over in bed, leaving a crew of surgeons standing around the operating table . . . that actors who spent years honing their craft would leave their public waiting anxiously for the curtain to rise. The fact that anyone could have such a disheartening view of humankind fills me with profound sadness.

Granted, such dire predictions are nothing new to Semco. I've been hearing them for 20 years, ever since we first proposed that people be allowed to work away from the office. Once again, our critics were wrong. Two decades later, we're not only still here, but we're thriving. Today, Semco employees work wherever they want—whether in Semco's satellite offices or "at home," which can encompass a myriad of locations, ranging from their literal home to a café or the park. Should they ever begin to feel out of touch, they take it upon themselves to meet up with someone—or spend some face time in the office.

Younger workers who've come of age in the era of Internet cafés and cell phones typically take to the concept of working "whenever, wherever" quite readily. Among seasoned workers, however, it frequently takes a little getting used to. I myself had a hard time not feeling self-conscious about working poolside in a pair of shorts when I first started working three half-days from home during the early 1980s. In the beginning, I would rush to pull on a pair of trousers whenever a messenger arrived with the office mail pouch. In my mind's eye, I pictured him returning to company headquarters, proclaiming that the boss was sunbathing while everyone else was busy toiling away on one of Brazil's sweltering summer days.

Eventually, I came to the conclusion that everyone already knew I worked at a garden table in my shorts with a stack of telex messages piled high by my side. Clearly, I was still getting my work done. So I stopped worrying about it. Soon, other Semco directors were taking a page from my playbook, working from home or wherever else their hearts desired. In time, the trend trickled down to middle management and eventually to regular employees.

Anyone who's had his or her eyes and ears open over the past decade and a half can readily tell that telecommuting is an inevitable part of our future. In 1990, four million people worked from somewhere other than a traditional office in the United States. By 2000, that number had mushroomed to 23.6 million telecommuters. Considering the unprecedented economic growth the United States enjoyed during the 1990s, it's safe to assume the work still got done.

This incredible growth in telecommuting came amid yet more dire predictions, this time that giving employees latitude in determining where they work would result in the demise of the traditional office. While it's true the number of people working elsewhere is expected to continue to increase as far as the eye can see, people need not worry that the traditional office will disappear completely. I tell you unequivocally that will never happen. In part, that's because there will always be a certain percentage of people who cannot work at home. Either they don't have the space or they have kids in the house or someone's always running a noisy appliance or they simply don't have the self-discipline to turn off the TV and get to work.

For those workers who really *can't* work at home but don't wish to be tethered to just one location, a decentralized system (such as Semco employs) with offices scattered around town is an effective solution. The advantages are numerous. Take, for example, the employee who has a dinner date planned with her husband and a group of friends. If she were to work a full afternoon at corporate headquarters before hopping into her car for the one-hour drive to the restaurant, she wouldn't arrive until 7:00 P.M. At Semco, she is free to leave headquarters at 3:00 P.M., take a leisurely drive to the satellite office nearest the restaurant, wrap up some unfinished business, and then saunter over to the restaurant just in time for dinner. She would be better equipped to enjoy her meal, having completed her work for the day, but without the stress of enduring rush hour traffic.

PUSHING THE BOUNDARIES

Semco's dedication to flexibility and balance doesn't end there. We are experimenting with a variety of management approaches, all of which are designed to return to people control of their own destinies. One particular proposition, dubbed "Up 'n' Down Pay" literally allows employees to manage their own pay. This approach is built around the assumption that allowing people to adjust their pay and work hours to their changing life situations will pay dividends all the way around.

This sort of program would allow people with temporary problems or family issues to scale back their work hours without derailing or endangering their careers. Take, for example, a mother who wishes to spend more time with her children. She could request that someone else assume 30 percent of her job duties for a designated time period. At the end of that time, she would then return to her full-time schedule.

Like many of our approaches, Semco's Retire-a-Little program sounds a little off-the-wall at first. However, it's carefully constructed to take life cycles and the curve of human health into account. Few people would argue that the peak of physical capability typically occurs during one's 20s and 30s. Likewise, one's health tends to take a downturn once someone passes the age of 60. At the same time, one's financial independence usually reaches its zenith between the age of 50 and 60, while idle time naturally peaks after 70. Basically, then, we can conclude that you don't have the money or leisure time to realize your dreams when you are most physically fit to pursue them. Conversely, you no longer have the required physical stamina for such pursuits when you have the most time and money to spare. Isn't that ironic?

At Semco, we believe the current system of work and retirement should be replaced with one that allows employees to better square their life cycle with their career cycle. Under our Retire-a-Little program, people are allowed to acquire from the company as much early retirement as they wish—provided they repay that time later. An employee may take Wednesday afternoons off, for example, to pursue those interests that would ordinarily be reserved for retirement. The company "sells" the employee that time by reducing take-home pay by a small amount. In turn, the employee receives a voucher for work to be performed after retirement.

Say employees took off 100 Wednesday afternoons. After retirement, they may redeem their vouchers by offering to work every Wednesday for two years in exchange for proportional pay. Essentially what they've done is exchanged early retirement for later work. When they're young enough to go rock climbing each Wednesday, they go rock climbing. In 10 years, when an arthritic knee or a bad back makes rock climbing too much of a risk, they'll spend their Wednesdays contemplating new products.

It's too early to worry about the what-ifs: What if the company no longer exists when these people reach retirement age? What if too many people show up for work that we no longer have? Sure, there are many reasons to hesitate before making such an innovative idea reality. But that's been the case with just about every other innovative idea we've put in place over the past two decades. Like everything else we do at Semco, Retire-a-Little is designed to push the boundaries and test the future. We'll worry about the potential consequences later.

Semco's Work 'n' Stop program allows employees to take a sabbatical of up to three years for any given purpose. An internal committee seeks out a

temporary replacement, either internally—in which case, the employee taking the break would be fairly certain of being able to reclaim the job at the
end of the sabbatical—or externally, in which case, returning to the employee's original job would be more problematic, but certainly not out of
the question.

To finance these sabbaticals, Semco allows employees to set aside a portion
of their monthly pay. The company acts as banker by keeping the money, but
releases it whenever employees feel they have enough to underwrite their
time off and want to make a withdrawal. For the employee, this program is a
golden opportunity to balance their work and personal life. For the company,
it pays for itself in productivity and longevity, not to mention decreased
turnover.

THE WHYWAY

At Semco, we believe that economic success requires replacing control and
structure with democracy in the workplace. As you've probably already gath-
ered, we place an immense amount of power in the hands of the workers.
With a show of hands, our employees can veto new product ideas or scrap
entire business ventures. When it comes right down to it, it's about trusting
our employees to be responsible adults. Think about it. People are considered
adults in their private lives, at the bank, at their children's schools, with family
and among friends, so why are they suddenly treated like adolescents at work?
Why can't workers be involved in choosing their own leaders? Why shouldn't
they manage themselves? Why can't they speak up—challenge, question, share
information openly?

If we have a cardinal strategy that forms the bedrock for all Semco practices, it's this: *Ask why*. Ask it all the time, ask it any day, every day, and always
ask it three times in a row. Employees must be free to question, to analyze,
and to investigate, and a company must be flexible enough to listen to the answers. Those habits are the key to longevity, growth, and profit.

Granted, constant questioning doesn't come naturally for most people. As
children, we question everything repeatedly, often driving our parents to the
point of exhaustion. As we mature, however, we are taught to set aside the
genuine impulse to question things. On the surface, the rationale for doing so
seems to make sense. After all, peppering someone with too many questions
may be perceived as rude. It can also be dangerous, tacitly implying that we're
ignorant or uninformed. In questioning something, we also run the risk of

discovering that everything we thought we knew we never really knew at all. Finally, there's the possibility that management will feel threatened by the prospect of employees who question continually.

Not so at Semco. In meetings, we address the same subject over and over again, asking "why" repeatedly. Nothing is ever carved in stone, either. Granted, we jot down generic ideas and broad numbers to enable us to better visualize the dimensions of a new product or service. But we throw those notes away. At the next meeting, we'll start over—without the benefit of the original notes. By so doing, we ensure that we do not fall into the trap of fixed assumptions. Instead, we are forced to reconsider all the variables. As a general rule, we at Semco despise written plans. The reason is simple. People will follow a plan like a Pied Piper—mindlessly, with no thought as to the final destination.

Many a new Semco executive has been heard to stammer: "But we already decided that at the last meeting!" or "Why are we going over this again, instead of forging ahead?" I don't deny that it's frustrating for them. I'm quite certain it is. But when they watch the process unfold, and if they listen to their colleagues asking "why," they'll see how our questioning strategy allows no stone to be left unturned.

Our business practices may be otherworldly, but so too are our profits. From 1994 to 2003, Semco increased its annual revenue from $35 million to $212 million. And we continue growing nearly 40 percent each year without any public investment. Had it been possible to invest $100,000 in Semco 20 years ago, that forward-thinking investor would now be sitting on a $5.4 million nest egg. My father's 90 employees have mushroomed to nearly 3,000. And we've moved from industrial manufacturing services to high technology without giving up any earlier business. We've accomplished all that with the company's largest shareholder—yours truly—rarely attending meetings and almost never making decisions.

It's because of those remarkable results achieved through the use of such unorthodox business practices that Semco has attracted such widespread attention. We've been profiled on dozens of TV programs and featured in hundreds of newspaper and magazine articles. Seventy-six universities feature case studies of Semco, while texts of our organization's practices are required reading at 271 other schools. Sixteen master's and doctoral candidates have made Semco the subject of their theses.

Hundreds of corporate leaders from around the world have visited our headquarters in São Paulo, hoping to gain some insight into what makes us tick. Six thousand people have written to us, and I've given nearly 300

speeches to companies, conferences, charitable groups, youth groups, and
universities, including Stanford, Harvard, MIT, the London School of Economics, and INSEAD. My first book about Semco, aptly titled *Maverick*
(Warner Books, 1993), ranked on the best-seller list in a dozen countries,
selling more than one million copies. Semco practices have been adopted at
schools, hospitals, police departments, and hundreds of other large and small
companies around the world. That's because Semco has what everyone else
wants—huge growth despite a fluctuating economy, unique market niches,
rising profits, highly motivated employees, low turnover, and diverse products and service areas.

SYNERGIES OF SEMCO

By now, you're probably asking yourself, "Just exactly what is it that Semco
does, anyway?" For years, I have deliberately resisted defining Semco for one
simple reason: Once you say what business you're in, you create boundaries
for your employees by restricting their thinking and giving them a valid reason to ignore new opportunities. "We're not in that business" will become
their mantra.

Instead of dictating Semco's identity, I let our employees shape it with
their individual efforts, interests, and initiatives. Still, I understand the need to
offer up some kind of definition, so (*deep breath*) here goes: Semco is a federation of businesses with a minimum common denominator. We are not mono-
lithic, yet there are common themes and threads uniting us all. All of our
business units are highly engineered, premium providers, and market leaders
in their niches. What's more, all were carefully chosen. We haven't ventured
into any of them by chance.

Semco is comprised of 10 companies, give or take. That answer may sound
deliberately vague, but the truth is that I really *can't* be more specific because
our business units quite literally come and go. Therefore, I'm not really sure
how many companies we have on any given day. We've had a minimum of
five for 20 years. We also have six Internet companies so I suppose we could
claim 16 units, but I'd rather not. After all, we don't know how many of those
will survive or in what form.

The first of our companies, an industrial machinery unit, is actually the
remnants of my father's original business. Founded to produce marine
pumps, the company eventually moved into manufacturing industrial mixers.
Currently, it produces only high-tech mixing equipment—the kind of com-

plex, engineered industrial mixers used in pharmaceutical manufacture and at candy factories.

SemcoBAC, a partnership with U.S.-based Baltimore Air Coil, makes cooling towers for commercial properties, while Cushman & Wakefield Semco handles facility management throughout Brazil and the rest of Latin America. Semco Johnson Controls came about as the result of an alliance with Johnson Controls, a $16 billion world leader in facility management. That particular business unit specializes in handling large properties like hospitals, airports, hotels, and major factories. Then there's ERM, which we added in 1996 as a result of our partnership with Environmental Resources Management, one of the world's premier environmental consulting companies. Finally, we have Semco Ventures, our high-tech ventures unit; SemcoHR, which manages HR activities for large companies; and SemcoRGIS, which manages inventory control for large global retailers, such as JCPenney and Wal-Mart, as well as Carrefour, Brazil's largest supermarket chain.

Just how did so many widely diverse industries come to be part of the same business? To the casual observer, they don't exactly stand out as complementary businesses. However, a closer look will reveal a hidden synergy that satisfied three basic criteria that Semco looks for whenever considering a new venture. First and foremost, we demand complexity, which usually means "highly engineered." Every business opportunity we venture into must have a high-entry barrier of complexity. Quite frankly, if a new business isn't difficult for us (and others) to break into, we're not interested.

In addition, we look to be the premium player in each and every market that we serve. Our goal is to offer a high-end product or service. Granted, that means we're always more expensive, but we provide the premium that stretches what the customer will pay. We also seek to fill a unique market niche, one that makes us a major player in any given industry. We believe this follows naturally from the first two requirements. We desire only to be in those businesses where our disappearance would cause our customers significant grief about which they would complain quite loudly. Sure, they'd survive. There's no doubt about that. But they'd have substantial difficulty moving on.

All of our products and services meet these three distinct criteria, and we bolster our strength by leveraging the power of our units. As a result, a number of clients have become customers of multiple Semco business units. Take Wal-Mart, for example. The retail giant has gradually become a customer of four of our businesses—we count their inventory, manage their cooling towers, administer their buildings and warehouses, and conduct environmental site investigation and remediation. Granted, this isn't unusual for us. A similar situation exists with General Motors and Unilever, as they too are customers of multiple Semco units. In each case, our objective remains the same—synergy. Whichever unit serves as the point of entry, it soon leads to business opportunities for the others.

Signing on with a client is usually our biggest hurdle because we are admittedly more expensive than our competitors. Once customers are on board, however, they are there to stay. We rarely have operational problems, we rarely abandon a customer, and we rarely have a customer leave us. I can count on my fingers the number of clients who have dropped us in 20 years of business. Our repeat business is so strong, in fact, that return customers represent an incredible 80 percent of our annual revenue.

CONCLUSION

So you see, Semco *is* different—so different, in fact, that Senator Macedo may very well have been justified in asking me what celestial plane I call home. By changing the rules—or eliminating them altogether—we encourage people to follow their interests and their instincts both in their personal lives and at work. We insist that our workers seek personal challenge and satisfaction *before* they attempt to meet the company's goals. We encourage people to ramble through their day or week, confident they will meander into new ideas and business opportunities. We embrace democracy and open communication, inciting questions and dissent in the workplace.

At Semco, we believe success is not measured only in profits and growth, but in helping our people achieve balance in their lives. Our people are free—free to work odd hours; free to work closer to their homes (even *at* their homes!); free to come to the office whenever *they* feel it's necessary; free to take off to the beach, the tennis court, or the concert hall in the middle of a weekday in exchange for working on a Sunday. In the end, it's all about the same thing—creating balance. When people have balance in their lives, they are better equipped to discover where their talents and interests lie and thus better able to merge their personal aspirations with the goals of the company.

A friend, William Ury, once told me what Semco was really advocating was "harnessing the wisdom of people." I couldn't have said it better myself. Semco's most precious asset *is* the wisdom of its workforce, and our success grows out of our employees' success. So far, that philosophy has served us well. Year after year, Semco has exhibited the kind of strong, consistent performance that leaves most other organizations wondering how they, too, could achieve a similar financial performance. What's more, after 50 years in business, we remain very proudly privately held with no plans to go public anytime in the foreseeable future. Rather than seeking outside investment, we believe we can take the wisdom of our people to the bank for decades to come.

In the meantime, we'll carry on, operating as we have for the past two decades—without a business plan, without a mission statement, and without a long-term budget. And no, it doesn't unnerve me to step back and see nothing on the company's horizon. The truth is I don't know where Semco is headed, and I don't want to know. I'm having too much fun watching Semco and its employees ramble through their days, running on instinct and opportunity, enjoying the kind of work/life balance that can be achieved only when employees are free to be whole people, and all the while turning in record profits.

At Semco, we don't play by the rules. We are unabashedly, unapologetically different, and we're proud of it. In fact, we revel in it. We've changed the way work works and improved the quality of our lives, and so can you. The workforce *does* need a wake-up call, and it's up to you to join the chorus and lend your voices (and your actions) to the cause. It's going to be quite an exciting ride.

CHAPTER 16

DIVERSITY'S NEXT FRONTIER: HARD-CORE INCLUSION

THE HARD STUFF OF A SOFT CONCEPT

ANDRÉS TAPIA

THE QUEST for a more diverse workforce in the United States and the increasing success of progressive companies in diversifying their head counts have resulted in a string of ironic, unintended consequences. White males have suddenly found themselves facing seemingly insurmountable barriers when it comes to feeling like part of the diversity story. As for white women, unbeknownst to them, they are increasingly in competition with women of color. Meanwhile, religiously conservative individuals are growing skittish about corporations being more open to gays and lesbians.

The reality is that a more diverse workforce is a more complex workforce. Most companies have been caught off-guard by the unspoken undercurrents as white females manage African-American males, who in turn manage white males, Latina women, and both immigrant and U.S.-born Asians, all of whom must ultimately deliver profit and loss (P&L) for an enterprise that is statistically still run by white males.

A more diverse workforce also means more diverse desires, beliefs, and behaviors posing increasingly more complex and profound challenges to human resources (HR). Granted, some of the more obvious ones—diversity hiring and training, for instance—have been on HR's radar screen for a while. However, there are other areas where HR has not yet awoken to the challenges a more diverse workforce brings to the status quo.

It turns out that the warm, let's-all-get-along connotations of inclusion are misleading. Inclusion is hard. Very hard. Harder than awareness. Harder than tolerance and sensitivity. Harder than diversity itself. Diversity is about getting a mix, and that is difficult enough when we take into account diversity sourcing, interviewing, hiring, and onboarding. But inclusion is about how to make the mix *work*. Now that we have increased diversity, how do we ensure that all individuals feel included in the corporation's overall community, regardless of whether they reflect the norms of the demographic group of which they are a part?

To achieve inclusive diversity, HR and business leaders must tackle four vital areas:

1. Answering the question: "Why is diversity vital for achieving our business objectives?"
2. Creating a cross-culturally competent organization.
3. Embedding diversity into the design, development, delivery, and communication of HR programs.
4. Addressing the unspoken taboos of diversity's undercurrents among various diverse groups.

Let's take a look at each of these in turn.

UNDERSTANDING WHY DIVERSITY IS IMPORTANT FOR ACHIEVING BUSINESS OBJECTIVES

Google the phrase *diversity in business,* and you'll get more than 41 million hits. Yet for all the talk about diversity in business, not many organizations are directly applying the implications of diversity to their business strategies. Without this connection, diversity as solely an "HR thing" will wither on the vine.

As with all business decisions, we must begin with the statistics:

- In 1950, 90 percent of the United States was white. Fast-forward a little less than 100 years to 2040, and you'll find just half of the United States

will be white. We are already more than half the way through this demographic shift with 30 percent of the population being people of color.[1]

- Hispanic and Asian populations in the United States will triple over the
  next 50 years.[2]
- The purchasing power of minorities already is $1.7 trillion. Latino pur-
  chasing power alone accounts for $600 billion. That's greater than the
  gross national product (GNP) of Mexico![3]
- By 2008, 70 percent of all new hires in the United States will be women
  and minorities.[4]
- Due to the ballooning number of baby boomers retiring in the next
  decade and the much smaller size of Generation X after them, there will
  be 10 to 28 million jobs that will not be filled.[5]

At this point, we need to ask: "So what?" Businesses that don't know how
to sell their products and services to this emerging marketplace will lose market share. And businesses that don't know how to attract and retain a more diverse workforce will be on the losing end of the war for talent.

Fortunately, a number of companies have been forward-thinking in their
approach to reaching this increasingly diverse population. Let's examine a
couple of them:

1. Nearly 10 years ago, Allstate decided to go after the growing and untapped Latino market, which tended to be underinsured or carry no insurance at all. They recruited a diverse workforce whose "good hands"
   looked like those they wanted to sell to. Then, they revamped their
   marketing materials to be compatible not only in language but also in
   culture. The results were nothing short of phenomenal. When last publicly reported in the 1990s, Allstate had 70 percent of the Latino market
   share in various markets in the country.[6] And it doesn't end there. The
   Latino market keeps growing and continues to be underpenetrated.
   When a senior professional at a rival insurance company heard the Allstate story told at a conference, she sighed and whispered, "We live with
   that statistic every day."
2. By raising the issue of diversity as a business imperative, a large hospital
   provider avoided a very costly error. The provider was designing waiting rooms in its new hospitals in the five fastest growing cities in the
   United States, four of which are growing due to diversity. Initially, they
   were designing with an assumption of a white family, where typically

just one or two individuals show up to wait while a loved one is wheeled into surgery. But when it's African-Americans, it could be six or seven. With Latinos, it's over a dozen! By taking this and a myriad of related issues into account, the provider is now poised to offer a diversity-based differentiator in the marketplace: cross-culturally competent health care.

These two companies are not alone. Business leaders across all industries are proclaiming the business importance of diversity. DuPont's president and CEO, John Krol, told a Conference Board audience, "We have proof diversity improves our business performance." A leader from Quaker Oats told the same crowd, "The talent and skills necessary to successfully drive our business are found in diverse people with different backgrounds." And Valerie Crane, executive vice president of Bank of America, drove the point home: "Bank of America treats diversity as a business imperative."[7]

However, Safeco's former CEO Mike McGavick takes it one step further. When he was CEO until his retirement in 2005 he doubled as the Seattle-based insurance company's chief diversity officer. McGavick, who is a white male, said, "Those who say 'give me the business case' have to be so out of touch. Corporate America is driving the diversity change the same way that President Truman led the way in desegregating the armed services."[8]

Before embarking on their diversity quest, corporations need to answer one vital question: "Why is diversity important to *us* specifically, given the industry we're in and the kind of company we are?" It won't be enough to simply regurgitate the demographic statistics or to say it's the right thing to do, as much as this is an important personal motivator for many leaders. They are going to have to make the connections between the statistics and what they mean to their business strategies for growth and better margins.

Only those who can answer by making hardwired links to their core business will be able to make the necessary investments to set the foundation for achieving sustainable diversity and inclusion. When companies do this, it has a remarkable effect of deescalating many of the contentious issues swarming around diversity. That's because employees, regardless of whether they are part of the majority or minority, see the relevance to their day-to-day responsibilities—a must-have to create an inclusive environment. It helps shift diversity from being about various constituencies to being about *the enterprise*. There cannot be inclusion without all employees knowing and believing that diversity is key to their business success.

CREATING A CROSS-CULTURALLY COMPETENT ORGANIZATION

Mention diversity and the need for training pops up almost immediately. Over the past 25 years, millions of American workers have experienced diversity training, resulting in significant change in how diversity is talked about and thought about in the corporate world. These efforts have yielded some outstanding stories of progress, yet most diversity practitioners would agree there is still a general lack of diversity competence throughout the workplace. The question is why.

While much of the progress made was right for the times, we must now rethink how these approaches are being implemented in today's work environment, particularly in the areas of training and organizational development. When there were few minorities and women in the workforce and blatant bias through slurs and inappropriate humor was common, it was necessary to begin addressing such issues through sensitivity training. Such mandates as zero-tolerance policies emanated from this era. This approach made an impact on workplace behavior as employees became more sensitized to their employers' expectations.

As a result, most explicit prejudice in the workplace has subsided. Regardless of what opinions people may hold, employees generally know what to say and what not to say. Compared to a decade ago, this is progress. Now, however, the time has come to take diversity learning to another, more powerful level.

The Faulty Paradigm of Tolerance and Sensitivity

The focus on tolerance and sensitivity has indeed been right for this past generation of diversity work. Coming out of the fight for civil rights and the transformative feminist movement, the influx of minorities and women into the workplace was full of dislocations, antagonisms, fear, and explicit prejudice. It has taken a generation to work out the old ways of exclusion, and women and minorities have begun to take their rightful places among white males in different fields and corporate positions, with white women making the greatest gains.

But while tolerance and sensitivity are good values to espouse, they are limited in their ability to foster a sustainable inclusive environment. Granted, tolerance and sensitivity are good antidotes to resistance and defensiveness toward those who are different, but it's a place of truce rather than truth. This approach is manifested in statements such as, "I won't resist you anymore," "I'll tolerate that you are here," "I'm okay, you're okay," "We'll agree to disagree," and "Live and let live." It's the answer to: "Why can't we all get along?" It's the voice of political correctness.

The tolerance and sensitivity approach also undermines inclusion because of its implied audience. Who is it that needs to be more tolerant and sensitive? The white heterosexual male, of course! This, in turn, immediately puts a significant portion of the community on the defensive.

While the current paradigm of tolerance and sensitivity has moved individuals and organizations along the diversity journey, we are now at a point of diminishing returns that do not move us toward greater inclusion. Today's companies need to make a paradigm shift toward a focus on *individual and organizational cross-cultural competence.*

The More Robust Paradigm of Cross-Cultural Competence

Let's begin with a clear definition of cross-cultural competence:

> The ability to discern and take into account one's own and others' worldviews, to be able to solve problems, make decisions, and resolve conflicts in ways that optimize cultural differences for better, longer-lasting, and more creative solutions.

Cross-cultural competence is a more sustainable approach to inclusion for various reasons. First, it's a competency rather than an attitude or stance. This is an important differentiation because competencies can be broken down into discrete, observable, and trainable behaviors and skills.

FOUR STAGES OF CROSS-CULTURAL COMPETENCE

Cross-cultural competence acknowledges, understands, and accepts cultural differences and uses the diverse experiences and perspectives of others to optimize results.

Stage I: Demonstrates an understanding of the definition and aspects of culture. Seeks to understand own culture and perspective, how it differs from others, and how culture and perspective can impact client work. Demonstrates an awareness of other cultures, diverse perspectives, styles, backgrounds, and worldviews in order to enhance contribution.

Stage II: Manages own biases and stereotypes and accepts cultural differences in styles, behaviors, beliefs, worldviews, and values. Reaches out to others with different backgrounds, perspectives, styles, and/or opinions to achieve optimal business results.

Stage III: Incorporates the diverse perspectives and talents of others to accomplish objectives and constructively addresses situations in which cultural differences are overlooked or not respected. Coaches others to be cross-culturally competent in questioning their assumptions about differences and shifting their thought processes and behaviors to culturally relevant perspectives.

Stage IV: Builds a cross-culturally competent organization by developing and supporting systems and processes that optimize the value of diverse cultures, backgrounds, skills, perspectives, and ideas. Shares cross-cultural competency innovations with thought leaders outside the firm.

In addition, cross-cultural competence is pragmatic and applicable to resolving daily diversity issues. Tolerance and sensitivity are not very helpful when facing a colleague whose cultural upbringing was very different from one's own. This is particularly evident when that colleague approaches a client dilemma in a way that *our* upbringing told us was wrong—and *their* upbringing told them was right. Cross-cultural competence provides language and concepts for approaching the differences skillfully—with an awareness of one's cultural preferences and how it may differ with another's—and then navigating the difference.

The cross-cultural paradigm also allows for a global diversity approach. "Tolerance and sensitivity" has a uniquely American feel that non-U.S. audiences can spot in a matter of minutes. But cross-cultural competence transcends the Americanization of diversity since it can be used to address diversity issues not only within demographic groups in one particular country, but also across countries: Americans and British, British and French, Canadians and Indians. It is also the same skill set required for navigating the combining of corporate cultures in mergers and acquisitions.

Finally, cross-cultural competence creates a level playing field. Who is the implied audience in need of more cross-cultural competence? Everyone. No group has an inherent advantage on being more cross-culturally competent than others.

With cross-cultural competence, recruiters will be less likely to fall into the trap of misreading a minority's lack of eye contact or modest description of their achievements. Managers will be better able to discern between a performance issue and a cross-cultural misunderstanding. Sales professionals will be better equipped to sell and negotiate with those who are culturally different from themselves. Executive leaders will not overlook women and minorities for top-level positions because they don't fit into a white male–influenced view of strong leadership. All this contributes to an authentic environment of inclusion.

Cross-cultural competence also means that HR professionals will be better able to look at the implications of diversity for programs that traditionally have not even been thought of as being culturally influenced, such as health care and retirement benefits, as well as the communications that surround them, a topic we turn to next.

EMBEDDING DIVERSITY INTO HUMAN RESOURCES PROGRAMS: HOW THEY ARE DESIGNED, DEVELOPED, DELIVERED, AND COMMUNICATED

Think of the last time you turned on your favorite TV show and one of the ads moved you—not only emotionally, but to action—to buy a product, go on a trip, or support a cause.

Marketers spend a lot of time and money figuring out how to reach you, whether you are a 20-something or a senior citizen; a millennial or a baby boomer; a man or a woman; a Latin American immigrant or a Texas cowboy. Marketers and advertisers have figured out not only how to reach you, but how to move you as well.

Marketers' approaches are based on a great deal of research data that reveals patterns in the way different demographic groups have a tendency to move, act, and believe. Of course, marketers know that not all members within these demographic groups move according to their group norm, but there is enough of a pattern for them to hit the broad mark time after time.

We need to ask how much of this applies to HR products and services. Different demographic groups tend to approach issues of health, wealth, and career in ways that are distinct. This has important implications for the design, development, and delivery of HR products and services. We need to start viewing talent as consumers of career opportunities and consumers of benefits. In other words, we must move into the *multicultural marketing* of job opportunities and HR benefits.

Consider 401(k) participation. Studies show that Latinos and blacks tend to undersave in their defined contribution plans for retirement, saving at a lower percentage rate than whites, *even when they earn the same amount of money*. One 2005 study by Ariel Capital Management, the largest minority-owned investment firm in the United States, and Charles Schwab reveals that the gap is 15 percent—only 65 percent of blacks in households earning more than $50,000 annually invest in stocks or mutual funds compared to 80 percent of whites in the same income bracket.[9]

Complex sociohistorical and sociocultural reasons are to blame. For example, cultural studies show that Latinos tend to have a shorter time horizon about the future than whites do, and African-Americans have been historically marginalized from participation in investment vehicles by the now-outlawed practice of redlining by financial institutions.

Since long-term investment is a way to create wealth for all, how do we create employee communications that tap into diverse attitudes toward savings and key behavioral drivers that would motivate more assertive planning for retirement years? I'm not just talking about having more diverse pictures in 401(k) materials or putting those same materials in another language. Rather, I'm advocating approaching the marketing of such plans in a cross-culturally competent way, creating communications that move diverse employees to action. Lest you think these are merely untested theories, we've been testing some of these cross-cultural approach ideas with our clients. In one pilot project at a medical institution conducted as part of Black History Month activities, though the sample size was small, 42 percent of a diverse group of attendees at a 401(k) workshop who were nonparticipants enrolled during the seminars.

There are similar issues that need to be further explored with the necessary cross-cultural competence, including diverse attitudes toward preventative health care, performance management, and engagement. This kind of deep embedding of diversity into HR processes is vital for creating sustainable inclusion.

ADDRESSING THE UNSPOKEN TABOOS OF DIVERSITY'S UNDERCURRENTS

Much needed attention has been paid to the classic diversity issues of race/ethnicity and gender in research and practice. Yet much still remains to be done in addressing glass-ceiling dynamics in corporations. Creating an inclusive environment demands that this work not stop. In this section, I want to focus on a couple of diversity undercurrents that tend to get less play, however. First is the issue of lesbians, gays, bisexuals, and transgendered (LGBT) in the workplace and how to best create an inclusive environment for them in a way that enables the corporation to navigate the polarizing shoals of today's culture wars. The other issue is that of the punching bag of diversity pugilists—the white male.

Creating Inclusion for LGBT

My name is Diana /
I am 39 years old/I love the work I do at Hewitt
and I consistently perform above expectations/
/I am a lesbian /
I am the same person I was before you read the previous sentence.
Diana in Atlanta

Last year, across our U.S. offices, lesbian, gay, bisexual, and transgendered associates, as well LGBT allies joined Diana in telling their stories publicly. The vehicle was a 130-square-foot display with 40 24-by-32-inch black-and-white posters, featuring photographs and essays called "Affirmations." They were exhibited in Hewitt's largest U.S.-based offices and posted on the corporate intranet.

The impact was quietly earth-shattering. Co-workers reflectively read the 300-word narratives after putting away their lunch trays. E-mails of support were sent. "I was on the verge of tears after reading the stories. They really brought to light what those in my family who are gay go through every day." "It's time for me to get involved as an ally in GALAA [Hewitt's LGBT affinity group]. No one should ever have to live his or her life in hiding." CEO Dale Gifford, a white male, helped set the tone. In the introduction to the Affirmations exhibit he stated, "These stories are about courage, often in the face of rejection, fear, and distrust. I believe that we can contribute our best to our teams, our projects, and our clients when we don't need to worry about hiding behind walls."

We know this inclusion strategy worked because we track LGBT engagement and experiences in our firmwide engagement survey.[10] And the reason we believe it worked is because the personal stories cut through the polemic. In each person's story—no matter how different it may be from our own—there was something that others could recognize. And that's the quest for meaning and self. This same approach can be used across all diverse groups. This kind of storytelling and personal connection is one of the keys to sustainable inclusion.

White Males: Vital for Achieving Diversity and Inclusion

White males make up the one group that frequently feels left out of the diversity discussion. And as long as they are, inclusion will never truly be achieved. White men represent a large part of corporate America, especially in the leadership ranks—nearly 10 million who need to be taken off the defensive and motivated to invest in the work of diversity.

White Men as Full Diversity Partners, a culture change consulting firm founded by Bill Proudman, posits that diversity initiatives that ignore the potential contributions of white males may only help foster the misconception that these efforts are nothing but a distraction.

While white males are significantly *more* likely than others to say that their companies are actively working to support diversity, engagement survey data tells us they are also significantly *less* likely to agree that they are personally included in their company's diversity efforts. Their engagement also tends to be lower than other groups.

That said, the paradigm shift from tolerance and sensitivity to cross-cultural competence in learning *does* have a positive effect for white males. Many report they feel as though a weight has been lifted when they explicitly hear they are no longer the implied *sole* audience that needs to get it. As one white male put it, "It was liberating, and for the first time I could see the potential really addressing diversity can have for our business without all the baggage of being the bad guy."

This then opens up some new space for minorities to see white males in a new light. In the sharing that happens under this paradigm shift, it's minorities who start having epiphanies about their own biases toward white males. In referring to her white male colleague who had chosen to share more about his own personal experiences, one African-American woman said, "I had no idea white men could feel vulnerable and not have all the answers. But he was so honest with me about his own challenges. It was eye-opening."

For diversity and inclusion to succeed and be sustainable, white males not only need to feel part of the story, but also need to emerge as diversity leaders. In places where they have done so already, their impact is profound and widespread.

WRAP-UP

A Hewitt study of how clients are preparing for tomorrow's workforce reveals a telling gap. While most have made diversity a priority and funded strategies and programs to attract and hire a more diverse workforce (getting the mix), they are not paying nearly the same attention to diversity retention (making the mix work).[11] In corporate America, the "revolving door syndrome" is particularly evident for women and minorities.[12] Until we see parity here, corporations will not have achieved inclusion.

Inclusion, the soft concept: Don't leave anyone out. Share. Be friendly. These are basic values we learned while still seated on our parents' knees. But for us as adult, competent, and successful professionals in the corporate world, they are the most elusive to implement. True, hard-core inclusion is very hard to achieve, but it's not impossible. For those who go for it, the competitive edge payoff will be insurmountable.

CHAPTER 17

THE DEMOCRATIC ENTERPRISE

LYNDA GRATTON

I am tempted to believe that what we call necessary institutions are often no more than institutions to which we have grown accustomed. In matters of social constitution, the field of possibilities is much more extensive than men living in their various societies are ready to imagine.

THESE WORDS—by French statesman and author Alexis de Tocqueville— were written in the early nineteenth century. Yet his voice resonates into the contemporary world of organizations. Indeed, we must ask ourselves, "How much of what we experience in organizations is there because we lack the imagination—or the courage—to see the world in a different way?"

If we increase the field of possibilities, what would we see? I view this issue through the lens of Warren Bennis, the contemporary philosopher and observer. Many years ago, he wrote in *Managing the Dream: Reflections on Leadership and Change* (Perseus Books Group), "It is possible that if managers and scientists continue to get their heads together in organizational revitalization, they might develop delightful organizations—just possibly."

When Bennis speaks of the "delightful organization," I believe he is referring to an organization that is democratic at heart—an organization where we have the imagination and courage to enable each and every employee to become the best they can be. Of course, enterprise democracy is both broader and deeper than the current notions of state democracy, which is based almost exclusively on the right to vote for a leader. This breadth and depth is revealed in the following six tenets, which serve to frame democracy in an organization.

Six Tenets of the Democratic Enterprise

1. The relationship between the organization and the individual is adult to adult.
2. Individuals are seen primarily as investors, actively building and deploying their human capital.
3. Individuals are able to develop their natures and express their diverse qualities.
4. Individuals are able to participate in determining the conditions of their association.
5. The liberty of some individuals is not at the expense of others.
6. Individuals have accountabilities and obligations both to themselves and to the organization.

To understand democracy, we must first understand citizens. After all, the great democracy of ancient Athens was defined by the behavior of its citizens. The same is true of enterprise democracy in that the eyes that we look through are the eyes of individual citizens. Let us consider the experiences of two particular citizens, Greg Grimshaw at British Petroleum (BP) and Stewart Kearney at British Telecom (BT). Granted, neither BP nor BT is a truly democratic enterprise, yet they are striving to adopt some of the tenets of democracy. In both companies, managers have the imagination to see the world differently and the courage to act.

THE TALE OF TWO CITIZENS

Scanning BP's employee portal, Greg Grimshaw notices his biweekly e-mail from myAgent. Earlier in the month, he had updated his online resume, myProfile, to include some of his recent experiences. Among other things, his experience profile lists "Deepwater/subsea engineering," "Petroleum engineering," and "Procurement—supply chain management." Not bad for someone who currently leads BP's e-HR capability! Next, he e-mails a number of colleagues, asking for feedback about his working style and competencies.

Opening the globally networked job portal myJobMarket, he sees 10 matches between his "dream job" and the current job vacancies. For Greg, taking control of his development started soon after he joined BP. Within three years, he had moved through several completely different jobs—starting as a petroleum engineer, then a reservoir engineer, before switching to offshore operations in engineering. By 1999, he joined the hundreds of people who were being trained in change management.

Come 2000, Greg found himself in discussions about yet another position—this time, a commercial role in BP's corporate center. While in the process of finalizing the role, Greg became intrigued by a listing on myAgent for a completely different role in the e-HR team. "I liked the sound of it, but I certainly did not fit the profile. I had no background in either IT or HR." That did not preclude him from applying for that job, however. As Greg explains, "In BP, we encourage people to achieve what they want, moving from one point to another. It is a zigzag rather than a straight line. There are very few things you learn in one job that you cannot apply to something else. For example, I managed to bring into the HR role all my offshore operations experience."

At the same time that Greg is scanning his e-mail, Stewart Kearney walks to his desk in his bright and spacious home office. One of many BT managers who work flexibly, he begins the day by talking with colleagues on the phone and working on an important strategy document for the next board meeting. After a few hours, satisfied with his draft, he takes a short break and reviews his calendar, noting that he has a telephone conference booked in the afternoon, after which he plans to catch up with some reading and online research. Granted, it was not always this easy. Stewart's initial first few months of home working were tough. "No one really understood what it was like to work from home, and there was not much in terms of support, and no advice." Around that time, however, a BT project team began experimenting with home-based working. As the trials began, so did the understanding of how to support people who chose to work flexibly.

For Stewart, the psychological aspects proved to be difficult at first. He had come from an environment in which being present was seen as an important precursor to success. Over time, however, he saw this attitude change: "In the end, I realized I was trusted, and this gave me a greater sense of responsibility. I came to realize the permission was being given, but nobody was saying it out loud as a set of rules. Instead, you have to learn the tacit rules by talking to other people."

Like other flexible workers at BT, Stewart had to make a clear and substantiated business case in support of his arrangement. In conversation with colleagues, he built a case for the business advantages of his working from home, the implications on the day-to-day running of his group, and the means by which problems could be addressed.

Stewart understood his personal needs, what would bring him joy, and how his potential could best be realized. At the same time, he has also acknowledged the consequences of his actions. As a flexible worker, he is aware that he may not achieve the senior roles to which he would have otherwise been exposed. But these are consequences he is prepared to accept in order to do what he knows is best for him, and ultimately, best for BT.

BUILDING BLOCKS OF THE DEMOCRATIC ENTERPRISE

These citizen tales are simply snapshots of the lives of two individuals. Yet within these tales, we see some of the core building blocks of the democratic enterprise.

At BT and BP alike, there is an emphasis on *individual autonomy*. Both Greg and Stewart were allowed to create an idea of what was important to them. Through introspection and discussions with others, they came to understand their strengths, what excited them, and what they found frustrating. By acknowledging their individuality, both organizations are supporting the first two tenets of the democratic enterprise: establishing an adult-to-adult relationship, and giving permission for employees to build and deploy their human capital.

Individual autonomy can be exercised only when there is choice and the freedom to act. This *organizational variety* is the second building block of enterprise democracy—the capacity to shape the world in which we work. We grow and become committed and excited in situations where we can express ourselves and through engaging with the world in many different ways. Like Greg, we do this by determining and shaping the jobs and projects on which we work, by crafting our training and development, and by having a voice in the rewards we receive. As did Stewart, we involve ourselves in decisions about where and when we work. By providing variety, BT and BP are fundamentally supporting the third and fourth tenets of the democratic enterprise—seeing their employees as sufficiently mature to make decisions and giving them the space to develop their natures and express their diverse qualities.

Building variety around job experiences, location, and time choice has been central to BT and BP. By doing so, they have supported individual choice and maximized commitment. Other companies have taken a different path to variety. At McKinsey, for example, the most significant work experiences are created through projects, rather than jobs. The employee portal, dubbed VOX, enables consultants from across the world to apply for any project, thus broadening their experience and skills. AstraZeneca, meanwhile, creates variety by providing employees with a wide choice of remuneration options. This enables employees to have the freedom to construct a package that is exactly right for them at exactly the right time. This is customization at its most powerful.

To understand the third building block we have to ask ourselves why organizations shy away from choice and freedom. Fundamentally, it's because we lack the courage to engage. We feel more comfortable and familiar with bureaucracies and hierarchies, with rules and prescriptions. The tenets seem too vague, too broad, too worrying.

In order to truly build the democratic enterprise, we must engage with the third building block: *shared purpose*. For it is shared purpose that contains and frames the democratic enterprise and supports the fifth and sixth tenets. The logic here is simple. Imagine your company not as a bureaucracy, but as a self-directed system. Forget the rules and hierarchies. Think instead of autonomous people operating in a context of freedom and choice. In this self-directed system, what holds the organization together? What stops it from deteriorating into the chaos of a band of separate people, each attempting to maximize his or her personal gain?

An important clue can be found in the self-directed systems of the natural world. Order emerges from chaos when there is a sense of direction, a sense of shared purpose. It emerges when the relationships between people are based on trust and authenticity. Order will emerge from chaos when there is sufficient information in the system for people to make the right decisions for themselves and for the organization.

Historically, we have built organizations on the premise that people will maximize their own self-interest. This is the point of departure for the bureaucracy and the rules and hierarchies that frame it. Imagine a company based on the premise that people can be trusted and that they will rarely maximize their own self-interest without considering the needs of others. This is the point of departure for the democratic enterprise.

THE TIME IS NOW

More than at any other time in history there exists a chance to create the democratic enterprise. The forces of change are strong. Globalization, demanding customers, and fast product cycles are all demanding flatter, less bureaucratic, and more agile companies. All these factors working concurrently provide us with fertile ground in which to create a more democratic way of working.

Beyond these structural challenges are other profound and inescapable forces of change, however. Demography, for example, will play an important role in the democratization of the enterprise. The entry of Generations X and Y into the workforce is expected to profoundly influence organizations over the next decade. Their preference for adult-to-adult relationships and their self-determination, autonomy, and technical savvy will trigger many of the tenets of the democratic enterprise. This generational force can only be strengthened and accentuated by the waves of technological invention that we are increasingly experiencing. Over the past decade, we have borne witness to the technological developments in platforms and software and how they have fundamentally changed the way we work. After all, advances in mobile networking and employee portals made possible the experiences of Greg and Stewart. And this is just the beginning.

What role can the HR function play in supporting the democratic enterprise and bringing it to fruition? Clearly, there is a broad leadership role of supporting the creation of a sense of shared purpose and a just and fair organization. But beyond this, there are two roles that are unique to the function.

The role of the creator of employee insight involves building an understanding of individuals based not on a one-size-fits-all approach, but rather on an acknowledgement of individual potential. This will require the creation of a whole set of competencies and skills that have not historically resided within the function—the skills of profiling individual aspirations and the techniques of understanding employee sacrifice, as well as employee motivations, skills that currently reside more within the marketing function than within HR.

The role of the builder of trials and experiments is essentially the basis of organizational variety. It took a courageous HR team at BT to try out home-based working at a time when computer support was underdeveloped. And it took a foresighted team at BP to experiment with opening up the internal labor market at a time when most companies placed strong control mechanisms on job moves. And yet without these early trials and experiments, the richness of variety we now see in these companies would never have been developed.

Demographics and technology have the power to accelerate the possibility of democracy. Many of the building blocks already are in place. All you need now is the imagination to dream and the courage to act. Welcome to citizenship!

PART IV

EMBRACE NEW AGE LEADERSHIP

STUNG BY the rash of corporate scandals that ripped a number of high-profile leaders out of the C-suite, and in some instances, into a prison cell, organizations have been forced to become increasingly fastidious in their quest for next generation leadership. Leaders of tomorrow must possess much more than strong ethical character, however, as they face a transformed workplace that's fraught with ever-changing challenges. No longer does workforce diversity refer solely to the color of an employee's skin, for example. These days, it can encompass age, sex, culture, religion, sexual orientation, or any one of a number of disparities. With more generations in the workforce then ever before, the potential for generational conflict alone is enormous. At the same time, the relationship between employee and employer has changed dramatically, with the growing contingent workforce representing the much looser and flexible bond that is quickly becoming the norm. To manage effectively in this new world, leaders must abandon the strategies of the past, even if they proved effective.

In this final section, the authors explain why these conditions create an unparalleled opportunity for new models of leadership. They stress the need for fewer dominant, self-interested leaders and more people of principle, vision, and humanity. Recognizing the need to create the conditions that unleash the spirit of the workforce, they make the case for adopting a model of coordinate and cultivate, rather than command and control. And as organizations seek to identify and groom future leaders, they advocate developing a leadership pipeline that extends all the way down to the front line and includes a broad spectrum of workers, including the substantially untapped female population.

CHAPTER 18

BUILDING TOMORROW'S LEADERSHIP PIPELINE

NOEL M. TICHY AND CHRISTOPHER M. DEROSE

THE COMPETITIVE workforce of the twenty-first century will be made up of knowledge workers, requiring leaders at all levels. Global competitiveness means that the winners will be those with a workforce that grows smarter every day, is aligned, and exhibits leadership from the front line to the executive suite. In this chapter we provide some benchmarks and guideposts for helping leaders develop the requisite pipeline.

Leadership pipelines became terribly broken in the 1990s and are still in disrepair today. The leading indicator of the wake-up call was the firing of CEOs for bad performance starting in the early 1990s. To name only a few: John Akers at IBM, Bob Stempel at General Motors, Bob Allen at AT&T, Echkard Pfieiffer at Compaq, Jill Baerd at Mattel. The other indicator of broken leadership pipelines in many companies is the number of outside hires for the CEO slot; Hewlett-Packard hired externally twice (Carly Fiorina and Mark Hurd); 3M twice (Jim McNerney and George Buckley). Boeing, IBM, Merck, Kodak, Motorola, Honeywell, and Home Depot all failed to produce internal leaders as well. These examples don't take into account another leadership failure, namely, lack of integrity, at Tyco, Enron, WorldCom, Imclone, HealthSouth, Adelphia, and many dot-com disasters. Those who rearchitect and rebuild pipelines for developing competent and courageous leaders first will have a tremendous competitive advantage.

As we dig deeper into the challenges, the solution for competing and having a globally competitive workforce at all levels starts at the top and flows to the frontline workers. The reason GE had Jeffrey Immelt (as well as numerous well-qualified alternatives, including Jim McNerney, now CEO of Boeing; Bob Nardelli, CEO of Home Depot; Bob Wright, a GE vice chairman) ready to step in as CEO is that a leadership pipeline for the twenty-first century was designed and created in the mid-1980s when Jack Welch was CEO and Noel Tichy was head of GE's development center, Crotonville. An internal team worked closely with Welch and vice chairman Larry Bossidy to come up with the new leadership pipeline.

THE GE LEADERSHIP PIPELINE: A BENCHMARK

The lessons from GE are relevant for most twenty-first-century corporations: Zero-base your current leadership pipeline and engage the CEO in rethinking what talent means in a very different future. Although lessons from the GE process may be true for many organizations, every company must adapt and create its own answer.

In 1986 Jack Welch challenged a team of leadership and talent experts at GE to answer the following question: to produce the next CEO for the year 2000, what should the leadership pipeline for GE look like from off-campus hires, through new managers, through functional leaders, to heads of businesses, to candidates for the CEO role? Welch knew that the road he traveled to become CEO would be irrelevant for his successor. GE would be a different company competing in a different world order. The pipeline, Welch admonished, could not be designed by looking in the rearview mirror.

The first step in the process of rearchitecting the pipeline was to outline the stages of leadership development at GE. Significant career transitions, such as moving from an individual contributor to a manager or from a manager to a functional leader, must be leveraged to develop people for new roles. Heated debates with Welch and other GE leaders led to an outline of the key career transitions and capabilities that would be needed for progression from one career stage to another.

GE'S LEADER/TEACHER PIPELINE

Phase 1: *Individual Contributors*—development activities for nearly 2,000 off-campus hires each year.

Phase 2: *New Manager*—development for approximately 2,000 first-time leaders of other professionals.

Phase 3: *Functional Leaders*—development for leaders of specialized functional staff such as HR, finance, manufacturing, marketing, and IT.

Phase 4: *Business Leader*—development for those running a business.

Phase 5: *Head of a Business*—development for those running GE's largest business groups; candidates for the corporate CEO position.

The second step in GE's rearchitecting process was identifying the developmental challenges at each career stage. Developing leadership capabilities, such as building teams, leading change, dealing with performance issues, and teaching GE's values, was weighted even more strongly than developing technical ability.

The fundamental leadership building blocks were similar across the company and across career stages, whether one is a 22-year-old engineer or the leader of a major business group. However, the complexity and level of mastery required is dramatically different for the 22-year-old engineer who must build a small team of other young engineers and teach them values versus the senior leader who has thousands of employees. The head of the business has the same task, build teams and teach values, but the scale and complexity is one-hundredfold more difficult.

With the career stages and development capabilities outlined, GE next identified developmental tools. As a rule of thumb, 80 percent of development is expected to occur on the job, with 20 percent coming from formal development or other experiences. This included coaching, external development opportunities, task force assignments, and many development opportunities at GE's management development center.

For future success, companies must build their entire pipeline following the steps just outlined. The remainder of the chapter provides some innovative benchmarks of leadership development early in the pipeline.

LEADERS WITH A TEACHABLE POINT OF VIEW

Leadership development cannot be reserved just for senior executives or high-potential midlevel managers. Historically, investment in frontline workers has been focused on building skills to perform tasks, consistent with the specialization of labor. In the future, these leaders will increasingly need to make judgments as they serve customers and deploy strategies. To do so, they must understand not only facts and skills but must have context on their companies' strategies and operations.

The first step in cultivating frontline leadership is an investment in these leaders to help them develop a teachable point of view (TPOV). Simply put, these leaders must understand the business strategies and ideas that will help their companies succeed in the market, the values and leadership behaviors required to execute these strategies, how to energize employees, and how to make difficult decisions. Only when they have these competencies will they be able to develop them in their teams.

Winning leaders need teachable points of view in four specific areas. (See Figure 18.1.)

1. *Ideas.* Great companies are built on central ideas. By passing the ideas to others and teaching others how to develop good ideas, leaders create organizations that are finely tuned toward delivering success.
2. *Values.* Winning leaders articulate values explicitly and shape values that support business ideas.

Figure 18.1
Teachable Points of View

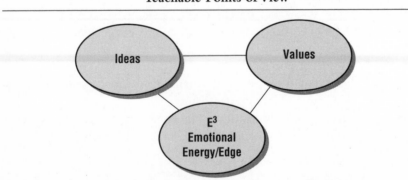

3. *Energy.* Winning leaders are motivated, and they motivate others about change and transition. Leaders energize others when they personally interact with them.
4. *Edge.* Leadership is about making tough yes/no decisions. Winning leaders face reality, and they make decisions about people, products, businesses, customers, and suppliers.

Intuit, the Mountain View, California–based software company, offers a good example of how to develop frontline leaders with a TPOV. Intuit brought together the leaders from across multiple call centers for an intense three-day workshop in which they were taught Intuit's strategies, core processes, and operational improvement efforts. Learning was not enough; the leaders then went through intensive preparation to be able to teach the strategies, values, core processes, and how to energize others.

A very rigorous three-day teaching process was designed for all the managers of the frontline leaders. Each manager conducted a disciplined, highly interactive workshop for groups of frontline leaders. No consultants or staff personnel were allowed to teach. At the end of the three days the frontline leaders had new concepts and tools for enhancing the effectiveness of their call center agents. The frontline leaders identified how they could better structure their work to deliver the business strategy, eliminate unnecessary activities, and reshape goal setting and performance management. The frontline leaders also engaged the agents to provide input on company-wide initiatives to streamline operational processes.

The key at Intuit is that leaders are teachers. By requiring the managers to be the teachers, the frontline leaders are taught by their bosses, who must not only internalize what they teach but reinforce it day in and day out. This is a lesson the military has known forever. Training at the Navy SEALS school is not taught by outside consultants and professors. Nor in medicine is a residency program taught by outsiders; it is the doctors teaching the new doctors and then supervising, reinforcing what is learned and taught. The Intuit training is not outsourced either, thus forcing managers to learn, internalize, and be personally equipped to teach. In our experience, when you do this, the teaching is better, more relevant, directly linked to the work, and reinforced day in and day out. When the process is highly interactive and there is mutual learning the leader/teachers keep improving as they learn as well. They create virtuous teaching cycles in which everyone learns and everyone teaches.

The frontline program at Intuit is the beginning of the company's pipeline. The emphasis on leaders developing leaders goes all the way up to Steve Bennett, CEO, who runs his own action-learning program for senior leaders. Six teams of six executives work on strategic initiatives for six months. These are CEO-owned projects with each team having a senior executive coach driving the leadership and team development agenda.

CAPITAL MARKETS TO THE FRONTLINE

Dell offers another example of investment in creating leaders at all levels. Today Dell is clearly one of the world's most successful technology companies, but in 1995 it looked far less promising. After three years of flat stock performance, Dell's inventories were swelling and its accounts receivable growth was outpacing revenue growth.

Dell wanted all of its employees to be leaders who are able to make good decisions that drive both growth and efficiency. As a result, everyone's performance is tied to a growth measure and to return on invested capital (ROIC). Early on, this required Dell's finance and treasury teams to teach thousands of employees at all levels of the company. People were taught how to calculate return on invested capital and to link their daily activities to ROIC performance. This line of sight propelled a double-digit turnaround in the share price over the next three years.

TEACHING CUSTOMER CENTRICITY TO THE FRONTLINE

Best Buy offers another benchmark of deliberately building frontline leadership. As part of a transformation strategy dubbed Customer Centricity, Best Buy has attempted to move away from mass market retailing by transferring decision making from its Minneapolis corporate office into the field. The company intends to create product and service solutions tailored to customer segments and customized to local market tastes. Whereas merchandising assortment was once consistent for a store regardless of whether it was in Kansas City or New York City, today local store general managers have far more influence in everything from assortment to store layout. However, Best Buy could not decentralize decision making without significant frontline development since each of its stores averages more than $35 million in annual revenue.

To enable frontline leaders to understand how the company operates and make better decisions, Best Buy has packaged expertise once embedded in corporate functions and made it accessible through training and technology across the company. For example, store design and visual merchandising principles are taught so that store leaders no longer put up paper signs or introduce product displays that impede traffic flow. Most important, Best Buy has taught its leaders to understand a basic profit and loss (P&L) statement and calculate the projected ROIC of changes made within the store.

When an employee has an idea, it is put through a rigorous testing methodology. First, within the individual store where the idea originates, store leaders partner with customer service associates to identify the intended customer and financial outcome of a new idea. Applying the scientific method, they concoct a hypothesis to test and verify in the coming days or weeks.

That is what happened when an employee in the company's Corona, California, outlet observed that his store was incurring monthly losses of $4,000 to $6,000 in damaged televisions. In all Best Buy stores, employees were told to use shrink-wrap to protect televisions that were shipped back to distribution centers for repair or return to the manufacturer. A front-line employee concluded flimsy shrink-wrap was not able to safeguard the televisions from bumping around and breaking while in transit. After researching options, he found a $50 tool that would take the same shrink-wrap and twist it into a sturdy rope that could hold the televisions securely on their palettes during shipment. Working with his manager, they tested the idea and after four months had completely eliminated damaged television charges. On a $50 investment, the self-initiation of this employee led to nearly 100,000 percent return for the single store in just the first year.

Teaching this idea testing approach to frontline leaders has created a common language and decision-making framework across the company. When an employee brings an idea to a manager, the manager can no longer dismiss it by saying "We've tried that already" or "I just don't think that will work." Instead, the manager can coach the employee and share potential pitfalls from prior experience. They have a fact-based dialogue with the employee and manager working together to shape the idea rather than shoot it down. This coaching creates tremendous development while simultaneously removing one of the biggest bottlenecks that companies face in fostering innovation. By providing frontline leaders and associates with a methodology for rapid experimentation, senior leadership attention isn't always needed to fuel a good idea.

Best Buy has seen the benefit of this not only for improving operations and controlling expense but, more importantly, for differentiating itself with customers. Best Buy is actively trying to appeal to female shoppers, a customer segment that is typically turned off by the noisy atmosphere and technical jargon of consumer electronics. Mothers usually shop in consumer electronics stores so they can purchase something for their families. Recognizing this, an employee suggested offering gift cards to kids under 18 who are having birthdays or who get all As on their report cards. Figuring that Mom will want to reward the kids on this special day, giving them a $5 gift card will be enough to lure Mom and the kids into a Best Buy store. This simple idea, which started with frontline employees, has had a massive return. Entering the store with a $5 gift card awarded for an excellent report card, a typical family spends $60 during a visit. Those who come in with birthday gift cards use them to kick-start average purchases of $160.

The initial investment in teaching employees about the business and providing them with a framework for leveraging their own ideas and creativity is generating business results and developing future leaders. Equally important, it is fostering commitment to the company so the leaders Best Buy develops will stay and grow there.

CREATING EMOTIONAL ENERGY AT THE FRONTLINES

Another aspect of the Best Buy story is the emphasis placed on engaging employees in the transformation. Just as the company cannot rely on a handful of people in corporate headquarters to build relationships with thousands of customers each day, store general managers cannot presume to have all of the best ideas within their own stores. Best Buy has recognized that its associates want to be involved in the business and want to see that they are actively contributing to their team's success. As one Best Buy field executive who leads dozens of stores and thousands of associates commented, "We unleash the power of our people and let them know they can make a difference by teaching them how to think, not just do what they're told." Consequently, Best Buy has invited all employees to contribute their ideas and energy to the transformation. Part of this has been a company-wide campaign labeled "What's Your Story?" that encourages managers to know employees on a personal basis. More than a slogan, managers are encouraged to understand employees' ambitions and unique talents so they can keep everyone energized.

This emphasis on understanding employees as individuals is consistent with the demographic shift under way to a post-boomer society. For a new generation of workers that views corporations with increased skepticism, and in an industry that averages more than 100 percent annual employee turnover, building personal relationships creates loyalty. Although Best Buy has encouraged these personal connections, it has also recognized that it cannot mandate them. The company campaigns have tried to galvanize attention to the need to build different relationships with employees but ultimately it falls to local store teams to do this in an authentic way. This generation of employees will be far more alienated by insincere rhetoric about taking an interest in individuals or inviting employees to contribute ideas. A Best Buy executive observed, "A lack of authenticity shines through in this environment. People will offer their ideas only if they trust the people they're sharing them with."

Best Buy's ability to teach and encourage store teams to engage individuals across its 700 outlets has translated into an outpouring of good ideas. Frontline associates, armed with information about customer segments and comprehending the business basics from their store P&L, are actively innovating.

CREATING VIRTUOUS TEACHING CYCLES

As Best Buy generates more and more creativity and customer insight from its frontline leaders, it has been confronted with the challenge of managing scale. With over 700 stores, it cannot easily facilitate a dialogue among all of its general managers, let alone its 90,000 associates. Best Buy is actively working to create two-way dialogue mechanisms between field associates and executive leaders, instead of one-way communication that used to come from corporate headquarters.

One-way command-and-control teaching creates vicious nonteaching cycles. The key DNA in a teaching organization is the virtuous teaching cycle (VTC), shown in Figure 18.2.

Like most companies, Best Buy is challenged to create VTCs in which leaders are open to learning even as they share their own teachable points of view. The ability to create VTCs is what differentiates companies that value

Figure 18.2
Virtuous Teaching Cycle

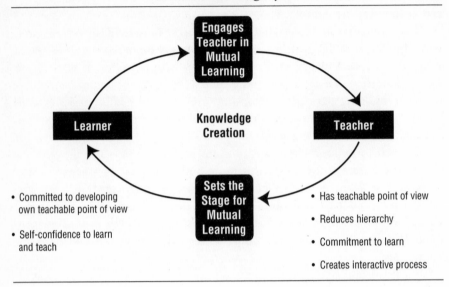

- Committed to developing own teachable point of view

- Self-confidence to learn and teach

Learner — **Knowledge Creation** — **Teacher**

Engages Teacher in Mutual Learning

Sets the Stage for Mutual Learning

- Has teachable point of view

- Reduces hierarchy

- Commitment to learn

- Creates interactive process

frontline leadership and work to actively develop these leaders. Leaders must welcome those at all levels to comment on the company's strategic initiatives and to engage in a dialogue so everyone can learn. Companies need this not only to hear about innovation but to validate that their strategies are translating into field execution. Most companies use traditional models of cascading strategies down the hierarchy. As messages travel, they may be distorted or midlevel manager behavior may not be consistent with the declared strategic intent. This has the effect of not only distorting execution but also role modeling undesired behaviors for frontline leaders.

This is what David Novak, CEO of Yum Brands, discovered when he attempted to deploy a multibranding strategy. Instead of offering customers just one choice in a restaurant, Yum wanted to combine two or more of its brands—Pizza Hut, Taco Bell, Long John Silver's, A&W, and KFC—under the same roof. If mom wanted chicken, she could have it while the kids ate tacos. As Novak was testing the idea with his franchise leaders, he got a rude awakening from one of his largest operators. The franchise requests for information, Novak learned, were being passed from person to person with long delays and little follow-through from Yum's corporate office. Novak had been working hard to create a frontline-focused culture and avoid arrogance in the executive ranks. He ultimately built a new operations team that was more focused on frontline requests and the company successfully deployed the multi-branding strategy. What Novak saw firsthand, however, is a disconnection between senior leadership rhetoric and frontline reality that trains many frontline leaders to be skeptical of the corporate office and less caring about their customers.

DIGITIZING VIRTUOUS TEACHING CYCLES

Trilogy Software, based in Austin, Texas, has developed a technology platform for providing direct feedback to frontline managers and mid-level managers. Recognizing that technology can be used to create a company-wide conversation, Trilogy implemented a multimedia platform, dubbed Leadership.com, that enables everyone in the company to hear directly from CEO Joe Liemandt. Moreover, it isn't only about the CEO broadcasting his message. More than 200 leaders at all levels in the company have shared their teachable points of view and used the platform's embedded survey technology to get feedback from others. This has enabled rapid idea testing and best-practice sharing. It has also ensured that frontline leaders actively participate in dialogues around major company changes.

Following the dot-com bust, Trilogy faced one such challenge. Liemandt foresaw the end of the enterprise computing business model that, up to 2000, had been built on multimillion-dollar sales to companies for technology that often didn't deliver. As Liemandt repositioned Trilogy to be a true business partner with its customers, he knew that moving his software development to India offered an opportunity to tap into a highly talented workforce with much lower costs for customers. When Trilogy made the announcement that development jobs would be moved overseas and those employed in the United States would need to find new jobs within Trilogy or look outside for work, employee resistance was anticipated. Unlike many companies, where gossip and griping occur around the watercooler and frontline managers are kept busy trying to keep their staff motivated, the dialogue at Trilogy played out publicly.

Using Leadership.com, employees openly complained about the off-shoring move and made strong assertions that perhaps the CEO and head HR jobs should be outsourced instead. Rather than censure the discussion, Liemandt watched as co-workers constructively debated the company's new strategy. When the discussion started to degenerate into a criticism of Trilogy's workforce in India, company employees rallied around shared values. An impassioned post from one manager in India followed a scathing comment about Indian employees' capabilities. The manager noted that employees in India woke up every day to come to work at Trilogy, not Trilogy India. Ultimately, the company moved its development operations and people came to accept that the new strategy offered growth opportunities instead of an inevitable decline in the company's core business.

The Trilogy case is an example of how technology can be used effectively to make leadership transparent. Frontline employees, software developers in Trilogy's case, didn't spend their time wondering what senior management thought or trying to decipher the new strategy. They heard directly from senior leaders online, and they responded. In the responses, those who participated also saw the company's values challenged and reaffirmed. As Jim Abolt, Trilogy's HR vice president, observed, the dialogue on Leadership.com did more to make Trilogy's values real and tangible to employees than any senior management speech or training class ever could.

THE PAYOFF

The twenty-first-century winners will be those that develop leaders at all levels. In a knowledge economy this means leaders who are teachers and are capable of developing other leaders. Organizations will need to invest in building virtuous teaching cycles throughout. Frontline leaders such as those at Intuit, Yum, and Best Buy will build the foundation of the leadership pipeline.

The most important role for the CEO is to ensure the long-term leadership pipeline for his/her institution. It starts with a commitment to do what Jack Welch did—systematically look at tomorrow's competitive environment and zero-base the thinking about what leaders are needed for tomorrow. This then leads to the architecture of a leadership pipeline from frontline to the candidates for the next CEO.

Once there is a framework for the leadership pipeline, the CEO needs to take the lead at ensuring that there is a series of developmental experiences, from primary position assignments to high-impact formal development programs. The day in, day out teaching is done by leaders at all levels, and the formal programs are built on an action-based learning platform, working real organizational issues, and are primarily taught by the leaders, not consultants or professors.

Finally, every opportunity is taken to create virtuous teaching cycles, whether it is with regard to the strategic planning process, the budgeting process, or the succession planning process. All of these are opportunities for making the organization smarter and more aligned, if they are built on virtuous teaching cycles.

CHAPTER 19

THE FUTURE OF WORK

FROM "COMMAND AND CONTROL" TO "COORDINATE AND CULTIVATE"

THOMAS W. MALONE

WE ARE now in the early stages of a profound increase in human freedom in business that may, in the long run, be as important for businesses as the change to democracies was for governments.

The key enabler for this remarkable change is information technology. By reducing the costs of communication, new technologies now make it possible for many more people, even in huge organizations, to have the information they need to make decisions for themselves, instead of just following orders from above. And so, for the first time in history, we can now have the economic benefits of very large organizations, such as economies of scale, without giving up the benefits of small ones—most notably, freedom, flexibility, motivation, and creativity.

Take eBay, for example. More than 430,000 people make their primary living as eBay sellers. If these people were employees, that would make

This chapter is adapted from Thomas W. Malone, *The Future of Work: How the New Order of Business Will Shape Your Organization, Your Management Style, and Your Life* (Boston: Harvard Business School Press, 2004). Reprinted by permission of Harvard Business School Publishing.

eBay the second largest private employer in the United States—after Wal-Mart and ahead of McDonald's. But they are not employees of eBay. They are essentially self-employed proprietors of their own retail stores. And as self-employed store owners, they have a huge amount of freedom. They decide for themselves what to sell, when to sell, and how to price. Even with all this freedom, they also have a huge global market for their products.

Of course, reduced communication costs will not always lead to this kind of decentralization. In places where the benefits of economies of scale and standardization are overwhelmingly important—as in some kinds of semiconductor manufacturing—we will probably see even more centralization. In our increasingly knowledge- and innovation-based economy, however, the benefits of decentralization—flexibility, freedom, creativity, and motivation—are becoming important in more and more places. In all those places, we should expect to see information technology leading to more and more decentralization.

In spite of these changes, most of us still have in our minds an old management model—that of "command and control." To manage effectively in this new world, we need a new model. We need to move from "command and control" to what I call "coordinate and cultivate."

To coordinate is to organize work so that good things happen, whether you are "in control" or not. And to cultivate is to bring out the best in a group of people through the right combination of controlling and letting go. So coordinating and cultivating are not the opposites of commanding and controlling. Rather, they include the broad set of management possibilities—from the completely centralized to the completely decentralized—of which commanding and controlling represent just one extreme possibility.

To cultivate something successfully, you need to understand and respect its natural tendencies at the same time as you try to shape it in ways you value. Managers cultivating organizations sometimes take drastic top-down actions, like closing divisions, for example. Other times, their main work centers around helping groups of people find and develop their natural strengths and desires.

By thinking of management in terms of coordinating and cultivating, you open up a whole new range of possibilities, freeing yourself from the old centralized mind-set. That is what it takes to be an effective manager today: the ability to move flexibly back and forth between centralized and decentralized thinking as the situation demands.

COORDINATING IS NOT ALWAYS CONTROLLING

Loosely speaking, coordinating simply means organizing work so that good results can occur. Of course, there are centralized, hierarchical ways of doing this. But there are many decentralized ways, too.

Some companies, for example, have very loose hierarchies in which bosses still exist but considerable decision-making authority is delegated to very low levels of the organization. Likewise, many management-consulting firms allow individual partners and consultants to make nearly all the operational decisions about a project to which they are assigned. AES, one of the world's largest electric power producers, lets low-level workers make critical multimillion-dollar decisions about such matters as acquiring new subsidiaries. This practice works, in part, because the people making decisions are required to ask for advice. Before making a critical decision, they get advice (often by e-mail) from many others, including senior managers.

In an even more extreme example, one of the most important computer operating systems in the world today—Linux—was written by a loosely coordinated hierarchy of thousands of volunteer programmers all over the world.

Some businesses go so far as to act like miniature democracies, where decisions are made through some kind of voting procedure. At W. L. Gore, the maker of Gore-Tex fabric, the chief executive does not select managers. Instead, people become managers only by recruiting enough other people from within the company to work for them. In Spain, meanwhile, the Mondragon Cooperative Corporation, a group of 150 companies operating in the financial, industrial, and distribution sectors, is owned by the workers. Consequently, they elect the equivalent of a board of directors and vote on other key issues.

The most extreme kind of decentralization occurs in markets. Many companies now outsource activities they used to perform inside—from manufacturing to sales to human resource management. In some cases, flexible webs of electronically connected freelancers—"e-lancers"—can even do the same things big companies used to do, but more effectively.

In other cases, large companies get many of the benefits of markets inside their own boundaries. Intel, for example, is considering letting individual salespeople and plant managers buy and sell "futures" for different Intel products among themselves in an internal electronic market. This could give the plants immediate and dynamic feedback about which products to make each day. What's more, the prices in the internal market also could help the salespeople continually fine-tune the prices they offer external customers.

COORDINATING REQUIRES CAPABILITIES, INCENTIVES, AND CONNECTIONS

Coordinating effectively requires the establishment of three key conditions that enable the actions of a group of people to produce good results: capabilities, incentives, and connections.

Capabilities

People must be capable of doing the things that need to be done. Traditional organizations use centrally managed personnel processes to get the right capabilities in place—through recruiting, promoting, training, and sometimes firing people. In decentralized organizations, capabilities are managed in very different ways. In loose hierarchies and democracies, for instance, many people evaluate candidates for recruiting or promotion, not just a few. In markets and very loose hierarchies (like the Linux organization), there often isn't even a clear boundary between "hired" and "fired." In principle, you can come and go at will. In practice, however, you won't actually do much work unless people trust your capabilities—because of your reputation, your credentials, or some other factor.

Incentives

Good outcomes require the right incentives. In some instances, these are financial incentives—a bigger salary or a fatter profit, for example. But there are many other kinds of incentives as well: status, recognition, access to information, or the opportunity to do enjoyable and fulfilling work. For incentives to help coordinate a group's actions, they must be coherent. If everyone has incompatible incentives, even a team of the most capable, motivated people won't achieve strong results. On the contrary, the various incentives must be tied to and support overarching goals shared by the entire group.

Connections

The final key to good coordination is strong connections between activities and information. Each different decision-making structure has its own characteristic kinds of connections. In general, as you move toward more decentralized ways of coordinating, horizontal peer-to-peer connections become more important, while vertical, top-down ones become less so.

Shared goals are critical to these connections—they provide the glue for the organization, bringing diverse activities together into a coherent whole. In a traditional organization, goals are set at the top by a small senior management group and communicated downward. As a manager of a more decentralized organization, however, you have a choice about how you set the goals that will tie activities together. You can be an *orchestrator* or a *facilitator*.[1] If you're an orchestrator, you have your own ideas about what the goals should be, and you try to guide people to adopt them. If you're a facilitator, in contrast, you don't try to get what *you* want. You merely help a group of people figure out for themselves what *they* want—and how to get it.

THE PARADOX OF STANDARDS

One of the best ways to coordinate decentralized organizations is to create incentives for individual action and standards for interaction.

Many people assume that rigid standards are incompatible with flexibility and decentralization. However, there is a paradox in decentralized coordination:

Rigid standards in the right parts of a system can enable much more flexibility and decentralization in other parts of the system.

In most markets, buyers and sellers are able to interact with each other freely and flexibly because they obey a set of standards. Prices are specified in standardized monetary currencies, and they have laws that establish the rights and responsibilities of each participant. Should a dispute arise, a legal system is available to resolve it. In traditional, centralized organizations, standards are much less important because bosses can simply tell people what to do. But when people make their own decentralized decisions, establishing coherent standards becomes critical. On the Internet, for example, rigid technical standards—in the form of the underlying Internet protocol (IP)—enable a tremendous amount of flexibility.

Similarly, one of the main responsibilities of managers in the future may be to define the standards and incentives the rest of the organization must follow. At times, they will be explicit, like the trading rules for an internal market at Intel. Other times, they may be unwritten, like the cultural norms at consulting firms. Either way, when these standards and incentives are in place, people throughout the organization can coordinate many things directly for themselves, without the need for any further intervention on the part of centralized managers.

PRINCIPLES FOR CULTIVATING ORGANIZATIONS

Thinking of your work as cultivating, not just controlling helps you get out of the mental boxes of the command-and-control mind-set. It enables you to be more flexible and open to possibilities. And it helps you realize that sometimes you need to control people carefully, while at other times you just need to gently nudge them in the right direction. Sometimes, you merely need to accept and encourage the direction they're already moving in, even if it isn't the precise direction *you'd* prefer.

Intuitively, most people understand this dynamic quite well. They know they can control *some* things, but they can't control *everything*. They know that people have minds of their own. And they know that sometimes you have to adapt to what *others* want in order to get what *you* want.

Still, the old command-and-control mind-set exerts a powerful influence on our thinking. It's easy to think there's something wrong with you if you aren't in control, for instance. And it's easy to think that if a problem pops up in your organization, the solution is to centralize control so it won't happen again. Such reactions, though natural, aren't always wise, however. Here, then, are some principles to help you remember the things you need to do when you are trying to cultivate, rather than control.

Harness People's Natural Tendencies

Any good salesperson, negotiator, or motivator knows that one of the best ways to get other people to do what you want is to show them how it will further their own goals. For instance, Dwight Eisenhower once defined leadership as "the art of getting someone else to do something you want done because he wants to do it."[2]

To successfully cultivate organizations, you may need to go further.

Instead of just harnessing other people's goals to your own, you may also need to adapt your goals to the goals and abilities of the people in your organization. Jim Schiro, the CEO of PricewaterhouseCoopers (PwC), who guided the merger of Price Waterhouse and Coopers & Lybrand, first articulated a goal that the combined firm should be "globally integrated."[3] Then, he tested this vision with people throughout the organization. In doing so, he found many employees were worried that focusing on being "globally integrated" as a general goal might lead the firm to become slow-moving and bureaucratic. As a result of these iterative discussions, the goal of being "globally integrated" was refined to being "intelligently integrated at the client interface." In other words, PwC would strive to excel at integrating its resources only when doing so was clearly in the client's best interest. By mixing top-down and democratic goal setting in this way, the firm arrived at a refined goal that was presumably much more compelling for its people.

Let a Thousand Flowers Bloom

Sometimes the best way to cultivate an organization is not to try to decide in advance, or at the top of the organization, which of several alternatives is best, but instead to let lots of different people try lots of different experiments. When something works well, you encourage it and give it more resources. When it doesn't, you let it die.

This approach is also part of the secret of innovation in market economies: many different companies can try out many different ideas at the same time without anyone on top telling them what to do. Granted, some of the ideas may be stupid or impossible or useless and there may be much duplication of effort. However, the inefficiency is a small price to pay for the significantly greater innovation.

Encourage Cross-Fertilization

In nature, cross-fertilization occurs only once in each generation of an organism. Since the "genes" of organizations are simply ideas about how to do things, however, they can be combined and recombined as often as organizational changes can occur. In cultivating innovation and creativity, therefore, one of the most important functions of new-style managers will be to cultivate the cross-fertilization of ideas by creating the right kinds of infrastructures and incentives for information exchange.

In studying one of the first large consulting companies to make extensive use of Lotus Notes, my MIT colleague, Wanda Orlikowksi, found that the consultants did not take advantage of the knowledge management aspects of the system because they had few incentives to do so.[4] They were evaluated at the end of the year on their billable hours, and any time spent learning to use or contributing to the system was not billable. At a more subtle level, Orlikowski observed that this organization, like so many others, was one in which people were rewarded for being the expert on something, for knowing things that others did not. Should we be surprised, therefore, that many people were reluctant to spend much effort putting the things they knew into an open database?

As a manager in a decentralized organization, one of your key jobs is to encourage this kind of cross-fertilization. To do this, you can't rely on any single simple technique. Rather, you need to think about a variety of different things at once: technology, culture, financial incentives, and others.

Improvise

You can't always plan everything from the top down, particularly if things are changing frequently and numerous people are making decisions. Rather, you must respond to unexpected problems. You must take advantage of new opportunities. You must improvise.

Of course, the more you know, the more you can try to anticipate and plan for these possibilities in advance. In situations that you already understand well, that may be the best course of action. In rapidly changing, decentralized environments, however, you're often better off heading out in the right direction with a general goal in mind, ready to respond creatively to whatever happens. Truth be told, lots of people already take this approach. They just don't realize it (or aren't willing to admit it).

THE PARADOX OF POWER

Like the paradox of standards, there is a similar paradox about cultivation:

Sometimes the best way to gain power is to give it away.

If you try to micromanage people, they will resist you. If they capitulate, they will lack the motivation to help you achieve your goals. If you give people power to make their own decisions, however, they will be more prone to support you. They will be more successful and so will you.

In the Linux project, Linus Torvalds gained power by giving it away to other programmers. Likewise, Dennis Bakke, CEO of AES, gained power by giving it away to employees. And Meg Whitman gained power at eBay by giving it away to customers. Granted, all of these people worked for new organizations that were unusually decentralized from the beginning. In general, it is not easy to find senior executives in large, traditional organizations who are willing to give up power. Decentralization, it seems, is more likely to spread through new companies that are decentralized from inception.

CONCLUSION

In 1600, few of Queen Elizabeth I's loyal subjects would have believed that someday all of Europe would be ruled by democratically elected governments and that the few remaining kings and queens would have only ceremonial roles.

Today, most people would not believe that something similar might be happening in business. But new technologies have made it possible. In the coming decades, the potential human benefits of freedom, flexibility, motivation, and creativity will make it almost inevitable in more and more business segments. To manage effectively in this new world, we need to change some of our deepest assumptions about management: from "command and control" to "coordinate and cultivate."

CHAPTER 20

WOMEN IN BUSINESS LEADERSHIP

WHAT COMPANIES OUGHT TO DO

SHEILA WELLINGTON

EVERY AUTUMN, my shelves seem ready to burst with the latest crop of books giving advice to women on rising to the top of the business heap. And it doesn't end there. New training programs sprout up, and women role-play themselves into exhaustion. They are instructed, cajoled, bullied, and motivated to find their voices, learn to negotiate, build relationships, dress right, talk right, and . . . yes, find mentors. Why? Because the number of women in the top business jobs is still minuscule. Women make up 5.2 percent of top earners in the Fortune 500, 13.6 percent of Fortune 500 board directors, and fewer than 16 percent of Fortune 500 corporate officers.

Given these facts, I wonder why the focus is almost exclusively on "fixing" the women. Someday in the mind-boggling morass of print aimed at improving women, I hope to see something new: a crop of books focused on "fixing" organizations by instructing them how to take advantage of the females who make up 47 percent of their existing workforce. Surely, women—who have outnumbered men in colleges and universities for some time and are entering law and medical schools in equal numbers—can't all be lacking commitment and the ability to manage their careers. There must be something that savvy business leaders could be doing better . . . or something that more than a few aspiring authors could be turning into print fodder.

While I'm holding my breath, let me make some modest proposals. Here's a once-over lightly about what companies can do to recruit and advance all the women who have entered their doors, gotten their badges, and are ready to use their talents to help their organizations, and themselves, succeed.

But first, a warning: Scattering a miscellany of programs through an organization in the hope that one or another will take root is no way to make change. Neither can running everybody through an inspirational training program. That is the "sheep-dip" method of change. It doesn't do much below the surface. A solid foundation is what making change is all about.

BUILDING A SOLID FOUNDATION

The first step in making an organization effective in managing its talent pool is mobilizing leadership support and making sure it's for real. Supporting women's careers entails more than issuing a memo announcing Women's History Month or letting everyone know that loyal old Jane has finally been promoted to vice president. Top leadership has to be on board and solidly committed. They must make it clear, time and again, that there's a business case for taking advantage of all talent, whatever shape, whatever color. Communication is key. Those who know the business world know that there's nothing more valuable to top executives than their time. So that's the investment that must be made—before a number of critical audiences, including the board of directors.

GETTING THE FACTS

The initial step—and the sine qua non—is finding out what's really going on with women in management. I am constantly amazed at the number of companies that don't analyze their own data or, worse yet, don't have a real sense of where most women executives are working in their organizations. Are women clustered in support positions, not involved in bringing in the bucks or engaging in the "business of the business"? Why? Is it really by choice?

Here's another question: Why are some companies able to recruit top women, while others apparently can't? Do company recruiters and executives recognize talent only when it looks like they look, talks like they talk, and graduates from the small group of colleges and universities they themselves attended? Sadly, some companies never seem to notice how their recruitment pool stacks up.

Furthermore, lots of organizations don't really know where women get stuck on the company career ladder. Usually it's approximately one-third down the pyramid of power, about three levels from the top. One would expect they'd be curious as to why this is going on. Because the majority of companies don't ask, however, they honestly don't know.

Similarly, when programs are put in place to take advantage of women's talent, results are often not tracked and the impact is frequently not evaluated. Why companies would throw away such a golden opportunity just doesn't make sense.

There are lots of other questions companies should be asking: At what point, from what levels, and why do women exit the organization? Furthermore, what would have kept them in their jobs in the first place? Yes, women tell HR they're going home. But do they really? And how long do they stay home? What organizations do they join when they reenter the workforce? Considerable research has documented that most women surface in different organizations, where they believe the playing field is more level or where they have more control over their lives.

In other words, businesses measure lots of things—nearly everything, in fact. Costs and profits are known to the penny and time is measured in nanoseconds, but when real information about women in management is sought, lots of men in management are surprised by the results.

WORKPLACE FLEXIBILITY IS NOT JUST A WOMAN'S ISSUE

Sixty percent of all marriages, including those of retired couples, are composed of two-career couples. And it isn't just women who value flexibility. Surveys of men and women in the workforce make this clear time and again. This point of view gets more pronounced with each new generation that enters the American workforce. Part-time work, the ability to work at home on occasion, schedule shifting, and temporary leaves are not really that hard to make happen. Not only is it a proven way to cut down on turnover, but it's also a proven way for companies to be a magnet for the increasing number of men *and* women who want to have both jobs and personal lives.

Most people—male and female—who take advantage of flexible work options are more than willing to be flexible in return. Grown-ups know that there are times when work must be the priority. Making that clear at the outset is important for employees and their bosses.

ACCOUNTABILITY

Nothing much is going to change for executive women unless progress—or the lack thereof—is measured and rewards follow results. Consider this advice from a leading CEO: "Hit them in the W-2 and their hearts and minds will follow." Whether it's dollars, or public praise, or seats on the 50-yard line, people respond to rewards, and they don't like criticism much. So track the results, measure the changes, and know it's a long-term effort. A few quick wins can be found, and there's always some low-hanging fruit. Keep in mind, however, that if it were that simple, the percentage of women in leadership wouldn't be hovering around 15 percent, year after year after year in virtually every sector of the U.S. economy.

DON'T BE SURPRISED BY BACKLASH

If you begin to make changes for women, don't be surprised to encounter backlash. It means you are succeeding. Backlash occurs only in response to change. So when the murmurs start that "women are taking over," here are a few things to do.

First of all, don't squelch complaints, and don't punish the resisters. Again, communication is key. Have top leaders communicate their commitment directly and praise those who have made progress in supporting the company's efforts. Hopefully, top managers will have been participants in the wins that have been achieved.

Make the facts of the situation known. Once again, publicize the numbers—as they were, and as they are. There's no doubt about it, the rumor mill will have overblown the numbers and percentages of women who have advanced.

Restate the business case—the dollars-and-cents reasons why advancing women is good for the company. Emphasize who your consumers are. Note some of the strategies your competitors have employed. A little competition gets the juices flowing and more people will get on board.

Whatever you do, make sure your team knows that advancing talent is not about arbitrary quotas and tokenism. Communicating this up front will help ensure that the organization hasn't committed these blunders in the first place. Emphasize the skills, the results, and the reasons why certain people have been promoted.

So there you have it: the primer on advancing women to leadership. Of course, this once-over lightly isn't going to help business leaders change the world. And when that hoped-for flurry of books commences, more information can and will be forthcoming. It goes without saying that a few pages cannot do justice to a complex and long-standing issue. But it's high time that the skill development focus shifts from what women ought to do to what companies ought to do. Only then can all those diversity mission statements be turned into mission accomplishments.

Women have gained entry to business careers and have almost achieved parity in the early management and professional pipelines. What is needed now is a focus on advancement and development.

In the commerce of the twenty-first century where knowledge and ideas have primacy, gender should not be a limitation.

CHAPTER 21

LEADERSHIP IN THE INTERNET AGE

MANAGING A DIVERSE
AND DISPERSED WORKFORCE

PATRICIA WALLACE

A leader is best when people barely know he exists; when his work is done, his aim fulfilled, they will say, "We did it ourselves."
                                                        —Lao-Tzu, 604 B.C.E.

CHINESE PHILOSOPHER Lao-Tzu knew nothing of the challenges a globalized and Net-centric world would present to modern leaders, but he recognized that talented people do their very best work when it is *their* work, not just an assignment handed down by the boss. Creating the conditions that unleash the workforce spirit that Lao-Tzu described and channeling it in the direction the leader wants to go was no small task then and it is far more complicated now. The workforce has been transformed in the Internet age, and the effective leader can no longer rely on past strategies.

NEW MEANINGS FOR DIVERSITY IN THE WORKFORCE

In the language of human resources, the term *diverse* typically refers to greater heterogeneity in demographic characteristics. Increasing ethnic diversity, for example, has been an important trend in organizations for several decades. Other kinds of demographic diversity are becoming critical elements as well. Age is a good example. People are living longer and choosing to work longer than ever. As a result, leaders have people working side by side who might have age differences of 50 or more years. A man born when Franklin Roosevelt was president might be on the same working team as a 20-year-old, whose living memory of presidents goes no further back than Bill Clinton. The differences in their knowledge base, life experiences, and values are substantial, even though they share the same ethnicity.

Cultural and religious differences in the workforce are also growing, and customs that were once embedded in the workplace in ways most people barely noticed are getting more scrutiny. The standard holiday season—from Thanksgiving in November to New Year's Day—has less meaning for many workers who celebrate other events, such as the Indian Diwali Festival in the fall or Ramadan, which is observed during the ninth month of the Muslim lunar calendar. Cultural and religious diversity brings many more fundamental issues to the surface that affect the workplace and how leaders behave. For example, finding jobs for relatives is expected in some cultures but considered scandalous nepotism in others.

DIVERSE EMPLOYMENT RELATIONSHIPS

Changing relationships between employees and employers contribute another twist to workforce diversity. Being employed by a particular organization once had a fairly narrow meaning that covered pay, benefits, personnel policies, job security, reporting lines, job responsibilities, performance evaluations, promotions, sick and vacation leave, retirement, and other aspects of the relationship. The arrangement created a trusted bond between employer and employee that may also have included a commitment to lifelong employment. I happened to be in Japan in the 1980s, when that kind of relationship was still common for college-educated men. A Sony engineer introduced himself to me by saying, "How do you do? I am Matsumoto; I belong to Sony," highlighting how potent that commitment can be. Matsumoto worked very hard, and he and his family socialized mainly with other Sony families, often at events sponsored by the company. Belonging to Sony was a job description, an honor, and a solid promise for a secure future for him. In return, Sony leaders could always count on Matsumoto to do his part.

That kind of employment bond and secure future was not very widespread then, even in Japan, but it has grown far less common during the Internet age. Today, people contribute their talents and skills to the company mission under many different arrangements. Enormous numbers of people are part of the contingent workforce, for example, having become independent contractors or "deployees." Some, particularly those with highly marketable skills, prefer this much looser and flexible bond with their employers, or clients, since they have more freedom to pick projects, working environments, and colleagues. In response to this trend, professional employee organizations have sprung up around the world to match deployees to organizations with a need for their skills.

Employment relationships for people in the same organization may also be more diverse because of corporate buyouts, mergers, outsourcing, and other business moves that mix people who signed on under different arrangements. When a university outsources the cafeteria and its workers to a restaurant chain, for example, deals may be struck to grandfather the people whose generous university benefits far exceed the typical restaurant employee. The two worker categories coexist, often doing the exact same work, albeit with quite different employment arrangements.

The workforce now includes a very diverse group of people working side by side, up and down the organization's hierarchy. Not only do they vary in terms of ethnicity, culture, religion, age, and other demographic characteristics, but they also have startlingly different kinds of employment arrangements. Thanks to globalization and the Internet, they may also be extremely dispersed around the globe.

WORKFORCE DISPERSION AND THE VIRTUAL EMPLOYEE

Struggling with soaring real estate prices, horrendous commutes, and the advantages of outsourcing and offshoring, managers at all levels have people on their teams who don't come to the office very often or have never even been there at all. This trend emerged from the Net's growing potential to support collaborative technologies and a virtual workplace. Along with all the other forms of heterogeneity, workforce diversity now also encompasses geography and physical presence.

This kind of workforce dispersion covers a range of situations, each of which presents different challenges for leaders. The occasional telecommuter who reports physically a few days a week is a growing arrangement, highly prized by many employees who have easy access to the Internet and electronic resources. Though the manager might have some difficulty scheduling face-to-face meetings, the employee interacts frequently enough with colleagues to maintain effective working relationships. The remote workers—whether on the other side of town or the far side of the globe—present much larger management challenges, in large part because they rarely, if ever, have face-to-face contact with managers and colleagues.

The advantages of remote work are many, both for worker and manager. The manager can draw on certain skills, such as legal or technical talent, for specific projects without having to hire locally or pay for travel. Meanwhile, the remote worker has the freedom to travel or remain home, relying on collaborative technologies to stay in touch. Yet remote work also presents many challenges, some of which are not easily overcome by improved technology.

Consider, for example, a global software company with developers in London, Boston, and Bangalore. On the positive side, workers can collectively work around the clock, so that bugs found by one team before close of business can be fixed by the next morning by people in a different time zone. They interact frequently via e-mail and occasionally use synchronous videoconferencing, when they can agree on a time.

Despite the increasingly sophisticated technologies, these teams have difficulty coordinating work and often they take longer to resolve problems than would a team whose members are collocated. People frequently develop strong and effective working relationships with those in the same physical location, but their relationships with remote workers are more fragile and easily disrupted. Research points to several reasons for this, including the fact that people in the same location communicate more efficiently and with more nonverbal nuances that speed understanding.

Besides all the nonverbal signals people use to communicate meaning, such as smiles, winks, grimaces, or shrugs, collocated team members share an awareness of presence, even when they are not in a face-to-face meeting. They know when a co-worker who has specialized knowledge is in the next office or taking a coffee break, so they can ask a quick question to resolve an issue immediately. "Got a second?" is a common question from co-workers who need information but don't want to wait for an e-mail response or arrange a Net meeting. Collaborative technology can be used to improve awareness of presence for remote workers, but far-flung time zones will continue to hinder the synchronized coordination that some projects require of their team members.

The dispersed workforce raises another challenge for managers involving personnel policies and compensation. Granted, multinational corporations have always dealt with disparities in pay, benefits, working environments, and the like. However, the Internet age adds a new ingredient. Now that people from different countries are being assigned to virtual teams, they develop closer relationships across national boundaries. Hence, disparities become more apparent and widely known.

THE CHALLENGE OF LEADERSHIP IN THE INTERNET AGE

Leadership in the Internet age—when the workforce has become so diverse and dispersed—calls for new approaches and new skills. The leader must first recognize that the composition, motivations, and nature of the workforce really *are* changing, and strategies that may have worked well in the past may not continue to be successful. This kind of adaptability carries some risk. After all, people with successful leadership track records may be reluctant to change. Therefore, they continue using the same approaches that served them well in the past.

One area in which leaders need far greater skills is in their use of the Internet itself. The dispersion of the workforce means leaders must be completely fluent and expert at communication via the Net, and they must fully grasp how the Net has transformed the nature of communication. The Net offers a convenient and inexpensive means to maintain contact and build a community among geographically dispersed workers. Its global reach enables the leader to communicate directly with people at all levels of the organization and also beyond its boundaries to other stakeholders.

However, the Net is quite a different communication medium compared to any that leaders have used in the past. It is a powerful amplifier of blunders and a reliable archive of messages thought to be deleted. An intemperate email to a few colleagues can be forwarded endlessly to the entire company and beyond—to shareholders, to the press, to competitors, even to law enforcement. The Net is also a leveler, since any employee can send messages to anyone inside or outside the organization. This supports flatter organizational structures and tends to make them so even when they were designed to be more hierarchical. Net-savvy leadership is a required skill, but it becomes even more challenging as the workforce becomes more diverse. For instance, the level of formality that employees might expect varies immensely. The marketing executive in California might be comfortable with an organization-wide message that opens with, "Hey guys . . . ," whereas a

Taiwanese manager might be taken aback by such informality, expecting something quite different.

Trust in the leader and in fellow co-workers has been and will continue to be a critical element that successful leaders must nurture. In the Internet age, however, the means to develop trust is changing. Again, an understanding of how information and telecommunications technologies can best be used and an appreciation of their limitations are needed. Research shows that people who never meet face-to-face have a far more difficult time establishing the kind of trust needed to build strong working relationships. Collaborative technologies help, but as Charles Handy, author of *The Hungry Spirit* (Broadway, 1998), observed, trust requires touch. It may seem odd in the age of the Internet for an organization to spend more on company picnics or annual conferences, but these events give far-flung and highly diverse workers the chance to build the personal bridges they need to work more smoothly together online.

Diversity in the workforce requires leaders to rethink incentives and rewards as well. What is valuable to the people in your organization, and how has that changed? A corner office is not very important for a worker who would prefer to telecommute and use a hot desk occasionally. A culturally and religiously diverse workforce may value flexibility in the choice of holidays. A knowledge worker for whom recognition by professional peers outside the company is more important than a pay raise may appreciate attendance at conferences or support for writing and publishing. Google, for example, offers extremely varied benefits and incentives for its employees, ranging from massage therapy and yoga to onsite child care and roller hockey. And engineers get 20 percent of their time to work on whatever projects interest them.

Successful leadership styles vary considerably, and no single style works for everyone all the time. The transformative leader, the one who becomes the magnetic focal point of an organization and energizes people through passionate commitment, is often the kind featured in the press. Daring and visionary, this person is often more of a spiritual leader than an operational manager. This approach can be enormously effective, but it can also fail badly. Take the charismatic leaders of the high-tech start-ups of the 1990s, for example. They could attract large sums from angel venture capitalists for operating expenses, while paying the workers—mostly young, tech-savvy college grads—mainly in stock options. When the venture funding dried up and stock values plummeted, that particular leadership style lost its appeal.

Lao-Tzu's best leader, described at the beginning of this chapter, is close to what is now called *systemic leadership*. This approach attempts to nurture leadership in every employee, rather than position it solely in the CEO and executive management team. It stresses the importance of helping each person become a responsible autonomous agent who can act independently and make decisions that contribute to the organization's goals. In the Internet age, it is the job of the CEO to find ways to build those capacities in each person, rather than leading the parade. In an age when the workforce is so dispersed and diverse, and very rapid decision making is needed on the ground, the most effective leadership may be the systemic kind. Though the CEO may take a more backseat role and may not be quoted in the press, the successful organization's workforce will be proud to say, "We did it ourselves."

CHAPTER 22

WORKFORCE DIVERSITY

A GLOBAL HR TOPIC THAT HAS ARRIVED

TED CHILDS

TODAY, WORKFORCE diversity is a global topic—a global workplace topic and a global marketplace topic. Any business that intends to be successful in this global arena must have a borderless view and an unyielding commitment to ensuring that workforce diversity is part of its day-to-day business conduct.

Success must also be measured as it pertains to a company's composition and its program content. A company's management team must ask itself, "Do we look like our customers, at all levels of our business? Do our programs reflect an understanding of the demand for talent in a competitive worldwide marketplace? Is our business culture one that fosters inclusiveness and tolerance in *each* country where we do business? And, most important, are we using workforce diversity issues to improve marketplace performance and grow shareholder value?"

To be successful, global companies must continue to look toward the future, not the past. And, I believe, CEOs, senior line and HR management,

---

and diversity leaders play a key role in that process. If we are to address the complex issues in the twenty-first century, such as the continuing core issues of race and gender, the growing issues of child and eldercare, the emerging issues of multiculturalism, tolerance of religious practices and the full inclusion of people with disabilities in the workplace, then diversity professionals must lead. They must lead because businesses cannot get there by themselves. Let me emphasize however that workforce diversity cannot be delegated. This must be a partnership. While the HR team plays the key staff role, total delegation from the top without active involvement is a recipe for failure.

IT'S ABOUT LEADERSHIP

There's a great deal of debate about the qualities needed for a successful diversity executive. "What attributes must a diversity executive have in order to be effective in corporations today?" is a question asked by experts and senior line executives. Others ask, "How can a diversity executive work in the corporate boardroom, but stay in touch with the various constituency groups and their needs, and still remain credible and effective?"

These are good questions, and there are many good answers that address them. During my 37-year IBM career, I've thought about these questions often and about the answers even more. Over and over again, I come to the same conclusion; it's about passion and leadership.

Do we exhibit leadership both in our personal approach to diversity and the policies we embrace for our company, and do we care about the outcome of the debates we engage in—do we hate to lose?

To answer these questions, I draw my response from two people that I have learned from and admire greatly. The first example comes from professional sports. The second example comes from business. Both are legends. I'm talking about Jackie Robinson of the Brooklyn Dodgers and Tom Watson Jr. of IBM.

"Life is not a spectator sport," said Robinson, who broke the baseball color barrier in 1947. "If you're going to spend your whole life in the grandstand just watching what goes on, in my opinion you're wasting your life."

And Robinson lived as he believed. While in the Army from 1942 to 1945, before baseball, Robinson challenged segregation at Camp (Fort) Hood. As he went through military channels stating his cause to superior officers, Robinson's protest led to desegregation at the camp. He also once faced and

defeated court-martial proceedings, after refusing to move to the back of an
Army bus when the driver gave the order. Robinson's protest, a legitimate
one, since Army regulations prohibited discrimination on government vehicles, eventually led to all charges being dismissed.

Robinson lays out a valuable lesson for diversity executives today. Our
work is not for spectators, but for those who thrive on change. Not for
change alone, but change that is a catalyst for improvement—creating
fairness when it doesn't exist, moving organizations from separate but
equal points of view to inclusiveness, and migrating people from conflict
to collaboration.

Diversity leaders can also learn from the leadership of Tom Watson Jr.
When it involved IBM, he also sought to live by his values as he led the business. In his book, *A Business and Its Beliefs* (McGraw-Hill, 1963), Watson said,
"If an organization is to meet the challenges of a changing world, it must be
prepared to change everything about itself except its basic beliefs as it moves
through corporate life. The only sacred cow in an organization should be its
basic philosophy of doing business."

And so, he identified three basic beliefs to serve as the cornerstone of
IBM's approach to business. They were:

1. Respect for the individual.
2. Service to the customer.
3. Excellence must be a way of life.

Watson led by these beliefs, reflecting his view of the values required to
lead a great company during the time in which he lived and worked. And he
walked the talk. In a personal meeting with Tom Watson in 1990, I asked him
why he wrote what I believe is America's first equal opportunity policy letter
in 1953—one year before the *Brown* U.S. Supreme Court decision integrating America's schools and 11 years before the Civil Rights Act. The letter
communicated his commitment to fairness and inclusion. Mr. Watson replied
that during negotiations with the governors of two Southern states regarding
the building of IBM plants, he told them that there would be no "separate
but equal" racial policies at IBM. To ensure the governors took him seriously,
he wrote a letter to his management team in 1953 and made the letter public.
As a result, he said, both governors responded by choosing payroll and tax
dollars over bad social policy—they chose progress.

The cornerstone in the partnership between senior line management and
diversity leadership, I believe, must be their passion about the people working

for their company and their customers. Leaders must help all people involved with their business understand that workforce diversity can be the bridge between the workplace and the marketplace. Passion is contagious, and when combined with leadership, the equation is very effective.

To achieve this convergence of passions, the most important quality for a diversity leader is the ability to motivate others to be part of the leadership on this subject, and see it as part of their personal day-to-day performance. A diversity leader must be able to draw others into the debate and be the catalyst who can convince others that helping to change the content and character of the workplace makes the team stronger and a better performer in the marketplace.

WHY IS DIVERSITY LEADERSHIP IMPORTANT?

The answer to why diversity leadership is important is simple: our work is not done. First, we have not solved the problems of gender and race. Women represent more than 50 percent of the world's population, but they're not 50 percent of our workforce and certainly have not achieved parity on our management and executive teams. They are, however, increasingly becoming members of our executive teams and owners of their own businesses. We must view them in a more important and inclusive context—as workforce talent and customers.

The issue of race has been a pivotal item in the United States since its founding. Today, driven by immigration patterns, the growing presence of people of color as citizens, business owners, and customers puts this issue on the social, business, and political agendas of many countries.

Second, the gay and lesbian workplace issue achieved legitimacy as a discussion topic in the past decade. The driving force was the debate around whether to offer domestic partner benefits. Although approximately 145 Fortune 500 companies offer domestic partner benefits today, many other companies don't.

While the domestic partner benefits issue is still a legitimate topic of discussion, we need to move forward within the lesbian, gay, bisexual, transgendered (LGBT) discussions to address issues of leadership. Do we have equivalent programs to attract, develop, and retain LGBT talent as we have done for women and people of color?

Are we being evenhanded? Are we just saying, well, gay and lesbian people work here, so we need to solve this benefits thing? Or do we see them as a part of our core business environment—employees, leaders, and customers? We must ask the same inclusion questions about our disabled community. Is our approach to disability anchored in sympathy, or is it based on respect for the individual and a high regard for *ability*?

Third, a key emerging issue is the concept of being global, whether we're in the United States, Europe, the Asia-Pacific region, Latin America, or Africa. When we look at our businesses, what do we see? Do we see a business that is limited to conducting its day-to-day operations in our country, or do we have a perspective about our company that crosses borders? What are our expectations about our business' conduct in other countries? Do we have a commitment to ensure fairness in the treatment of women, people with disabilities, gays and lesbians, and ethnic minorities—no matter where we do business?

Are we taking steps to understand the workforce diversity legislation in each country where we do business? Is our company in compliance with the expectations of the legislation in each country where we do business?

A HERITAGE OF LEADERSHIP

IBM is committed to building a workforce as broad and diversified as the customer base it serves in 165 countries. Reflective of this customer base, we have a broad definition of diversity. In addition to race, gender, and physical disabilities, it includes human differences such as culture, lifestyle, age, religion, economic status, sexual orientation, gender identity and expression, marital status, thought, and geography.

We consider diversity a business imperative as fundamental as delivering superior technologies in the marketplace. And to ensure that talented people can contribute at the highest possible level, our company insists on a workplace that is free of discrimination and harassment and full of opportunity for all people.

At IBM, diversity is comprised of the following three areas: equal opportunity, affirmative action, and work/life balance. The common denominator is access to the workplace—access through an environment free of harassment in a workplace that provides the tools to eliminate disadvantage, and a workplace that understands that work/life balance makes it possible for employees to come to work and be productive.

From its inception more than a century ago, IBM has embraced workforce diversity as a fundamental value. IBM's commitment to workforce diversity can be traced back to 1899, when we hired our first women and black employees—20 years before women's suffrage and 10 years before the founding of the National Association for the Advancement of Colored People (NAACP) and 36 years after the signing of the Emancipation Proclamation.

And part of that heritage is the fact that eight IBM chairmen have acknowledged the importance of workforce diversity to our business, to our culture, to the marketplace, and finally, as a cornerstone to our IBM values.

Under the leadership of IBM chairman and CEO Sam Palmisano, IBM's values have been redefined and drive everything we do. They are:

- Dedication to every client's success.
- Innovation that matters—for our company and for the world.
- Trust and personal responsibility in all relationships.

It's clear to me that IBM's leaders, in every generation, believed that diversity was right for the company no matter what the prevailing issues of the day mandated. That kind of leadership didn't just happen. It sprang from our shared beliefs and values, and from the efforts of our visionary founders to infuse every aspect of our business conduct with the deeply held convictions of IBMers. And, that type of leadership begins with the CEO and the leadership team.

When Sam Palmisano, IBM's eighth CEO, took over the helm of IBM in 2002, not only did he have the responsibility for heading up one of the world's leading global technology companies, but he was also entrusted with ensuring that IBM continued its commitment to diversity.

This was no trivial matter, as each of Palmisano's predecessors had personalized his commitment to building an inclusive IBM community where talent was the common denominator. After more than a century of small victories, IBM's record in diversity is unassailable—one that is unmatched by any other company in its industry. The forward-thinking vision of the company's CEOs has put IBM at the forefront of promoting diversity, challenging institutional barriers that preclude a more inclusive community.

And so, what is the future of diversity at IBM and where is it heading? According to Palmisano, the lesson that IBM draws from a century of leadership in diversity is to stay true to the company's shared values. The marketplace demands it, and it's what we believe—and have always believed—is the right thing to do.

GLOBAL DIVERSITY WINNING PLAYS

Today at IBM, we're attacking diversity issues through innovation and actions that we call winning plays. These winning plays are distinctive and allow us to execute globally, and compete locally.

Here are some examples:

- Building on what was America's premier corporate commitment to basic child and dependent care initiatives in the 1980s/1990s to creating IBM's $50 Million Global Work/Life Fund Strategy in 2000–2006. We remain the only company to have such a strategy, which includes 74 child care center relationships around the globe.
- Creating eight executive task forces in 1995 (Asian, black, Hispanic, Native American, gay/lesbian (currently named gay/lesbian/bisexual/transgendered), people with disabilities, men, and women) to each look at IBM through the lens of its group and answer these four questions: What is required for your group to feel welcomed and valued here? What can IBM, in partnership with your group, do to maximize your productivity? What decisions can IBM make to influence the buying decisions of your group? What outside organizations that represent the interests of your group should IBM have a relationship with?
- Growing our investment in our supplier diversity program from $370 million in 1995 to $1.3 billion in 2003 in the United States and $263 million outside the United States.
- Helping to address the digital divide through programs like our signature initiatives including Reinventing Education; Native American, Black Family, and La Familia Technology Weeks; and Exploring Interests in Technology and Engineering (EXITE) camps for middle-school girls.
- Showcasing our assistive technology at the California State University Northridge (CSUN) Conference and subsequently in six Global Accessibility Centers.
- Incorporating the eight constituencies mentioned earlier into our advertising and marketing campaigns—which speaks to advocacy.

The business of workforce diversity is constantly evolving, and presents us with new and different challenges, especially as businesses become more global.

One major winning play we are developing at IBM is a global workforce strategy that will span 2004 through 2010. This strategy will address the growing equal opportunity legislation taking shape around the world, play a positive role in shaping the debate about global sourcing, and respond to the growing variety of multicultural/ethnic minority issues becoming a dominant factor in the labor market.

When we look at the landscape, we are confident we will maintain a path of innovation and leadership. Every year we demonstrate our willingness to solve new challenges. In Canada, for example, we developed separate washing facilities for our Muslim employees who need to cleanse their feet before they pray—over 100 employees use the facilities daily. In Brazil, as a result of our EXITE camp, a 16-year-old girl opened a bakery business.

For IBM, maintaining the integration of our global diversity initiatives within the mainstream of the corporation is crucial to our future success in the information technology industry.

Diversity is becoming a key factor in helping to define leadership in today's marketplace. Workforce diversity is about effectively reaching customers and markets. As a company we are clearer than ever before about our values and our commitment to diversity.

I know we have some very tough and challenging diversity issues today. I also know the world is smaller today than it was when I was a boy growing up in Springfield, Massachusetts. But one thought has guided me during my lifetime: My mother continues to tell me to always set high goals. She says, "Never reach for the mountaintop—if you fall, you may fall to the bottom of the mountain. Always reach for the stars; if you miss you may land on the mountaintop." We still have several mountaintops worth pursuing.

If reaching the stars will help our companies have the most diverse, talented workforce we can assemble in our respective marketplaces—then it is a goal our shareholders, customers, and employees deserve that we pursue.

CHAPTER 23

ORGANIZATION AS
NATURE INTENDED

HUMAN UNIVERSALS AND
THE EMPLOYMENT EXPERIENCE

NIGEL NICHOLSON

THE PRECEDING chapters in this volume have provided a diverse richness of ideas, inspiration, and insight on the startling new world that is opening up before us wrought by globalization, technological innovation, and
cultural development. In the face of the momentous challenges of our age, we
find remarkable new conditions for business practice. Yet we must remind
ourselves how much remains unchanged in our world—not the least of
which is the single most important factor in management and organization:
human nature.

As we explore the question of how to approach new management challenges, in this chapter I draw on the most radical new thinking in the social
sciences, ideas that come from evolutionary psychology as applied to the field
of business.[1] Their implications are profound, urging an unfashionable caution
in our assumptions about change. This does not imply pessimism, however, for
the ideas point in clear directions with regard to what may and may not be
possible in terms of human adaptation to a transforming world economy.

Without getting too philosophical, we should consider what it means to
talk of an unchanging human nature. When we look at how far we have
come from the brutality of previous ages or how management culture has advanced in the last millennium, it is easy to conclude that humans are capable

of endless self-reinvention. Even today, however, barbarity persists in many societies. On our global doorstep, sweatshops and primitive organizational practices are widely to be found. Although progress feels like an irreversible ratchet, we can also backtrack. Civilization can retreat under the pressure of war, famine, and extremism. And good firms, like good people, can turn bad. Luckily, the converse is also true. People and organizations can be reformed, but only by adopting measures that take human nature into account. Utopian aspirations are insufficient and will be disappointed at whatever level they are entertained if not accompanied by smart practices that are designed with our evolved psychology in mind.

THE NEW DARWINISM: ITS STARTLING MESSAGE

We may have taken ourselves out of the Stone Age, but we haven't taken the Stone Age out of ourselves. For all our brilliant inventiveness and amazing advances in ways of living and working over the past millennia, we remain hunter-gatherers in mind and body. No consistent selective pressures have been applied and too little time has passed since we ceased to live on the savanna for any fundamental evolution to have occurred to our basic psychological architecture. As a result, our minds are hardwired in ways that to this day govern human behavior—including how we act in organizations. Understanding these inborn dispositions is useful for managers, especially as they try to adapt their organizations to a changing business environment. In this chapter, I discuss four elements of human nature[2]—thinking and feeling, interpersonal relationships, organizational and cultural forms, and human types and differences—along with their implications for organizations approaching some of the managerial challenges that have figured most prominently in this volume. These challenges include finding and developing leaders, managing in knowledge economies, the challenge of diversity, virtuality and new forms of organization, and twenty-first-century values and cultures.

THE NATURE OF HUMAN NATURE: KEY ELEMENTS

Thinking and Feeling

The thoughts and emotions that best served human beings living on the savanna were programmed into their psyches and continue to drive behavior today. In the uncertain world of our ancestors, those who survived were in touch with their emotional radar and instincts at all times. Today, emotions remain the first screen through which all information is received, but often with less trust and confidence. Sometimes in business we try to dispense with emotion in favor of rational analysis. In our recent major study of financial traders in the City of London[3] it was apparent that the injunction to traders not to let their feelings intrude in their supremely rational task was futile. Granted, the best traders learn to manage their emotions, but emotions can never be abolished. From our earliest origins we humans have survived the harsh elements by striving to avoid loss. We evolved under conditions where life was fragile and a single loss of resource or opportunity could threaten our very existence. Our minds retain this set today. On trading floors, for example, it can induce gambling to chase losses, the typical pattern for so-called rogue traders. The best managers of traders are alert to this and have rules and procedures to counter it. Another evolutionary characteristic is that our thinking rarely proceeds in straight logical lines, but rather progresses by flashes of intuition and judgment in ways that were really helpful in the simpler and more fluid world of a tribal existence. The crunch comes in contemporary life when we are calculating risks, thinking about probabilities, and making any kind of complex judgments. Routinely one can see executives pulled into lousy decisions through their intuitions and irrational judgment calls, who then make matters worse by struggling to cover them up in an attempt to avert loss.

Interpersonal Relationships

We evolved and were psychologically equipped for communal living in a world where we would have had few interactions with strangers of any kind. The communities in which we evolved were modest in size and exhibited the full diversity of human psychological types, yet were bonded by ties of kinship and alliance (that is, a clan). This made us friendly, loyal, deeply concerned with reputation, gossipy, and, frankly, clannish. We were fiercely resentful of cheaters and protective of our group against external threats. All of this worked well in regulating tribal societies, but in the modern world, it produced Enron. It generates corruption in many high and low places, defensive solidarity, and discrimination of all sorts. In today's world, it also throws us into dilemmas of trust. We trust strangers too readily, treating them as if they were part of our community. When one of them lets us down, we flip—mistrusting almost everyone. That's because our mind and spirit are still locked into the assumptions of a communal world that scarcely exists in the developed world, except in fragments.

Organizational and Cultural Forms

We were designed not only for communal living, but also for communities of a circumscribed size and shape. It has been discovered that the brain size of monkeys and apes is directly related to the size of their troop. In other words, their mental capacity is for a network size where they can relate with some familiarity to every member of the group. Humans, with our big craniums, have a capacity of around 150. This is the size within which it is possible to maintain a sense of organic community. Many businesses have learned this lesson, keeping unit size small and familiar. We also like hierarchy—ranking is one way evolution gives advantage to the best genes in the pool. Tribal hierarchies are characteristically fluid and informal, which is how they work best, but in modern organizational life we have resorted more often to rigid bureaucratic orders, which appeal to our status striving. This has many dysfunctional consequences in organizational life.

Human Types and Differences

Humans have also evolved to have many hardwired differences, both between individuals and between groups. Naturally, one of the most important is the inborn difference between the sexes. This remains highly controversial but it is increasingly accepted that men and women often have different preferences in their ways of working, relating, and even thinking. While we do many things very much the same, it is often with a different nuance or approach. This applies to status competition, for example. Men tend to prefer the tournament culture of corporate career development more than women, who tend to be much more attracted to networks of inclusion and exclusion. The other major source of human differences lies in inborn characteristics: ability, personality, and physical constitution. Evolutionary psychology suggests that people are born with these set predispositions, which crystallize with age. Some people are more dominant than others. Some are more optimistic. Some like math better than poetry. People can compensate for these underlying dispositions with education and training, but there is little point in their trying to completely restructure these deep-rooted inclinations. Fortunately, these inclinations are the source of the most rewarding aspects of social life— an almost infinite matrix of opportunities for roles to play and people to associate with. They also underpin varieties of leadership and followership.

Now let us consider, briefly, how these forces of human nature play out when applied to five key themes in transforming economies.

FINDING AND DEVELOPING LEADERS

As the war for talent intensifies, companies are ever more urgent in their search for an instant—and sometimes magical—solution to leadership. Leadership is not a single thing, however. It is an ever-changing challenge—a continuous stream of different situations that need to be led. Thus, different leadership processes or styles are needed, according to the nature of the leadership role and the events surrounding it. Wartime and peacetime leaders need different attributes, for example. Likewise, transforming and consolidating organizations need contrasting approaches from their CEOs. We must have either supremely adaptable leaders or different people for different roles and times. We see organizations becoming increasingly diverse in their structures and operating strategies. This provides unparalleled opportunities for new kinds and styles of leadership. Thus, there are as many types of leaders as there are leadership situations. The important thing is to match the personality profile of the leader with the demands of the situation.

But what if the personalities we need to lead do not have the desire to do so? Behavior genetics—the study of inborn differences in human attributes—tells us that we grow up to desire very different roles and lifestyles. The *desire* to lead is perhaps the most important attribute to leadership. However, many people, including in some cases people who have been thrust into leadership roles, just have no drive to lead!

Moreover, there is a risk in our transforming world that leadership roles in many major corporations are becoming increasingly unattractive—fraught with poor work/life balance, increasing forests of regulation, and greater personal risks of failure. Perhaps the real risk is that the only people sufficiently driven to accept these costs are precisely the kinds of leaders we want fewer of—those who are dominant, self-interested, and tough, for example, when the leaders we want more of are people of principle, vision, and humanity. The answer lies in helping reform organizations so they can attract and retain more of the people we want to lead them.

MANAGING IN KNOWLEDGE ECONOMIES

The shift from work organized around mechanized processes to environments where information exchange is the dominant principle offers new opportunities and challenges. The reduced constraints of this environment have features that hearken back to the more open and fluid working world of our preagrarian ancestors. This means we can do away with much of the rigidity that has characterized traditional industries. Yet the human propensity for emotions to supplant reason, for friendliness to undermine impartiality, for gossip to prevail over authorized communications, all hold the danger that knowledge organizations will still become networks of influence, politics, personal bias, and unofficial tournaments for status and advantage, much like a tribal community. Fortunately, these same properties also hold the potential for positive benefits, such as flair, flexibility, and fun. The question is, what do we want? Can we have our cake and eat it, too? Can we have organizations run on rational grounds with the fluidity and freedom that we know brings out the best in people? Yes, we can, but we will need smart management practices and systems.

Unfortunately, some knowledge-based organizations—many medium-sized professional firms, charities, trade unions, finance firms, educational institutions, and the like—are badly managed. In large part, that's because they lack a coherent concept of management and employ few people who are prepared to forgo any portion of their professional practice for the responsibility of managing other people. These organizations fail the test of being organic communities where a full diversity of human types and interests can be found, including people who relish the responsibilities of management. The tendency for birds of a feather to flock together is a by-product of both our clannishness and the freedom in modern economies for people of like mind to gravitate toward each other in work and play. Thus, we must take deliberate steps to foster diversity and prevent monocultures from stifling creativity and much-needed difference.

THE CHALLENGE OF DIVERSITY

We tend to think of diversity in terms of obvious social categories, such as race, age, and gender. Even when you have what appears to be a healthy variation in these factors, however, an organization can still lack the full diversity of human types that makes for the most creative and effective communities. The risk of developing clusters of excessively homogeneous thinking has always been a feature of large corporations that organize on functional grounds. A principle source of difficulty for human resource professionals has been that they are often dealing with tribes from finance, production, or marketing who have an unsympathetic cast of mind to them and to each other. Of course, age, race, and gender are also subject to clustering, but the problem of discrimination in contemporary business is less naked prejudice than people self-selecting to be with their kin. It is also the product of what in the language of equal opportunity is called indirect discrimination. This occurs in subtle ways. One of the most pervasive is the growing phenomenon of networking as a means of adapting to organizational complexity. Along with this phenomenon comes a set of special problems. Women and men network in different ways, for example, and women often find the male politically based networks of influence hard to penetrate. Naturally, this can be to their disadvantage. Ethnic minorities face a similar problem. Even where they are actively encouraged to participate in organizational life, they frequently lack the confidence, will, or opportunity to engage in the networks of power. Thus, organizations need to take steps to enhance diversity at all levels and stimulate dynamism by helping people participate in organic networks of association.

VIRTUALITY AND NEW FORMS OF ORGANIZATION

Clearly, we live in an age where it is possible to do deals without seeing people and to organize via the Internet. Yet it is at our peril that we ignore the basic human need for physical presence, face-to-face contact, and visibility. Even if such contact occurs infrequently, it is a means of keeping organizations tangible and human. It is important here to distinguish between the different actions that make organizations function. Many of them can be done virtually—factual information exchange, discussion of ideas, brokering deals, and, up to a point, making decisions. The gap that cannot be filled so easily is in forming and building of relationships. People who try to manage by e-mail know firsthand how easy it is to have trust wobbles, unexpected fights, and misapprehended motives. That said, it is not impossible to cultivate a feeling of friendship with people you never meet. For real bonding, however, you need real presence. The irreducible qualities of teamwork that are the most valuable to an organization are also those that are most rewarding and sustainable. Intimacy of this sort does not mean we need to cling to traditional forms. Quite the contrary. New models of organization—with partial outsourcing, new kinds of alliance and integration, and temporary and networked structures—all need to be linked by effective relationships. We can use new technology to help build creative new ways of organizing that bring out the best in our people, but only if we also foster close working relationships.

TWENTY-FIRST-CENTURY VALUES AND CULTURES

It has become clear that the humanistic values of work organization—first voiced in the nineteenth century by the Quaker reformers and others, followed by the "human relations" scholars of the mid twentieth century who criticized the soullessness of technology-centered management—are now accepted by just about every thinking business leader as the only viable model for today's business. The only form of sustainable and inimitable competitive advantage a firm can have is its culture. Only the magnetism of strong values, flourishing talent, innovative mind-sets, empowering practices, and celebrated success will attract and retain the best people. And there is something more—the firm needs to have the internal dynamic of cohesion and acceptance—a family spirit, if you will—in which people feel respected, cared about, and given the chance to show they can make a difference. Drawing upon and diffusing the feeling of kinship throughout the business, family firms outperform nonfamily firms time and again.[4] They do so by rising above the rational-economic and entering the domain of true community. The best of them connect with organizational values linked to our social origins—identifying with what they produce or serve, being intent on maintaining continuity over generations and not treating the business as a mere disposable asset, and fostering a spirit of kinship throughout the business. Granted, falling birthrates are going to make the family business model harder to sustain in the future, but when one looks at the companies for which most people want to work,[5] they have the same family ethos: high involvement, recognition, empowerment, and concern for their staff as people, not just as employees. Indeed, what has been one of the fastest-growing organizations in the world—the Australian-based travel agency, Flight Centre Ltd.—has achieved staggering growth by building upon the ideas of evolutionary psychology, inspired by my *Harvard Business Review* article,[6] to organize around "families, villages, and tribes."[7]

CONCLUDING IMPLICATIONS

As we have seen, the evolutionary perspective is not a recipe for pessimism. Quite the contrary, a deeper understanding of the human animal can help us shed our utopian delusions and point us toward new adaptive strategies that are in harmony with the essence of what it means to be a human being.

Thus, we can extract from it a few simple lessons for twenty-first-century management:

- Create the spirit of true community as if you were an extended kinship model, keeping unit size small enough that you can mentally put your arms around it.
- Foster new models of leadership, especially those driven by values of stewardship and service to the business as a community.
- Promote organic diversity on what I call the "Duke Ellington principle": It doesn't matter what color, gender, or age you are; all that matters is: do you love the music and can you play the music?
- Keep managing face-to-face—MBWA: manage by wandering about.
- Learn how to learn from failure—face up to the weaknesses inherent in human decision making and compensate for them.
- Create a positive and celebratory ethos in the firm—honor achievements, identity, and history.
- Remember, you cannot become the best just by outspending others in the war for talent. The best firms punch above their weight, taking ordinary people and finding magical capabilities in them.

Management is a mixture of art and science. The new Darwinism is providing the latter. As the Flight Centre example shows, all it takes is people with vision, flair, and courage to apply insights, to consider the implications of evolutionary psychology in approaching contemporary management problems. In Chapter 15 you would have read about Ricardo Semler, CEO of the Brazilian company Semco, which has been organized around principles that are consistent with evolutionary psychology. In organizing Semco, Ricardo Semler eschewed management texts in favor of finding the natural way of managing. The result has been a highly successful self-organizing communitarian system built of small, flexible subunits.

Notes

PREFACE

1. Willi Leibfritz, "Retiring Later Makes Sense," *OECD Observer*, January 13, 2003.

2. *The Challenge of Age: The Change Agenda*, Chartered Institute for Personnel and Development, November 2003.

3. Nancy R. Lockwood, "The Aging Workforce," *HR* Magazine, December 2003.

4. *Future of Work Overview*, New Zealand Department of Labour, 2002.

5. *The American Workplace 2003*, Employment Policy Foundation.

6. Susan F. Martin, "Heavy Traffic," *Brookings Review*, Fall 2001.

7. *Employer Perspectives on Global Sourcing*, Hewitt Associates, 2004, and also see Robert Gandossy and Tina Kao, "Overseas Connections," *Across the Board*, November/December 2004.

8. "Innovation: Remote Working in the Net-Centric Company," The Economist Intelligence Unit Executive Briefing, July 15, 2003.

9. "Global Survey Predicts Upsurge in Telework," International Telework Association & Council (ITAC) *Telework News*, issue 3.3, Summer 2003.

10. Chuck Salter, "Solving the Real Productivity Crisis," *Fast Company*, January 2004.

11. Michael J. Weiss, "To Be About to Be," *American Demographics*, September 1, 2003.

12. Catherine Loughlin and Julian Barling, "Young Workers' Work Values, Attitudes, and Behaviours," *Journal of Occupational and Organizational Psychology*, November 2001.

13. Peter Schwartz, *Inevitable Surprises: Thinking Ahead in a Time of Turbulence* (New York: Gotham Books, 2003).

14. Paul Temple, "No Retirement for Boomers," *Workforce*, July 2000.

15. Stephanie Armour, "Higher Pay May Be Layoff Target," *USA Today*, June 22, 2003.

16. *The Challenge of Age: The Change Agenda*, Chartered Institute for Personnel and Development, November 2003.

17. *Facts on Women at Work*, International Labour Organization, 2003.

18. Mitra Toossi, "Labor Force Projections to 2014: Retiring Boomers," *Monthly Labor Review*, November 2005.

19. *The Social Situation in the European Union 2003*, European Commission, 2003.

20. *Meeting the Challenges of Tomorrow's Workforce*.

21. Society for Human Resource Management and *The Wall Street Journal* Job Recovery Survey, 2003.

22. June 2004 interview with Elaine Dixon, director, organizational development and training, and Erich Wilson, director, compensation, PacifiCorp.

23. Ken Dytchwald, Tamara Erickson, and Bob Morison, "It's Time to Retire Retirement," *Harvard Business Review*, March 2004.

24. Eric Bonabeau, and Valdis Krebs, "Model Behavior," *Optimize*, October 2002.

25. Mark Niesse, "Home Depot Seeks Older Workers for Jobs," Associated Press Online, February 6, 2004.

26. Dytchwald et al., "It's Time to Retire Retirement."

27. Joe Mullich, "Hiring without Limits," *Workforce Management*, August 2002.

28. Ricardo Semler, *The Seven-Day Weekend* (New York: Penguin Group, 2004).

29. Chuck Salter, "Calling JetBlue," *Fast Company*, May 2004.

30. Semler, *The Seven-Day Weekend*.

31. James Ware, and Charles Grantham, "The Future of Work," *Journal of Facilities Management* (September 2003).

32. "A Different Track," *Chief Executive*, May 2004.

33. Thomas W. Malone, *The Future of Work*, (Boston: Harvard Business School Press, 2004).

34. Ibid.

35. Ibid.

36. Semler, *Seven-Day Weekend*.

37. Malone, *Future of Work*.

INTRODUCTION   Abundance, Asia, and Automation

1. Drucker first discusses the broad concept of "knowledge work" in his 1959 book, *Landmarks of Tomorrow* (Transaction Publishers), though his first

apparent use of the term is in Peter Drucker, "The Next Decade in Management," *Dun's Review and Modern Industry* 74 (December 1959). For the paragraph's first quotation, I've relied on the always excellent work of Richard Donkin and his October 30, 2002, *Financial Times* article, "Employees as Investors." The second and third quotations come from Peter Drucker, "The Age of Social Transformation," *Atlantic Monthly* (November 1994). For some of Drucker's latest thoughts on the subject, see Peter Drucker, "The Next Society," *The Economist* (November 1, 2003), in which he defines knowledge workers as "people with considerable theoretical knowledge and learning: doctors, lawyers, accountants, chemical engineers."

2. Staples 2003 Annual Report; Staples Corporate Overview (available at www.corporate-ir.net/ireye/ir_site.zhtml?ticker=PR_96244&script=2100); "PETsMART Reports Second Quarter 2003 Results," PETsMART 2003 Annual Report (August 28, 2003).

3. Gregg Easterbrook, *The Progress Paradox: How Life Gets Better While People Feel Worse* (New York: Random House, 2003), 6. Easterbrook's smart book also contains a collection of other statistics that confirm the shift from scarcity to abundance.

4. Data are from the U.S. Bureau of Transportation Statistics' 2001 National Household Travel Survey, available at www.bts.gov.

5. John De Graaf, David Wann, and Thomas H. Naylor, *Affluenza: The All-Consuming Epidemic* (San Francisco: Berrett-Koehler, 2002), 32. See also data at www.selfstorage.org.

6. Polly LaBarre, "How to Lead a Rich Life," *Fast Company*, March 2003.

7. Virginia Postrel, *The Substance of Style: How the Rise of Aesthetic Value Is Remaking Culture, Commerce, and Consciousness* (New York: Harper-Collins, 2003). More Postrel: "But, more important, aesthetics is also becoming more prominent relative to other goods. When we decide how next to spend our time or money, considering what we already have and the costs and benefits of various alternatives, 'look and feel' is likely to top our list. We don't want more food, or even more restaurant meals—we're already maxed out. Instead, we want tastier, more interesting food in an appealing environment. It's a move from physical quantity to intangible, emotional quality."

8. Andrew Delbanco, *The Real American Dream: A Meditation on Hope* (Cambridge, MA: Harvard University Press, 1999), 113.

9. Robert William Fogel, *The Fourth Great Awakening and the Future of Egalitarianism* (Chicago: University of Chicago Press, 2000), 3.

10. "Wax Buildup," *American Demographics*, March 2002.

11. Rachel Konrad, "Job Exports May Imperil U.S. Programmers," Associated Press, July 13, 2003.

12. Pankaj Mishra, "India: On the Downswing of Software Outsourcing," *Asia Computer Weekly*, January 13, 2003.

13. Khozem Merchant, "GE Champions India's World Class Services," *Financial Times*, June 3, 2003.

14. Amy Waldman, "More 'Can I Help You?' Jobs Migrate from U.S. to India," *New York Times*, May 11, 2003; Joanna Slater, "Calling India . . . Why Wall Street Is Dialing Overseas for Research," *Wall Street Journal*, October 2, 2003.

15. Pete Engardio, Aaron Bernstein, and Manjeet Kriplani, "Is Your Job Next?" *Business Week*, February 3, 2003; Merchant, "GE Champions"; "Sun Chief to Woo India in Software War," Reuters, March 4, 2003; Eric Auchard, "One in 10 Tech Jobs May Move Overseas, Report Says," Reuters, July 30, 2003; Steven Greenhouse, "I.B.M. Explores Shift of White-Collar Jobs Overseas," *New York Times*, July 22, 2003; Bruce Einhorn, "High Tech in China," *BusinessWeek*, October 28, 2002.

16. Engardio et al., "Is Your Job Next?"

17. Auchard, "One in 10 Tech Jobs"; "Outsourcing to Usurp More U.S. Jobs," CNET News.com, August 31, 2003; Paul Taylor, "Outsourcing of IT Jobs Predicted to Continue," *Financial Times*, March 17, 2004.

18. John C. McCarthy, with Amy Dash, Heather Liddell, Christine Ferrusi Ross, and Bruce D. Temkin, "3.3 Million U.S. Services Jobs to Go Offshore," *Forrester Research Brief*, November 11, 2002; Mark Gongloff, "U.S. Jobs Jumping Ship," *CNN/Money*, March 13, 2003.

19. George Monbiot, "The Flight to India," *Guardian*, October 21, 2003; Moumita Bakshi, "Over 1 Million Jobs in Europe Moving Out," *The Hindu*, September 3, 2004.

20. "Not So Smart," *Economist*, January 30, 2003.

21. Rudy Chelminski, "This Time It's Personal," *Wired*, October 2001.

22. Robert Rizzo, "Deep Junior and Kasparov Play to a Draw," *Chess Life*, June 2003.

23. Steven Levy, "Man vs. Machine: Checkmate," *Newsweek*, July 21, 2003.

24. A similar pattern occurred the year before when another chess champion, Vladimir Kramnik, played another computer, Deep Fritz, in a Persian Gulf contest that promoters dubbed "Brains in Bahrain." Kramnik went into the sixth game with a lead, but at a critical juncture, instead of playing a conventional move, Kramnik attempted one that he felt was more creative and aesthetic. The fool. It cost him the game—and ulti-

mately the match. Said Kramnik of his loss, "At least I played like a man." (Daniel King, "Kramnik and Fritz Play to a Standoff," *Chess Life*, February 2003).

25. Chelminski, "This Time It's Personal."

26. Paul Hoffman, "Who's Best at Chess? For Now, It's Neither Man Nor Machine," *New York Times*, February 8, 2003.

27. "The Best and the Brightest," *Esquire*, December 2002.

28. "Software That Writes Software," *Futurist Update*, March 2003.

29. Laura Landro, "Going Online to Make Life-and-Death Decisions," *Wall Street Journal*, October 10, 2002.

30. Laura Landro, "Please Get the Doctor Online Now," *Wall Street Journal*, May 22, 2003; "Patient, Heal Thyself," *Wired*, April 2001.

31. Jennifer Lee, "Dot-Com, Esquire: Legal Guidance, Lawyer Optional," *New York Times*, February 22, 2001.

CHAPTER 3   Human Capital Investments for Pareto-Optimal Returns

1. Service firms are typically at the higher end of this range.

2. All personal and company information is deidentified and aggregated prior to analysis to protect confidentiality of such information.

3. CFROI is a registered trademark in the United States and other countries (excluding the United Kingdom) of CSFB HOLT and/or its affiliates.

CHAPTER 4   Using Workforce Analytics to Make Strategic Talent Decisons

1. "The High Cost of Disengaged Employees," *Gallup Management Journal*, April 15, 2002.

2. F. F. Reiccheld and T. Teal, *The Loyalty Effect: The Hidden Force behind Growth, Profits, and Lasting Value* (Boston: Harvard Business School Press, 1996).

3. "What Your Disaffected Workers Cost," *Gallup Management Journal*, March 15, 2001.

4. *Driving Employee Performance and Retention through Engagement*, Corporate Leadership Council, 2005.

CHAPTER 5 Cutting Through the Fog

1. Peter Cappelli, "Will There Really Be a Labor Shortage?," *Organization Dynamics*, August 2003.

2. Roger Martin, "Capital vs. Talent: The Battle That's Reshaping Business," *Harvard Business Review*, July 2003.

3. Jeffrey Pfeffer, *Competitive Advantage through People* (Boston: Harvard Business School Press, 1994) and *Hidden Value: How Great Companies Achieve Extraordinary Results with Ordinary People*, (Boston: Harvard Business School Press, 2000); Jon Katzenbach, *Peak Performance: Aligning the Hearts and Minds of Your Employees* (Boston: Harvard Business School Press, 2002); Bruce Pfau, *The Human Capital Edge* (New York: McGraw-Hill, 2002).

CHAPTER 6 Staffing for the Future

1. U.S. Bureau of Labor Statistics.

2. *American Workplace Report 2004*, Employment Policy Foundation.

3. Interview with Dave DeLong, May 11, 2005.

4. *Facts on Women at Work*, International Labour Organization, 2003.

5. Thomas L. Friedman, *The World Is Flat: A Brief History of the Twenty-First Century* (New York: Farrar, Straus, & Giroux, 2005), 38.

6. Kelly Services, September 2002 survey.

7. Interview with Daniel Pink, March 30, 2005.

8. R. Martin and M. Moldoveanu, "Capital versus Talent: The Battle That's Reshaping Business," *Harvard Business Review*, July 2003.

9. Hewitt Associates, Engagement Data.

10. Manpower, Inc. Manpower Employment Outlook Survey, March 15, 2005.

11. HR Focus, "How a Talent Management Plan Can Anchor Your Company's Future," Yahoo.com, October 2004.

12. See James Ware and Charles Grantham, "The Future of Work: Changing Patterns of Workforce Management and Their Impact on the Workplace," *Journal of Facilities Management*, September 2003.

13. Esther V. Rudis, *The CEO Challenge 2004* (New York: The Conference Board, 2004).

14. *Preparing for the Workforce of Tomorrow*, Hewitt Associates Timely Topic Survey Report, February 2004.

15. Interview with Allan Schweyer, March 25, 2005.

16. Kevin Wheeler, "Reframing Traditional Workforce Planning," *ER Exchange,* January 12, 2005.

17. Interview with Home Depot's Cindy Milburn, April 2005.

18. Interview with Home Depot's Tim Crow, April 2005.

19. "How Google Searches—For Talent," *BusinessWeek Online.*

20. Interview with Capital One's John Ansted, June 29, 2005.

21. For more on this see Friedman, *World Is Flat*; Richard Florida, *The Flight of the Creative Class: The New Global Competition for Talent* (New York: HarperBusiness, 2005); John Hagel III and John Seely Brown, *The Only Sustainable Advantage: Why Business Strategy Depends on Productive Friction and Dynamic Specialization* (Boston: Harvard Business School Press, 2005).

22. Ricardo Semler, *The Seven-Day Weekend* (New York: Penguin Group, 2004).

23. Thomas W. Malone, *The Future of Work* (Boston: Harvard Business School Press, 2004).

24. Alison Stein Wellner, "EDS Reinvents Its Workforce," *Workforce Management Online,* November 2004.

25. Leslie Gross Klaff, "New Internal Hiring Systems Reduce Cost and Boost Morale," *Workforce Management Online,* March 2004.

26. Malone, *Future of Work.*

27. For more on high potentials, see Hewitt's recent report "Putting Your Finger on the Talent Pulse."

28. Chuck Slater, "Solving the Real Productivity Crisis," *Fast Company,* January 2004.

29. Nidhi Verma, "Making the Most of Virtual Working," *World@Work,* Q2 2005.

30. Interview with Daniel Pink, March 30, 2005.

31. James Ware and Charles Grantham, "The Future of Work: Changing Patterns of Workforce Management and Their Impact on the Workplace," *Journal of Facilities Management,* September 2003.

32. Interviews with Capital One's Shyam Giridharadas, June 29, 2005.

CHAPTER 7   How an Evolving Psychological Contract Is Changing Workforce Flexibility

1. For a review of the debate on these numbers, see S. Cohany, "Workers in Alternative Employment Relationships," *Monthly Labor Review,* October 1996, 31–45.

2. For a review of European work on the psychological contract and well-being of temporary workers, see N. De Kuyper, K. Isaksson, and H. De Witte, eds., *Employment Contracts and Well-Being among European Workers* (Hampshire, UK: Ashgate Publishing, 2005).

CHAPTER 8   Leading the Knowledge Nomad

1. See Yukl (1989); Bass and Avolio (1994); Burns (1978); Barling, Weber, and Kelloway (1996).

2. See Bass (1999).

3. See Drucker (1959) and Shea (1987).

4. It is important to note that the relationship between organizational commitment and positive outcomes, for both the organizational and individuals, is not unequivocally desirable—even though, for many reasons, it is often highly desirable. As with many positive states, there can also be too much of a good thing, as when, for instance, commitment involves a loss of personal freedom and choice. Furthermore, researchers have argued that an excess of commitment can be maladaptive to both individuals and organizations. Whyte (1956) suggests the possibility of a "shadow side" to excessive commitment, a possibility further explored by Randall (1987) and others. Although interesting and important to examine, this shadow side of organizational commitment seems to be the exception rather than the rule. Maladaptive outcomes of commitment identified in the literature seem to occur when commitment is excessive. The more typical scenario is for individuals to choose to be committed to the organizations they join and for commitment to have positive effects for both the organization and its members (Pfeffer, 1998).

5. See Hackett, Bycio, and Hausdorf (1994); Meyer, Allen, and Smith (1993); Somers (1995); Bashaw and Grant (1994); Munene (1995); Pearce (1993).

6. See Ainsworth, Blehar, Waters, and Wall (1978); Bowlby (1982).

7. Interestingly, while there is a perception that worker mobility is on the rise, empirical evidence examining trends in worker mobility—specifically the perceived decline in job tenure—is mixed (Auer and Cazes 2000; Marcotte 1999). For example, there has not been an observable increase in the number of employees with tenure of less than one year (Jaeger and Stevens 1998). Still, there is some evidence that there was a slight decline, in the aggregate, in job stability in the early 1990s (Neumark, Polsky, and Hansen

1997). But regardless of whether mobility is actually on the rise, the perception that it is fuels assumptions about the direction of organizational commitment. The critical point here is that the perceptions of an inverse relationship between worker mobility and organizational commitment may be just that: perceptions.

8. See Merton (1948); Rosenthal and Jacobson (1992).

9. To be sure, one of the most important advances in the organizational commitment literature has been the articulation and investigation of different forms of commitment. For example, scholars have begun to differentiate between "continuance commitment," "affective organizational commitment," and "normative organizational commitment." It is critical to note, however, that even when a particular form of commitment is focused on a worker's staying in an organization, assumptions about commitment and mobility can still leak into the other forms of commitment. In Meyer and Allen's (1991, 1997) typology, for example, continuance commitment is often discussed as the form of commitment most concerned with whether a worker stays in an organization. But it is instructive to look at the operationalizations of their two other forms of commitment: affective and normative organizational commitment. Both of these presume that organizational commitment and intent to remain in the organization are one and the same. Affective commitment is measured by items such as, "I would be very happy to spend the rest of my career in this organization" and "I think I could easily become as attached to another organization as I am to this one." Among the measures of normative commitment: "I do not feel any obligation to remain with my current employer."

10. These two companies were matched for industrial niche: commercial Internet software and complex Internet-enabled services. Two corporate recruiters reviewed the field site companies and evaluated the degree to which these companies would be recruiting from the same pool of workers. Both reported that the skills, background, and employment prospects of the employees in each of the two field site companies were very similar.

11. Pittinsky (2001) found that the intersection of commitments—the compatibilities as well as the conflicts—is a better predictor of turnover than any one commitment alone. For example, the compatibility of family commitments and organizational commitment can be more important to whether one stays in an organization than family commitment alone or organizational commitment alone. Moreover, some very committed people leave organizations because of conflicts, not because of low levels of commitment in any absolute sense.

12. First, we randomly selected a target sample of employees from the companies' telephone directories; this provided us comprehensive and up-to-date lists of employees. Second, we sent a general e-mail announcement requesting survey participation. Third, midway through the survey period, we sent a follow-up request to employees in the targeted sample who had not yet completed the survey. Fourth, during the final three days of research, we left a flyer requesting participation from employees in the targeted sample.

13. We provided the research contacts at each of the field sites with the survey sample's distribution of gender, age, geography (whether on-site or working in the field), and job function. No systematic differences between the sample and the target population, above and beyond what would be expected with random sampling, were uncovered.

14. Use of this scale is a conservative approach because, as noted earlier, commitment scales, including Meyer and Allen's Organizational Commitment Scale, are often operationalized in a way that frames commitment as a reason for staying in or leaving an organization. Thus the deck is, in some sense, stacked toward finding a relationship. In this light, the lack of relationship predicted and observed in our research is even more compelling.

15. Participants generated a career history—including their previous employing organizations, dates of employment, geographic locations of employment, and organizational roles—to help ensure the accuracy of responses for this self-report measure of past mobility. The alternative methodology, a developmental study following a cohort of workers over their careers, was not possible for practical reasons.

16. First measure: $\alpha = .84$: $r = .007$, $p = .94$; second measure: $r = -.07$, $p = .42$.

17. $\alpha = .78$: $r = .05$, $p = .54$.

18. Age was partialed out in these analyses. As a result, age was found to be related to both commitment and mobility; it drove a correlation between the two variables independent of a distinct relationship between them. Interestingly, age was related to commitment, but not in the direction commonly assumed. Younger workers were found to have a higher commitment to the organization than older workers.

19. $r = -.29$, $p = .001$.

20. Because the hypothesis is one of no relationship between commitment and mobility, we took four methodological precautions. First, we conducted a power analysis, which revealed that, based on the range of effect sizes reported in the commitment literature (for example, Mathieu and Zajac,

1990), our study sample size was large enough to detect an effect at a power of 90 percent. Second, we examined the relationship between commitment and mobility from four different perspectives. Third, to avoid drawing premature conclusions from a single set of analyses, we used multiple measures. Fourth, we asked a second researcher to examine the data and run similar analyses, with the expectation of finding statistically significant inverse relationships between commitment and mobility measures.

21. See Pittinsky (2001).

22. See Levine and Pittinsky (1997).

23. See Hackman (2002), for a rich discussion of teams in their organizational contexts.

24. See Baker (2001).

25. See Baker (2001).

26. See Baker (2001).

27. See Baker (2001).

CHAPTER 9 What Happened to the "New Deal" with Employees?

1. See Peter Cappelli, *The New Deal at Work: Managing the Market-Driven Workforce* (Boston: Harvard Business School Press, 1999).

2. See Peter Cappelli, "Contemporary Employment Practices in Historical Perspective," in *Corporate Responsibility and Human Capital,* ed. Margaret Blair and Thomas A. Kochan (Washington, D.C.: Brookings Institution, 2000).

3. See Sandford M. Jacoby, *Modern Manors: Welfare Capitalism Since the New Deal* (Princeton, NJ: Princeton University Press, 1997); Stuart Brandes, *American Welfare Capitalism, 1880–1940* (Chicago: University of Chicago Press, 1976); Daniel Nelson, *Managers and Workers: Origins of the New Factory System in the United States, 1880–1920* (Madison: University of Wisconsin Press, 1995).

4. Not everyone thought that these arrangements were necessarily better for employees than the previous, more market-driven era because employees gave up control for security. In the former system, the argument goes, at least employees had more autonomy. See Stephen A. Marglin, "What Do Bosses Do? The Origins and Functions in Hierarchy in Capitalist Production," *Review of Radical Political Economics* 6 (2) (1974): 60–112.

5. A detailed guide to these practices is Sumner H. Slichter, James J. Healy, and E. Robert Livernash, *The Impact of Collective Bargaining on Management* (Washington, D.C.: Brookings Institution, 1960). An analysis of the decline of that system is Thomas A. Kochan, Harry C. Katz, and Robert B. McKersie, *The Transformation of Industrial Relations* (New York: Basic Books, 1984).

6. The classic study of managerial capitalism is A. A. Berle and Gardner Means, *The Modern Corporation* (New York: Macmillan, 1932).

7. See, for example, Rosabeth Moss Kanter, *Men and Women of the Corporation* (New York: Basic Books, 1977); C. Wright Mills, *The American Middle Class* (New York: Oxford University Press, 1953); William H. Whyte, *The Organization Man* (New York: Simon & Schuster, 1956).

8. This case is argued persuasively in D. Quinn Mills, *The IBM Lesson: The Profitable Art of Full Employment* (New York: Times Books, 1988).

9. The rise of these pressures from the investor community is perhaps the most important development in the world of business in a generation. See Michael Useem, *Investor Capitalism* (New York: Basic Books, 1996).

10. U.S. Department of Labor, *Guide to Responsible Restructuring* (Washington, D.C.: Government Printing Office, 1995).

11. Even if we focus just on the private sector and leave out the roughly 11 percent of the workforce who are self-employed, in farming, or other jobs that do not fit the model of working for an employer, organizations still had to be a certain size before it is efficient to have systems of internal development and training, job ladders, and other arrangements associated with long-term commitments. Seven percent of private sector employees work in establishments with fewer than five employees, and 44 percent are in establishments with fewer than 100. One researcher calculated that organizations need a minimum of 500 employees to make formal compensation systems feasible. See Robert S. Smith, "Comparable Worth: Limited Coverage and the Exacerbation of Inequality," *Industrial and Labor Relations Review* 41 (2) (January 1988): 227–239. Another argued that only about 40 percent of U.S. employees were in firms large enough and old enough to even have a reputation in their community, something that he saw as necessary to make the implicit contracts that were behind internalized employment practices operate. See Walter Y. Oi, "The Fixed Costs of Specialized Labor," in *The Measurement of Labor Cost*, ed. Jack Tippelt (Chicago: University of Chicago Press, 1983). Even within those organizations, the lifetime commitment model was generally a phenomenon for

managerial workers who typically constituted about one-fifth of a company's workforce. If we define the workforce that ever had the lifetime, career-based employment system as managerial employees in firms large enough to have reputations, a rough estimate would be about 10 percent of the private sector workforce.

12. For an explicit comparison, see Peter Cappelli, "Examining Managerial Displacement," *Academy of Management Journal* 35 (1) (March 1992): 203–217.

13. Olivier J. Blanchard, "Explaining European Unemployment," *NBER Reporter* (Summer 2004), special section: 6–9.

14. Steven Hipple, "Contingent Work," *Monthly Labor Review* (March 2001): 3–27.

15. These surveys are discussed in Richard S. Belous, *The Contingent Economy* (Washington, D.C.: National Planning Association, 1989).

16. HR Executive Review, *Implementing the New Employment Contract* (New York: Conference Board, 1997).

17. See American Management Association, *Survey on Downsizing, Job Elimination, and Job Creation* (New York: American Management Association, 1996).

18. See American Management Association, *Survey on Downszing.*

19. Daniel Rodriguez and Madeline Zavodny, "Changes in the Age and Education Profile of Displaced Workers," *Industrial & Labor Relations Review* 56 (3) (April 2003): 498–510.

20. Henry S. Farber, "Has the Rate of Job Loss Increased in the Nineties?" (Princeton University, Industrial Relations Section Working Paper no. 394, January 1998).

21. Steven G. Allen, Robert L. Clark, and Sylvester J. Schieber, "Have Jobs Become Less Stable in the 1990s? Evidence from Employer Data," in *On the Job: Is Long Term Employment a Thing of the Past?*, ed. David Neumark (New York: Russell Sage Foundation, 2002).

22. See Daniel Polsky, "Changing Consequences of Job Separations in the United States," *Industrial and Labor Relations Review* 52 (4) (July 1999): 565–580 for this result. The other two studies are Annette D. Bernhardt, Martina Morris, Mark S. Handcock, and Marc A. Scott, "Trends in Job Instability and Wages for Young Adult Men," *Journal of Labor Economics* 17 (4), Part 2 (October 1999): S65–S126 and Robert G. Valetta, "Has Job Security in the U.S. Declined?," *Federal Reserve Bank of San Francisco Weekly Letter*, No. 96-07 (February 16, 1996).

23. Bernhardt et al., "Trends in Job Instability."

24. See Christopher J. Ruhm, "Secular Changes in the Work and Retirement Patterns of Older Men," *Journal of Human Resources* 30 (2) (Spring 1995): 362–385.

25. H. S. Farber, *The Changing Face of Job Loss in the United States, 1981–1995* (Princeton, NJ: Princeton University Industrial Relations Section, 1997).

26. David Neumark, Daniel Polsky, and Daniel Hansen, "Has Job Stability Declined Yet? New Evidence for the 1990s," *Journal of Labor Economics* 17 (4), Part 2 (October 1999): S29–S64.

27. Allison J. Wellington, "Changes in the Male/Female Wage Gap 1976–85," *Journal of Human Resources* 28 (2) (Spring 1993): 383–411.

28. "Employee Tenure, Table 4," U.S. Bureau of Labor Statistics, 2004. www.bls.gov/news.release/tenure.t01.htm.

29. "Executive Update," *T+D* 56 (12) (December 2002).

30. Peter Cappelli and Monika Hamori, "The Path to the Top: Changes in the Attributes and Careers of Corporate Executives, 1980 to 2001," *Harvard Business Review* 83 (1) (January 2005): 25–32.

31. Peter Gottschalk and Robert Moffitt, "Welfare Dependence: Concepts, Measures, and Trends," *American Economic Review* 84 (2) (May 1994): 38–42.

32. Ann Huff Stevens, "Changes in Earnings Instability and Job Loss," *Industrial & Labor Relations Review* 55 (1) (October 2001): 60–78.

33. Steffanie L. Wilk and Elizabeth A. Craig, "Should I Stay or Should I Go? Occupational Matching and Internal and External Mobility," Wharton School Department of Management, working paper, Philadelphia, 1998.

34. Claire Brown, ed., *The Competitive Semiconductor Manufacturing Human Resources Project* (Berkeley: University of California Press, 1997).

35. Keith W. Chauvin, "Firm-Specific Wage Growth and Changes in the Labor Market for Managers," *Managerial and Decision Economics* 15 (1) (January/February 1994): 21–37.

36. David Marcotte, "Evidence of a Fall in the Wage Premium for Job Security," Center for Governmental Studies, Northern Illinois University, 1994.

37. Daniel Polsky, "Changing Consequences of Job Separation in the United States," *Industrial & Labor Relations Review* 52 (4) (July 1999): 565–580.

38. Thanks to Steve Gross, then of Hay Associates, for providing Peter Cappelli with these unpublished figures in 1996.

39. Sandra O'Neal, "Recent Trends in Compensation Practices: Presentation to the Board of Governors of the Federal Reserve," Valhalla, NY: Towers, Perrin, October 1997.

40. U.S. Bureau of Labor Statistics Employee Benefits Surveys, 1989–1997.

41. For a description of these plans across the Fortune 500 and their relationships to firm performance, see Angela G. Morgan and Annette B. Poulsen, "Linking Pay to Performance—Compensation Proposals in the S&P 500," *Journal of Financial Economics* (December 2001).

42. K. C. O'Shaughnessy, David I. Levine, and Peter Cappelli, "Changes in Management Pay Structures, 1986–1992 and Rising Returns to Skill," working paper, University of California at Berkeley Institute of Industrial Relations, 1998.

43. Jeffrey A. Williamson and Brian H. Kleiner, "The Use of Stock Options in Compensation Packages," *Management Research News* 27 (4/5) (2004): 31.

44. See Peter Cappelli, Laurie Bassi, David Knoke, Harry Katz, Paul Osterman, and Michael Useem, *Change at Work* (New York: Oxford University Press, 1997).

45. Richard A. Ippolito, "Toward Explaining the Growth of Defined Contribution Plans," *Industrial Relations* 34 (1) (January 1995): 1–20.

46. Leora Friedberg and Michael T. Owyang, "Not Your Father's Pension Plan: The Rise of 401(k) and Other Defined Contribution Plans," *Review, Federal Reserve Bank of St. Louis* 84 (1) (January/February 2002): 23–25.

47. Lewis M. Segal and Daniel G. Sullivan, "The Growth of Temporary Services Work," *Journal of Economic Perspectives* 11 (2) (Spring 1997): 117–136. The estimates of temporary help in particular count only employees working for agencies, but estimates that include temps working directly for employers might double the total number of temps, from 2 to 4 percent of the workforce.

48. Consider, for example, a company that outsources janitorial or other lower-level jobs to a vendor. The janitors may still have full-time jobs, albeit now with a vendor. But the likelihood of being able to advance to any position outside of janitorial work may well be reduced.

49. Sara L. Rynes, Marc O. Orlitzky, and Robert Bretz Jr., "Experienced Hiring versus College Recruiting: Practices and Emerging Trends," *Personnel Psychology* 50 (2) (Summer 1997): 309–339.

50. See Cappelli, *New Deal at Work*, Chapter 6.

51. See Cappelli, *New Deal at Work*, 215.

52. William Ocasio, "Institutionalized Action and Corporate Governance: The Reliance on Rules of CEO Succession," *Administrative Science Quarterly* 44 (2) (June 99): 384–416.

53. Kevin J. Murphy and Ján Zábojník, "CEO Pay and Appointments: A Market-Based Explanation for Recent Trends," *American Economic Review* 94 (2) (May 2004): 192–196.

54. Jill L. Constantine and David Neumark, "Training and Growth of Wage Inequality," *Industrial Relations* 35 (4) (October 1996): 491–510.

55. This material is reviewed in Cappelli, *New Deal at Work*, Chapter 6.

56. See Paul Osterman, "Skills, Training, and Work Organization in American Establishments," *Industrial Relations* 34 (2) (April 1995): 125–146.

57. There are now many studies reporting this result, but the first one appears to be Jone L. Pearce, "Toward an Organizational Behavior of Contract Laborers: Psychological Involvement and Effects on Employee Co-Workers," *Academy of Management Journal* 36 (5) (October 1993): 1082–1092.

CHAPTER 10   Human Capital Relationship Management

1. Trevor Merriden, "Capital One: With Employees Keeping Stress Diaries, Capital One Aims to Cut Staff Churn," *Human Resources*, May 2003.

2. "Softening the Sell," *Employee Benefits*, September 2004.

3. Betty Sosnin, "Getting Personal," *HR* Magazine, June 2005.

4. Ulrike Wiehr, *Customer Relationship Management at Capital One (UK)*, INSEAD Case, 2003.

5. For a more detailed description see Chapter 3 in this volume.

6. Samuel Greengard, "Analyze This," *Workforce*, June 2003.

7. "Take Control: Motivating Employees to Take Personal Responsibility for Their Retirement Savings," Hewitt Associates teleconference, February 9, 2005.

8. Tom Starner, "Qualcomm: An Inside Job," *Human Resource Executive*, January 19, 2005.

9. "Build Your Own Health Plan Options for Employees at Dell," PowerPoint presentation by Liz Hill, global benefits, Dell, presented at The Gathering Conference, Hewitt Associates, 2004.

10. Fay Hansen, "The Turnover Myth," *Workforce Management*, June 2005.

CHAPTER 11   Getting the "New" Newcomer Connected and Productive Quickly

1. Sources: U.S. Department of Labor Report 02-531, "Employee Tenure in 2002," and Report 02-497, "Number of Jobs Held, Labor Market Activity, and Earnings Growth among Younger Baby Boomers—Results from More than Two Decades of a Longitudinal Survey." www.bls.gov.

2. These numbers are for external hires—internal transfers get up to speed about twice as fast. The entire report "Mellon Learning Curve Research Study" was published in November 2003 and can be obtained at www.mellon.com.

3. For example, see S. P. Borgatti, and R. Cross, "A Relational View of Information Seeking and Learning in Social Networks," *Management Science* 49 (4) (2003): 432–445.

CHAPTER 13   Managing Workforce Challenges in India's IT Industry

1. Lee Iacocca and William Novak, *Iacocca: An Autobiography* (New York: Bantam, 1988).

2. Douglas Lavin, "Globalization Goes Upscale," *The Wall Street Journal* Online, February 1, 2002.

3. Rowan Gibson, *Rethinking the Future*. London: Nicholas Brealey Publishing, 1996.

4. Jerry Useem, "Jim Collins on Tough Calls," *Fortune*, June 27, 2005.

CHAPTER 16   Diversity's Next Frontier: Hard-Core Inclusion

1. U.S. Census Bureau.

2. Ibid.

3. Zelig Council of Economic Development.

4. U.S. Department of Labor.

5. Ibid.

6. Allstate statistic.

7. Various Conference Board publications on diversity.

8. Speech by Mike McGavick, Safeco CEO to Conference Board Business Diversity Council at Safeco, March 7, 2005.

9. Ariel Capital Management/Charles Schwab study, July 2005.

10. Hewitt engagement survey. Survey recipients are given an option to self-identify their sexual orientation. We are then able to do a data cut of all the data by sexual orientation. Those who identify as LGBT are offered about a dozen additional questions specifically about their LGBT experience in the corporation.

11. Hewitt Timely Topics survey: "Preparing for the Workforce of Tomorrow," February 2004.

12. Nancy R. Lockwood, "Workplace Diversity: Leveraging the Power of Difference for Competitive Advantage." *SHRM Research Quarterly*, 2005.

CHAPTER 19   The Future of Work

1. For previous uses of the term *orchestrator* in this same sense, see John Hagel III, Scott Durchslag, and John Seely Brown, "Orchestrating Loosely Coupled Business Processes: The Secret to Successful Collaboration," in *Reflections on Web Services: A Compendium of Working Papers*, Warburg Pincus Technical Report 1, no. 1 (August 2002): 62–76; John Hagel III, *Out of the Box: Strategies for Achieving Profits Today and Growth Tomorrow Through Web Services* (Boston: Harvard Business School Press, 2002), 114–116.

2. *American Speaker* (Washington, D.C.: Georgetown Publishing House, 1994), QUO/23.

3. Douglas Ready, "Mobilizing Collective Ambition: How Effective Top Teams Lead Enterprise-Wide Change" (Working paper, International Consortium for Executive Development Research [ICEDR], Lexington, Massachusetts, July 2002).

4. Wanda J. Orlikowski, "Learning from Notes: Organizational Issues in Groupware Implementation," in *Proceedings of the 1992 ACM Conference on Computer-Supported Cooperative Work, November 1–4, 1992, Toronto, Ontario, Canada*, ed. Marilyn Mantel and Ronald M. Baecker, 362–369.

CHAPTER 23   Organization as Nature Intended

1. See N. Nicholson, "How Hardwired Is Human Behavior?," *Harvard Business Review* 76, no. 4 (July/August 1998): 134–147; N. Nicholson, *Managing the Human Animal* (London: Thomson/Texere, 2000).

2. Readers can see other sources for more detailed accounts. See, for example, S. Pinker, *How the Mind Works* (New York: W.W. Norton, 1997).

3. M. Fenton-O'Creevy, N. Nicholson, E. Soane, and P. Willman, *Traders: Risks, Decisions and Management in Financial Markets* (Oxford: Oxford University Press, 2005).

4. See N. Nicholson, and A. Björnberg, "Familiness: Fatal Flaw or Inimitable Advantage?," *Families in Business* (March 2004): 52–54.

5. As listed annually in *Fortune* magazine in the United States, and the *Sunday Times* in the UK.

6. N. Nicholson, "How Hardwired Is Human Behavior?"

7. M. Johnson, *Family, Village, Tribe: The Story of the Flight Centre Ltd.* (Sydney, Australia: Random House, 2005).

ABOUT THE CONTRIBUTORS

Max H. Bazerman

In addition to being the Straus Professor at the Harvard Business School, Max Bazerman is formally affiliated with the Kennedy School of Government, the Psychology Department, the Center for Basic Research in the Social Sciences, the Harvard University Center on the Environment, and the Program on Negotiation. In his prior position at the Kellogg School of Northwestern University, Bazerman was the founder and director of the Kellogg Environmental Research Center. He is currently on the board of a number of organizations. Bazerman's research focuses on decision making in negotiation, and improving decision making, organizations, nations, and society. He is the author or coauthor of more than 150 research articles and chapters, and the author, coauthor, or coeditor of 11 books, including the following recently published books: *Judgment in Managerial Decision Making* (John Wiley & Sons, now in its sixth edition); *Negotiation, Decision Making and Conflict Management* (Edward Elgar Publishers, 2005, available in three volumes); *Predictable Surprises* (Harvard Business School Press, 2004, with Michael Watkins); and *You Can't Enlarge the Pie: The Psychology of Ineffective Government* (Basic Books, 2001, with J. Baron and K. Shonk). He is the Academic Editor of *The Negotiation Newsletter*; a member of the editorial boards of the *American Behavioral Scientist, Journal of Management and Governance, Mind and Society*, and *Journal of Behavioral Finance*; and a member of the international advisory board of the *Negotiation Journal*. Bazerman was profiled by *The Organization Frontier* in 1993 as the leading management expert on the topics of negotiation and decision making. In 2002 and 2004, he was named one of the top 40 authors, speakers, and teachers of management by *Executive Excellence*. While at Kellogg, he was named "Teacher of the Year" by the Executive Masters Program of the Kellogg School. In 2003, Bazerman received the Everett Mendelsohn Excellence in Mentoring Award from Harvard University's Graduate School of Arts and Sciences. Later in 2006, Bazerman will receive an honorary doctorate from the University of London (London Business School). His professional activities include projects with Abbott, Aetna, Alcar, Alcoa, Allstate, Ameritech, Amgen, Asian Development Bank, AstraZeneca, AT&T, Aventis, BASF, Bayer, Becton Dickenson, Boston Scientific, Bristol-Myers Squibb, *BusinessWeek*, Celtic Insurance, Chevron, *Chicago Tribune*, City of Chicago, Deloitte & Touche, Dial, Ernst & Young, First Chicago, Gemini Consulting, General Motors, Harris Bank, Home Depot, Hyatt Hotels, IBM, John Hancock, Johnson & Johnson, Kohler, KPMG, Lucent, The May Company, McKinsey, Merrill Lynch, Monitor, Motorola, National Association of Broadcasters, The Nature Conservancy, PricewaterhouseCoopers, R. P. Scherer, Sara Lee, Siemens, Sprint, Sulzermedica, Unicredito, Union Bank of Switzerland, Wilson Sporting Goods, Xerox, Young Presidents Organization, World Bank, and Zurich Insurance. Bazerman's consulting, teaching, and lecturing have occurred throughout the world, including Argentina, Australia, Austria, Barbados, Belgium, Brazil, Chile, Costa Rica, Ecuador, England, France, India, Israel, Italy, Malaysia, the Netherlands, Peru, the Philippines, Puerto Rico, Singapore, South Africa, South Korea, Switzerland, and Thailand.

Rocio Bonet

Rocio Bonet is a PhD candidate in the Management Department at the Wharton School of the University of Pennsylvania. She received her MS degree in Economics, Management, and Finance from the University Pompeu Fabra in Barcelona and her BA in Business Administration from the University of Zaragoza, Spain. Her research interests are human resource management and individual career development with a special focus on the effect that organizations have on individual careers. She is also interested in studying the effects of human resource practices on employee welfare, in particular on wage growth and promotions. Bonet is a special sworn employee for the U.S. Census Bureau where she is investigating the effect of new organizational practices on employees. She is also interested in the study of corporate governance, with special interest in the role of the board of directors on executive compensation and its effect on organizational performance.

Bob Campbell

Bob Campbell is Hewitt's global practice leader for consulting in Building a High Performance Workforce, helping organizations create high performance cultures focused on business-critical results and talent management as a competitive advantage. Campbell has over 20 years of experience as a management consultant working with companies in North America, Europe, and Asia to design and implement high-impact performance management, leadership development, career progression/management, and strategic staffing. Campbell has also managed human resources planning and development in major pharmaceutical, manufacturing, and retail organizations. Some of Campbell's clients include Allstate Corporation, American Express Company, HMSHost Corporation, Intuit Inc., and Weyerhaeuser Company. Campbell has BS and MS degrees from Syracuse University and an MBA from the University of Pittsburgh.

Peter Cappelli

Peter Cappelli is the George W. Taylor Professor of Management and director, Center for Human Resources, at the Wharton School of the University of Pennsylvania. Cappelli has a BS in Industrial Relations from Cornell University and a PhD in Labor Economics from Oxford, where he was a Fulbright Scholar. He is also a research associate at the National Bureau of Economic Research. Cappelli is recognized as one of the world's most important authorities on human capital. His research has examined changes in the workplace and their effects on employers. He is particularly interested in changes in the ways organizations recruit, manage talent, and appraise and manage performance. His latest book, *Ambition: The New Path to the Top*, examines the changing models for corporate careers.

Ted Childs

Ted Childs is IBM's Vice President, Global Workforce Diversity, with worldwide responsibility for workforce diversity programs and policies. He is a graduate of West Virginia State College and a member of the board of directors and a past president of the University's Foundation. He is also a member of the Executive Leadership Council and The Conference Board's Work Force Diversity Council. Childs has served on various councils, including the New York State Governor's Advisory Council on Child Care, the National Council of Jewish Women's Work Family Advisory Board, the White House Conference on Aging, the Family Reunion "V," and the U.S. Treasury Secretary's Working Group on Child Care. He has received numerous awards including "25 Men Friends of the Family" and Diversity Awards 2000 for Excellence in Diversity, both from *Working Mother* magazine; lifetime achievement awards from the National Association of Child Care Resource and Referral Agencies and *Savoy* magazine and the Women and Diversity Leadership Summit; a Corporate Leadership Award from the Human Rights Campaign; the Alumni Leadership Award from the Thurgood Marshall Scholarship Fund; and the Work/Life Legacy Award from the Families and Work Institute. Childs has also received honorary doctor of humane letters degrees from Pace University, West Virginia State College, and Our Lady of the Elms College and is a fellow in the National Academy of Human Resources.

Rob Cross

Rob Cross is an assistant professor of management at the University of Virginia, where he is the director of the Network Roundtable, a consortium of 45 organizations sponsoring research on network applications to critical management issues. His research focuses on how relationships and informal networks in organizations can be analyzed and improved to promote competitive advantage, organizational flexibility, innovation, customer retention and profitability, leadership effectiveness, talent management, and quality of work life. Cross has worked directly with more than 80 strategically important networks across a wide range of well-known organizations in consulting, pharmaceuticals, software, electronics and computer manufacturers, consumer products, financial services, petroleum, heavy equipment manufacturing, chemicals, and government. Ideas emerging from his research have resulted in two books, four book chapters, and 23 articles, several of which have won awards. In addition to top scholarly outlets, his work has been published in *Harvard Business Review, Sloan Management Review, California Management Review, Academy of Management Executive*, and *Organizational Dynamics*. His most recent book, *The Hidden Power of Social Networks* (Harvard Business School Publishing, 2004), has been featured in venues such as *The Financial Times, Time* magazine, *The Wall Street Journal, CIO, Inc.*, and *Fast Company*. Cross holds a PhD from Boston University and a BS and MBA from the University of Virginia. He speaks, consults, and conducts executive education both domestically and internationally.

Christopher M. DeRose

Christopher DeRose is an active researcher and consultant in the area of organizational change and leadership. He assists business leaders to improve their organization's growth and profitability while concurrently developing the next generation of leadership. He has been an associate of the University of Michigan Ross Business School's Global Business Partnership, a consortium of leading multinational corporations, since 1989. He also teaches executive education with Noel Tichy at the Business School. Additionally, DeRose is a partner with Action Learning Associates, a consulting firm specializing in development and delivery of CEO-driven, large-scale transformation. He has consulted and taught around the world with companies such as Royal Dutch/Shell, Ford Motor Company, Intel, 3M, and HP. His research and consultation in the areas of leadership, organizational change, and growth have taken place in the automotive, telecommunications, publishing, e-commerce, software, financial services, biotechnology, pharmaceutical, energy, semiconductor, retail, and beverage industries. DeRose has co-authored book chapters, development handbooks, and articles for publications such as *Fortune* magazine, *Training & Development, Journal of Cost Management*, and *Australian Human Resources Journal*. Prior to becoming a consultant, DeRose worked in the financial services industry and led a sales organization in Japan. He received both undergraduate and graduate degrees from the University of Michigan.

Robert P. Gandossy

Robert Gandossy is a global practice leader for Talent and Organization Consulting for Hewitt Associates. He has special expertise in improving organizational effectiveness, human resource strategy, leadership, managing large-scale change, mergers and acquisitions (M&A), and increasing growth through innovation. Prior to joining Hewitt Associates, Gandossy was a senior management consultant for a number of years at a general management consulting firm in Cambridge, Massachusetts. Some of his consulting clients include American Express, IBM, Pfizer, and Verizon. He has written over 50 articles and five books on a variety of subjects including HR strategy, M&A, performance improvement, innovation and change, and business ethics. Gandossy's newest book, *Leadership and Governance from the Inside Out* (John Wiley & Sons, 2004), which he co-edited with Jeff Sonnenfeld, is a collection of perspectives on the challenges, problems, and potential solutions associated with corporate governance in today's business world. Jamie Dimon, president of JP Morgan Chase, called it "the best collection . . . of influential opinion leaders;" Jeff Immelt, CEO of General Electric, said it was "a thoughtful framework for rebuilding trust in business"; and Doug Conant, CEO of Campbell Soup, called it "superbly crafted, thought-provoking, and compelling." He is also the co-editor of the book *Human Resources in the 21st Century* (John Wiley & Sons, 2003), featuring chapters by the world's thought leaders in leadership and human resources. Gandossy is coauthor of the book *Leading the Way: Three Truths from the Top Companies for Leaders* (John Wiley & Sons, 2004). David Cote, CEO of Honeywell, said the book offers "actionable insights" and the authors "focus on the things that matter"; Robert Nardelli, CEO of Home Depot, said the book provides "useful insights"; and Susan

Peters, Vice President for Executive Development at GE, called it a "must read for all leaders." His book *Bad Business* (Basic Books, 1985) was called a "masterful job" by Tom Peters and "high drama and a fascinating story" by Rosabeth Moss Kanter. Gandossy has been a speaker for a number of groups including Harvard Business School, Human Resources Planning Society, The Wharton School, Tom Peters Group, Yale Law School, Yale's School of Organization and Management, WorldatWork, SHRM, American Management Association, and The Conference Board. He has spoken to audiences all over the world including Hong Kong, Singapore, Shanghai, New Delhi, Paris, London, and Brussels. Gandossy holds a BS degree from Harpur College and a PhD degree from Yale University, where he specialized in the study of organizational behavior.

Lynda Gratton

Lynda Gratton is Professor of Management Practice at London Business School, where she directs the school's executive program, Human Resource Strategy in Transforming Organizations. Over the past decade Gratton has led The Leading Edge Research Consortium (www.london.edu/lerc), a major research initiative involving companies such as Hewlett-Packard and Citibank. The initial results from the research were published by Oxford University Press in 2000 in the book *Strategic Human Resource Management: Corporate Rhetoric and Human Reality*. In *Living Strategy: Putting People at the Heart of Corporate Purpose*, published by FT/Prentice Hall in 2000, Gratton called for a more strategic approach to people management. The book has been translated into seven languages and was voted one of the 20 most influential books by American CEOs. More recently she has addressed the issue of organizational purpose in *The Democratic Enterprise: Liberating Your Business with Freedom, Flexibility and Commitment*, published by FT/Prentice Hall in 2004. Gratton is acknowledged as one of the world's most influential thinkers in HR strategy. She serves on the advisory boards of Exult and the Concours Group and consults to a wide range of multinational companies including Shell, Unilever, Royal Bank of Scotland, and HP. In 2004 she was appointed a research fellow of the Advanced Institute of Management in the United Kingdom (www.aim-research.org) and is a visiting professor at the Center for Human Resource Strategy at Michigan Business School.

David E. Guest

David E. Guest received his first degree in psychology and sociology from Birmingham University and PhD in Occupational Psychology from London

University. After postgraduate research, he became a research officer in the Department of Occupational Psychology at Birkbeck College. He then spent three years as behavioral science adviser to British Rail before joining the London School of Economics in 1972. He moved to Birkbeck in 1990 and for 10 years was Professor of Occupational Psychology and head of the Department of Organizational Psychology. During that period he had a spell as a governor of Birkbeck and as pro-vice master with responsibility for information and learning technology. Guest moved to King's College in 2000, where until September 2005 he was head of the Department of Management and deputy head of the School of Social Science and Public Policy. He has written and researched extensively in the areas of human resources management, employment relations and the psychological contract, motivation and commitment, and careers. He is a member of the editorial advisory board of a number of journals and a Council Member of the Tavistock Institute. He is a member of the SDO Commissioning Board and of the Sector Skill Development Agency Academic Advisory Group. He has worked closely with a range of companies including Shell, IBM, HSBC, Hong Kong MTRC, as well as with the National Health Services and a number of government departments. His current research is concerned with the relationship between human resources management and performance in the private and public sectors, the individualization of employment relations and the role of the psychological contract, flexibility and employment contracts, partnership at work, and the future of the career.

Helen Handfield-Jones

Helen Handfield-Jones helps companies build a stronger talent pool by teaching senior leaders how to assess, develop, and recruit the leadership talent their company needs to reach its aspirations. She co-wrote *The War for Talent* (Harvard Business School Publishing, 2001) and co-led McKinsey & Company's groundbreaking research on this topic in 1997. She helps the senior executive team conduct more effective talent reviews and succession planning processes and accelerate the development of their high-potential leaders, advising more than 70 clients around the world, including Pfizer, Owens Corning, Whirlpool, Bell Canada Enterprises, Alcan, and CPR. At the board level, she helps directors strengthen their value-added role by improving the way they do CEO evaluation, CEO succession planning, and leadership talent review. She is a regular part of the faculty of the Directors Education Program offered by the Institute of Corporate Directors and the Rotman School of Management in Canada. Prior to starting her own consulting practice, she spent 12 years as a consultant with McKinsey & Company. She graduated as the gold medalist from the MBA program at the Ivey School of Business at the University of Western Ontario in 1990.

Tina Kao

Tina Kao is a senior consultant in the Talent and Organization Consulting Practice in Hewitt Associates' New Jersey Center. She helps organizations design and implement people strategies and systems that support business objectives. Global talent management, change and transition management, HR strategy, recruitment and sourcing, merger and acquisition integration, culture assessment, and organization design are among her areas of specialization. Most recently her work has been in the area of global sourcing—helping clients think through the organizational and people implications of moving work and talent across the globe. Kao is a member of the Insights and Innovation team for Hewitt, a thought leadership group dedicated to cutting-edge research and ideas on people and business. Her work on critical talent and HR issues has appeared in a number of journals, including *Across the Board*, *Worldat Work Journal*, *Human Resource Executive*, and *Human Resource Planning*. Kao's previous work experiences include: HR generalist for a Fortune 500 investment banking firm, marketing and communications specialist for a major agribusiness company in Taiwan, and history teacher in Brooklyn, New York.

Kao graduated with high honors from Brown University with a BA in History. She earned an MBA from Yale University School of Management with a focus on business strategy and leadership.

Edward E. Lawler III

Edward E. Lawler III is the Distinguished Professor of Business and Director of the Center for Effective Organizations in the Marshall School of Business at the University of Southern California. He joined USC in 1978 and during 1979 founded and became director of the University's Center for Effective Organizations. He has consulted with over 100 organizations on employee involvement, organizational change, and compensation and has been honored as a top contributor to the fields of organizational development, organizational behavior, and compensation. The author of more than 300 articles and 35 books, his articles have appeared in leading academic journals as well as *Fortune*, *Harvard Business Review*, and leading newspapers including *USA Today* and *The Financial Times*. His most recent books include *Rewarding Excellence* (Jossey-Bass, 2000); *Corporate Boards: New Strategies for Adding Value at the*

Top (Jossey-Bass, 2001); *Organizing for High Performance* (Jossey-Bass, 2001); *Treat People Right* (Jossey-Bass, 2003); *Creating a Strategic Human Resources Organization* (Stanford Press, 2003); *Human Resources Business Process Outsourcing* (Jossey-Bass, 2004); *Achieving Strategic Excellence: An Assessment of Human Resource Organizations* (Stanford Press, 2006); and *Built to Change* (Jossey-Bass, 2006).

Thomas W. Malone

Thomas W. Malone is the Patrick J. McGovern Professor of Management at the MIT Sloan School of Management. He is also the founder and director of the MIT Center for Coordination Science and was one of the two founding codirectors of the MIT initiative on Inventing the Organizations of the 21st Century. Malone teaches classes on leadership and information technology, and his research focuses on how new organizations can be designed to take advantage of the possibilities provided by information technology. His research over the past two decades is summarized in his book *The Future of Work: How the New Order of Business Will Shape Your Organization, Your Management Style, and Your Life* (Harvard Business School Press, 2004). Malone has also published over 50 articles, research papers, and book chapters; he is an inventor with 11 patents; and he is the coeditor of three additional books: *Coordination Theory and Collaboration Technology* (Erlbaum, 2001); *Inventing the Organizations of the 21st Century* (MIT Press, 2003); and *Organizing Business Knowledge: The MIT Process Handbook* (MIT Press, 2003). Malone has been a co-founder of three software companies and has consulted and served as a board member for a number of other organizations. His background includes work as a research scientist at Xerox Palo Alto Research Center (PARC), a PhD from Stanford University, and degrees in applied mathematics, engineering, and psychology.

N. R. Narayana Murthy

N. R. Narayana Murthy (education: BE Electrical 1967, University of Mysore; M. Tech. 1969, Indian Institute of Technology, Kanpur, India) is the chairman and chief mentor of Infosys Technologies Limited, a global information technology (IT) consulting and software services provider, headquartered in Bangalore, India. Murthy served as the CEO of Infosys for 20 years and under his leadership, Infosys was listed on NASDAQ (INFY) in 1999. In March 2002, he handed over the reins of the company to fellow co-founder, Nandan M. Nilekani. Murthy is the chairman of the governing body of both the Indian Institute of Information Technology, Bangalore, and the Indian

Institute of Management, Ahmedabad. He is a member of the Board of Overseers of the University of Pennsylvania's Wharton School, Cornell University Board of Trustees, Singapore Management University Board of Trustees, INSEAD's board of directors, and the Asian Institute of Management's board of governors. He is also a member of the advisory boards and councils of various universities—such as the William F. Achtmeyer Center for Global Leadership at the Tuck School of Business, Dartmouth University; the Corporate Governance initiative at the Harvard Business School; and the Yale University President's Council on International Activities. Murthy has led key corporate governance initiatives in India. He was the chairman of the committee on Corporate Governance appointed by the Securities and Exchange Board of India (SEBI) in 2003. Murthy serves as an independent director on the board of the DBS Bank, Singapore, the largest government-owned bank in Singapore. He is a member of the Asia Pacific Advisory Board of British Telecommunications plc., and a member of the Board of New Delhi Television Ltd. (NDTV), India. He also serves as a director on the Central Board of the Reserve Bank of India, as a member of the Prime Minister's Council on Trade and Industry, and as a member of the board of directors of the United Nations Foundation. He is an IT adviser to several Asian countries. Murthy has been the recipient of numerous awards and honors. *The Economist* ranked him 8th in the list of the 15 most admired global leaders (2005). He was ranked 28th among the world's most respected business leaders by *The Financial Times* (2005). He topped the Economic Times Corporate Dossier list of India's most powerful CEOs for two consecutive years—2004 and 2005. The *Time* magazine "Global Tech Influentials" list (August 2004) identified Murthy as one of the 10 leaders who are helping shape the future of technology. He was the first recipient of the Indo-French Forum Medal (in the year 2003), awarded by the Indo-French Forum, in recognition of his role in promoting Indo-French ties. He was voted the World Entrepreneur of the Year—2003 by Ernst & Young. He was one of the two people named as Asia's Businessmen of the Year for 2003 by *Fortune* magazine. In 2001, he was named by *Time*/CNN as one of the 25 most influential global executives, a group selected for their lasting influence in creating new industries and reshaping markets. He was awarded the Max Schmidheiny Liberty 2001 prize (Switzerland), in recognition of his promotion of individual responsibility and liberty. In 1999, *BusinessWeek* named him one of their nine Entrepreneurs of the Year, and he was featured in *BusinessWeek*'s "The Stars of Asia" for three successive years—1998, 1999, and 2000. The Queensland University of Technology (Brisbane, Australia) conferred an honorary doctorate on Murthy in 2005. He has also received honorary doctorates from several well-known universities in India.

Nigel Nicholson

Nigel Nicholson is a Professor of Organizational Behavior at London Business School, where he conducts research and teaches on leadership, family business, and interpersonal skills. Nicholson studied psychology, followed by a PhD in Work and Organizational Psychology. He joined the Social and Applied Psychology Unit at the University of Sheffield where he worked on issues of labor management relations, industrial conflict, organizational change, innovation, and management career mobility. He moved to London Business School in 1990, where in addition to two periods as Organizational Behavior Chairman he has been Research Dean, a Deputy Dean, and member of the Governing Body. He has been a distinguished visitor at universities in the United States, Germany, Canada, and Australia, and a fellow of the British Academy of Management and the British Psychological Society. He has been honored for his contribution to theory and method by the Academy of Management in the United States. Since 1996 a key mission of Nicholson has been to pioneer the introduction of the powerful and radical ideas of evolutionary psychology to the world of business, through a stream of publications and presentations, including most notably his *Harvard Business Review* articles in 1998 and 2003, and book in 2000. Areas of his recent research and writing include personality and executive development, risk and decision making in finance, careers, organizational change, expatriate adjustment, and leadership skills. In these and other areas he has published more than 15 books and 200 articles for academic and practitioner audiences. In teaching, Nicholson has created a number of initiatives, including the Proteus Program, a totally new kind of experiential program for top leaders. He also directs the school's longest-running open enrollment program, High Performance People Skills for Leaders, as well as a number of company-specific programs.

Salvatore Parise

Salvatore Parise is an Assistant Professor in the Technology, Operations, and Information Management Division at Babson College. His research focuses primarily on using organizational network analysis to understand innovation, worker performance, lost and critical knowledge, cultural differences, and talent management. His other research work focuses on knowledge management, strategic alliances, and electronic commerce. Parise works in several research centers, including Working Knowledge at Babson College and The

Network Roundtable at the University of Virginia. He is also an assistant director of the e-commerce research group at Babson. He has worked directly with managers and executives across a wide range of industries, including consulting, technology, consumer products, financial services, petroleum, and government. His research has been published in the *Sloan Management Review*, *Academy of Management Executive*, *IBM Systems Journal*, and *Journal of Management Education*. Prior to obtaining his Doctorate in Business at Boston University, Parise was an engineer and research manager at IBM.

Jeffrey Pfeffer

Jeffrey Pfeffer is the Thomas D. Dee II Professor of Organizational Behavior in the Graduate School of Business at Stanford University, where he has taught since 1979. He is the author or co-author of 11 books, including *The Knowing-Doing Gap, Managing with Power, The Human Equation: Building Profits by Putting People First, Hard Facts, Dangerous Half-Truths, and Total Nonsense: Profiting from Evidence-Based Management*. He has also had published more than 100 articles and book chapters. Pfeffer has served on the faculties of the business schools at the University of Illinois and the University of California at Berkeley, and was a visiting professor at the Harvard Business School. He currently serves on the board of directors of SonoSite, Audible Magic, and Uni-Cru. He also writes a monthly column for *Business 2.0* entitled "The Human Factor." Pfeffer received his BS in Administration and Management Science and his MS in Industrial Administration from Carnegie-Mellon University. He obtained his PhD in Business Administration from the Stanford Graduate School of Business. Pfeffer has taught executive seminars in 27 countries throughout the world in addition to lecturing in management development programs and consulting for many companies, associations, and universities in the United States. Pfeffer is a member and fellow of the Academy of Management and a member of the Industrial Relations Research Association. He has won the Richard D. Irwin award for Scholarly Contributions to Management as well as several awards for books and articles.

Daniel H. Pink

Daniel H. Pink is the best-selling author of two influential business books. *A Whole New Mind* (Penguin Group, 2005), his latest book, charts the rise of right-brain thinking in modern economies and explores the six abilities people will need to master in an outsourced and automated world. Reviewers have described the book as "an audacious and powerful work," "a profound read," "right on the money," and "a miracle." Several publications named it one of the best business books of 2005. In 2006, translated editions will appear in 12 languages. Pink's first book, *Free Agent Nation* (Warner Books, 2001), about the rise of people working for themselves, was a *Washington Post* nonfiction best seller and a business best seller in the United States and Canada. *Publishers Weekly* said that the book "has become a cornerstone of employee-management relations." Pink's articles on work, technology, and economic transformation have appeared in *The New York Times*, *Wired*, *Harvard Business Review*, and other publications. He also lectures these subjects to corporations, universities, and associations around the world.

Todd L. Pittinsky

Todd L. Pittinsky is an assistant professor at the John F. Kennedy School of Government and a core faculty member at Harvard's Center for Public Leadership. Pittinsky's research focuses on the psychological science of leadership and on the nature of allophilia (love of the other) in intergroup relations. Pittinsky earned his BA from Yale University, his MA in Psychology from Harvard University, and a PhD in Organizational Behavior jointly from the Harvard Graduate School of Arts and Sciences and the Harvard Business School. Pittinsky is a lead investigator of the National Leadership Index (NLI), an annual national study of confidence in public and private sector leadership. The NLI—online at www.ksg.harvard.edu/leadership/nli/—is conducted in collaboration with *U.S. News & World Report* and Yankelovich. He has published studies in leading academic journals, including *American Behavioral Scientist*, *Psychological Science*, and the *Journal of Social Issues*. Pittinsky is also the author of two case studies for the Harvard Business School Press and co-author of a book on work-family diversity with Dr. James A. Levine (Addison Wesley, 1999). Pittinsky teaches three graduate-level courses at Harvard: an advanced seminar on leadership studies, a course on diversity and leadership, and a field research methods course. Pittinsky also teaches in the Kennedy School's Executive Programs, the leading executive education program for public sector leaders, and has offered advanced undergraduate seminars at Harvard College. Prior to joining the Harvard faculty, Pittinsky worked as a senior researcher for the Families and Work Institute, where he led several foundation-funded research projects. Pittinsky has worked professionally for several other nonprofit organizations, including the School of the 21st Century Foundation and a United Way child care center. He has also worked for several for-profit companies, including Netscape Communications Corporation and KPMG Peat Marwick LLP. Pittinsky has served as a consultant to General Motors, Bright Horizons, Catalyst, Netscape Communications Corporation, Opsware, and Triumvirate Environmental. In 1990, Pittinsky received Yale University's President's Award for Outstanding Community Service. In 1998, he received the George S. Dively '29 Award for Distinguished Research from the Harvard Business School. In 2000, he was awarded the Eliot Merit Fellowship for the Social Sciences from Harvard University. In 2003, Pittinsky was selected to represent Harvard in the Young Faculty Leaders forum, a group of 34 faculty members selected from America's leading universities.

Samir J. Raza

Samir Raza is a senior consultant at Hewitt Associates, leading the Shareholder Value initiative with the Corporate Finance group. He is also leading research development of the Human Capital Foresight project, leveraging over a decade of management consulting experience with clients in North America, Europe, and Asia, and research experience with academic institutions. Raza has been a frequent speaker at conferences and business schools on topics related to organizational strategies for economic value creation. He has written several articles on shareholder value and human capital management: "The Path to Value: A Capital Markets' Perspective," 1997; Linking Employee Engagement to Business Results, Wachovia Bank Research Project, 1999; "CFO Survey—Shareholder Value Alignment," 2000; "A Market Based Approach for Goal Setting," 2002; "Human Capital Foresight—Framework and Empirical Foundations," 2005; and "Optimizing Human Capital Investments for Superior Shareholder Returns," published in *Valuation Issues Journal*, February 2006. Raza has an undergraduate degree in systems and industrial engineering and a graduate degree in economics.

Keith Rollag

Keith Rollag is currently an Assistant Professor of Management at Babson College. His research focuses primarily on newcomer socialization, training, organizational culture, social networks, and leadership development. His most recent publication, "Getting New Hires Up to Speed Quickly," co-authored with Salvatore Parise and Rob Cross, appeared in the 2005 Winter Issue of *MIT/Sloan Management Review*. His research has also been published in the *Journal of Organizational Behavior* and *Journal of Management Education* and has been featured in *Harvard Management Update, Stanford Social Innovation Review, Contingent Workforce Strategies, Wired News, IEEE Spectrum, New Venture Development*, and the *Boston Business Journal*. Recently, he was the sole recipient of the 2005 New Educator Award from the Organizational Behavior Teaching

Society, a national organization focused on management education. Prior to obtaining his PhD in Industrial Engineering from Stanford University, he was a product development manager at Procter & Gamble.

Caryn Rowe

As a Global Marketing Leader at Hewitt Associates, Caryn Rowe brings a strong understanding of the clients, services, and human resource programs and operations to the HR outsourcing and consulting arena. Over the years Rowe has developed Hewitt's strategy, content, and scope, for their client-oriented marketing and client events. Rowe has managed many of its large clients, like BP and DaimlerChrysler, which have used a broad range of Hewitt's consulting and outsourcing services. Most recently, Rowe played a leadership role in the Hewitt-Exult merger and the development of their market strategies for HR outsourcing. Rowe has accumulated an extraordinary amount of experience in human resources. Her areas of expertise are in assessing clients' needs and desired results, and designing HR outsourcing solutions. Rowe is notably seasoned in the area of integrating human resources plans, policy design, and outsourcing. Rowe is known for her client orientation and the way she partners with clients to target solving their problems. Prior to Hewitt Associates, Rowe spent 10 years at a Fortune 100 company as the director of employee benefits. Her experience includes strategic planning, design, and implementation of HR plans. She also has extensive experience working with and negotiating in union environments. Rowe holds a BS in Physiology from the University of Michigan, and a master's degree in Human Resources from National Louis University.

Betsy Scheffel

Betsy Scheffel is a senior consultant in the Talent and Organization Consulting Practice in Hewitt's Connecticut Center. She has a broad consulting background that focuses on leading large projects in the areas of creating human resource strategy, building high performance organizations, and designing and implementing broad reward strategies. She has worked with clients to create talent management strategies, realign their human resource functions to better serve the business, and design and implement programs that engage the workforce. Prior to joining Hewitt, she worked for another major consulting firm. Scheffel earned a BA from Dartmouth College.

Matt Schuyler

Matt Schuyler joined Capital One in April 2002 as the Senior Vice President of Human Resources and was promoted to Executive Vice President in December 2003. Schuyler has experience in all facets of HR management, including organizational design, recruitment, and retention strategies. Under Schuyler's direction, Capital One's Human Resources organization provides talent, integration, and infrastructure to Capital One on a worldwide basis. It also works to effectively allocate talent throughout the company, and it employs pay and benefit programs that reward associates for performance and value creation. The Human Resources organization is comprised of more than 650 associates spanning four countries: the United States, the United Kingdom, France, and South Africa. Prior to joining Capital One, Schuyler was the Vice President of Human Resources with Cisco Systems, Inc. Prior to Cisco he was a partner in the Global Human Resources group at PricewaterhouseCoopers. In this capacity he was responsible for multifaceted global human resource programs and projects, recruitment of talent, and the development and design of comprehensive global human resource strategies, including merger integration, change integration, and cost-effectiveness. A native of Pennsylvania, Schuyler holds an MBA from the University of Michigan in Organizational Behavior and HR Management and a Bachelor of Science in Accounting from Pennsylvania State University. He is a member of the Society of Human Resource Management, Society of International Human Resource Management, Chicago Museum of Modern Art, and the Penn State Alumni Association.

Ricardo Semler

Ricardo Semler, 46, president of Semco, the Brazilian machinery manufacturer and service provider, is internationally renowned as the creator of the world's most unusual workplace. Semler's management philosophy of empowering employees and looking at corporate structures in new ways is a serious challenge to the ingrained model of the corporate pyramid. His book describing his management philosophy, *Turning the Tables*, was on Brazil's best seller list for more than 200 weeks and saw 51 printings. His first article in the *Harvard Business Review*, "Managing without Managers," provoked intense discussion among senior managers worldwide and is one of the most reprinted articles in the journal's history (77,000). *Harvard Business Review* also published his articles "Why My Former Employees Still Work for Me" in January/February 1994 and "How We Went Digital without a Strategy" in September/October 2000, making him the *journal's* most published Latin American author. *Turning the Tables* was released in the United States as *Maverick: The Success Story Behind the World's Most Unusual Workplace*, shaping American business dialogue as Semler described how he spurred his company to 900 percent growth in 10 years and increased Semco's industry ranking from 56th to 4th in machinery and reaching number one positions in all of the service industries in which Semco is active. Semco has gone from 100 to nearly 3,000 employees in the interim. *Maverick* has since been published in 23 languages, including Japanese and Chinese, and has sold more than 1.1 million copies. It reached best seller status in the United Kingdom, Australia, France, Switzerland, Austria, and Holland. His new book, *The Seven-Day Weekend*, is published by Penguin in the United States and by Random House in the United Kingdom, where it is a best seller. An influential leader, Semler has been profiled in more than 260 magazines and newspapers, including *The Wall Street Journal*, *The Financial Times*, and *Fortune*. He was also profiled in *Time*'s special edition, *Time 100*, which is published every 20 years to highlight future leaders around the globe. The World Economic Forum in Switzerland named him one of the Global Leaders of Tomorrow. He has appeared on television and radio on four continents and has lectured some 500 times to audiences around the world. He also consults with major companies, including some of the largest car companies, cable channels, and telecom firms. *CIO* magazine, using an elite jury that included Tom Peters, Jim Champy, and Michael Hammer, selected Semco as the only Latin American company among the most successfully reengineered companies in the world. The BBC included Semco in "Reengineering the Business," a series focusing on the world's five most successful management structures. In 2004, CNN, BBC, and France's M6 sent crews for multiday filming at the company. Semler was twice named Brazil's Business Leader of the Year, and *America Economia* (*The Wall Street Journal*'s Spanish-language magazine) named him Latin American Businessman of the Year. A graduate of Harvard Business School, Semler speaks five languages fluently. He was vice president of the Federation of Industries of Brazil and a board member of the SOS Atlantic Forest, Brazil's foremost environmental defense organization.

Semler has:

- Been chosen by 24 percent of university graduates in Brazil as the "boss for whom they would most like to work."
- Been the subject of 19 TV specials around the globe.
- Given nearly 500 lectures.
- Served as consultant to the Discovery Channel, NASA, GM, and Wilson.
- Given workshops with Peter Drucker, Tom Peters, John Naisbitt, and C.K. Prahalad.

- Spoken to a crowd of 8,500 people in a basketball stadium in Sydney, Australia, with Lee Iacocca in 1999.
- Shared a podium with George Bush, Valéry Giscard d'Estaing, Lord Carrington, and George Soros.
- Spoken by invitation of David Rockefeller to the 100 Wealthiest Clients of Chase at the Paris Ritz Hotel.
- Spoken to the Club of Rome, Club of Paris, International Monetary Fund, World Bank, Jewish National Congress, and Arab Counsel
- Consistently maintained Semco's place on the list of the 10 most sought-after jobs by young managers and university students in Brazil.

Semler's newest nonprofit project is a cutting-edge school experiment based on three years of intensive study and visits by sociologists and educators to over 200 schools around the globe. The school and its institute, both named Lumiar (to shed light) have an ambitious goal: to help redesign education for the new century. Semler is currently a Visiting Scholar at Harvard University, and teaches leadership at MIT.

Margaret J. Shih

Margaret Shih has been an Assistant Professor of Organizational Psychology at the University of Michigan since 2000. Shih earned her undergraduate degree from Stanford University. From there, she went on to complete her PhD at Harvard University. She is co-author of "Knowledge Nomads: Organizational Commitment and Worker Mobility in Positive Perspective," published in *American Behavioral Scientist* (February 2004).

Andrés Tapia

Andrés Tapia is Hewitt Associates' chief diversity officer, responsible for leading the company in its internal and external diversity vision. Working closely with Hewitt's CEO on business and people strategies, he developed a three-pronged strategy to increase value to each of the firm's stakeholders: associates, clients, investors, and communities through diversity and inclusion. Using his training and experience in journalism, history, political science, and HR he has created innovative approaches to the firm's attraction, retention, and development strategies to foster an inclusive working environment. This includes shifting the diversity paradigm from one being based on tolerance and sensitivity to one based on cross-cultural competence. Working with current national and global demographic trends, he also focuses on the implications of varying world views around health, wealth, and performance by the growing number of diverse groups in the workplace. Prior to this role, Tapia worked for six years as a performance and knowledge management leader for several of Hewitt's lines of business. Tapia has also created several ground-breaking and high-impact diversity learning and communications programs and is a master trainer for Hewitt's internal diversity/cross-cultural learning. In addition, he is one of the founders of Hewitt's Latino and Hispanic employee network (LAHA). Tapia has worked at CSC Index and Andersen Consulting (now Accenture) doing performance consulting, instructional design, and technical writing. He has experience as a journalist, with articles on social issue trends in the United States, Latin America, and his native Peru appearing in publications such as the *Baltimore Sun, Chicago Tribune, San Francisco Chronicle, Voçe* (Brazil), and *Hemispheres* magazine. He holds a BA in History with an emphasis in journalism and political science from Northwestern University.

Noel M. Tichy

Noel M. Tichy is a Professor of Organizational Behavior and Human Resource Management at the Stephen M. Ross School of Business at the University of Michigan, where he is the director of the Global Business Partnership. Recently, he led the launch of the Global Corporate Citizenship Initiative in partnership with General Electric and Proctor & Gamble, designed to create a national model for partnership opportunities between business and society emphasizing free enterprise and democratic principles. Between 1985 and 1987, Tichy was Manager of Management Education for General Electric, where he directed its worldwide development efforts at Crotonville. Prior to joining the Michigan Faculty he served for nine years on the Columbia University Business School faculty. Tichy is the author of numerous books and articles. His most recent books are *The Ethical Challenge* (Jossey-Bass, 2003, with Andy McGill) and *The Cycle of Leadership: How Winning Leaders Teach Their Organizations to Win* (HarperCollins, 2002, with Nancy Cardwell). He wrote *The Leadership Engine: How Winning Companies Build Leaders at Every Level* (HarperCollins, 1997, with Eli Cohen), named one of the top 10 business books in 1997 by *BusinessWeek*. He is coauthor of *Every Business Is a Growth Business* (with Ram Charan), published October 1998 (Random House). In addition, Tichy is the co-author of *Control Your Destiny or Someone Else Will: How Jack Welch is Making General Electric the World's Most Competitive Company* (HarperBusiness, 1994, with Stratford Sherman). Tichy has long been regarded as a staple of management literacy as noted by his rating as one of the "Top 10 Management Gurus" by *BusinessWeek* and *Business 2.0*. He has served on the editorial boards of the

Academy of Management Review, Organizational Dynamics, Journal of Business Research, and *Journal of Business Strategy* and was the founding editor in chief of *Human Resource Management*. Tichy consults widely in both the business and public sectors. He is a senior partner in Action Learning Associates. His clients have included Best Buy, General Electric, PepsiCo, Coca-Cola, General Motors, Nokia, Nomura Securities, 3M, Daimler-Benz, and Royal Dutch/Shell.

Elissa Tucker

Elissa Tucker is a senior consultant in the Research Practice at Hewitt Associates. Tucker leads large-scale research studies on a wide array of talent management topics and is an expert on workforce trends. Tucker's published Hewitt papers include: *Next-Generation Talent Management: Insights on How Workforce Trends Are Changing the Face of Talent Management, Driving Firm Performance Through People Management, 21st Century Corporations, Becoming a Generation X Employer of Choice*, and *The IT Talent Environment*. Among her published survey reports are: *Improving Organizational Speed and Agility* and *Paying for Performance*, which was produced in conjunction with the *Worldat-Work*. Previously, Tucker conducted data analysis for "The 100 Best Companies to Work for in America" study for *Fortune* magazine and co-authored Hewitt's survey report, *The People Practices of the 100 Best Companies to Work for in America*. Tucker earned a BA degree in social and cultural anthropology from Lawrence University.

Mark C. Ubelhart

Mark C. Ubelhart is the Value-Based Management (VBM) Practice Leader for Hewitt Associates LLC. With 30 years of consulting experience in corporate finance and executive compensation, Ubelhart served as vice president and division administrator of corporate financial consulting for a major money center bank before joining Hewitt. He holds a BA in economics from Dartmouth College, where he earned Phi Beta Kappa honors, and an MBA in finance from the University of Chicago. Previous articles include "Case Studies of Shareholder-Value Incentives," *ACA Journal*, 1994; Business Strategy, Performance Measurement, and Compensation," *Journal of Applied Corporate Finance*, 1985; and "Measuring the Immeasurable," *Shareholder Value* magazine, 2000.

Nidhi Verma

Nidhi Verma is a senior consultant in the Talent and Organization Consulting practice at Hewitt Associates. In this position, she provides consulting and thought leadership in the area of talent management and strategic directions of the human resources function. Verma has experience in both external consulting and internal HR and change-management roles and has consulted with a diverse range of clients in the United States, United Kingdom, and Asia. She consults on a wide spectrum of people and organizational development areas, specifically talent and leadership development, performance improvement, and change management. Verma has focused on supporting organizational change and transformation with effective and practical people solutions. Verma is a member of the Insights and Innovation team for Hewitt, a thought leadership group dedicated to cutting-edge research and ideas on people and business challenges. Her research work on significant talent and leadership issues has appeared in a number of leading journals. Prior to joining Hewitt, Verma worked as a consultant with Clark Consulting and Arthur Andersen and as an HR practitioner with General Electric. Verma holds a master's degree in leadership and adult learning from Teachers College, Columbia University, and a master's degree in personnel management from the Tata Institute of Social Sciences, Mumbai.

Patricia Wallace

Patricia Wallace is the Senior Director, Information Technology and Distance Education at the Johns Hopkins University Center for Talented Youth. She earned her PhD in psychology at the University of Texas at Austin, and also holds an MS in Computer Systems Management. Wallace's career has spanned the disciplines of information technology and psychology, as a chief information officer, faculty member, and adviser on IT architecture and strategy, distance education, online communities, and knowledge management. She is the author of many articles and several books including *The Internet in the Workplace* (Cambridge University Press, 2004) and *The Psychology of the Internet* (Cambridge University Press, 1999), which has been translated into eight other languages including Japanese and Chinese. Other recent publications include *Psych Online* (McGraw-Hill, 1998), *PRISM* (Interactive CD-ROM, McGraw-Hill, 1998), and a chapter in the Educause Leadership Strategies Series, *Information Alchemy: The Art and Science of Knowledge Management*. She has been principal investigator on several major grants involving multimedia, software development, and distance learning, with funding from Annenberg/Corporation for Public Broadcasting, Toyota USA Foundation, and AT&T Foundation. Wallace's work is featured in the media often, including *USA Today, The Wall Street Journal, The Washington Post, Baltimore Sun, Japan Times,* APA *Monitor,* MSNBC, CNN, ZDTV, various National Public Radio stations, Voice of America, Source Report, Maryland Public TV, and Australian National Public Radio.

Michael D. Watkins

Michael Watkins is a leading expert on the acceleration of leadership transitions, and author of the international best seller *The First 90 Days: Critical Success Strategies for New Leaders at All Levels* (Harvard Business School Press, 2003). He is a Professor of Practice at INSEAD, the leading European business school, and the founding partner of Genesis Advisers, a leadership strategy consultancy. His current book, *Shaping the Game: The New Leader's Guide to Effective Negotiating*, is being published by the Harvard Business School Press in the spring of 2006. Watkins is coauthor of *Right from the Start: Taking Charge in a New Leadership Role* (1999) and *Predictable Surprises: The Disasters You Should Have Seen Coming and How to Prevent Them* (2004) (a *Strategy + Business* best business book of 2004); author of *Breakthrough Business Negotiation: A Toolbox for Managers* (2002) (winner of a CPR Institute book prize 2002); and content expert for *Leadership Transitions*, Harvard Business School Publishing's award-winning e-learning system. He is also the author of other books on leadership and many articles, including publications in *Harvard Business Review*, *Sloan Management Review*, *Leadership Quarterly*, *Executive Update*, and *Negotiation Journal*. A native of Canada, Watkins received a degree in electrical engineering from the University of Waterloo, did graduate work at the University of Western Ontario, and completed his PhD in Decision Sciences at Harvard University. Between 1991 and 1996, he was a professor at Harvard's Kennedy School of Government. From 1996 to 2003 he was a professor at the Harvard Business School and taught negotiation in the Senior Executive Program at the Program on Negotiation at Harvard Law School.

Sheila Wellington

After a decade of outstanding leadership as president of Catalyst, the nation's premier nonprofit research and advisory organization on women's private sector leadership, Sheila Wellington was appointed Clinical Professor of Management at the New York University/Stern School of Business in September 2003. Prior to joining Catalyst, Wellington served for six years as Secretary of Yale, the second woman to be appointed as a Yale University officer. Previously, she worked in the public health arena for more than 20 years, serving on the faculty of Yale Medical School and as director of two major mental health facilities. As she was leaving for Catalyst in 1993, the mayor of New Haven presented her with the keys to the city, the first such honor ever given to a Yale University officer. Wellington is the author of *Be Your Own Mentor*, published by Random House in 2001. She is a trustee of the Nuveen Select Portfolios and has served on presidential, federal, and state commissions. Wellington received the Distinguished Alumnus Award from the Yale School of Public Health in 2002, was inducted into the National Academy of Human Resources, and serves on the board of the United Way of America. Wellington also serves on the boards of the Institute for Women's Policy Research, the Transitions Network, and the New York City Commission on Women's Issues. A Phi Beta Kappa graduate of Wellesley College, Wellington received concurrent master's degrees in public health and in urban studies from Yale.

INDEX